MUSCOGEE DAUGHTER

AMERICAN INDIAN LIVES

Series Editors

Kimberly Blaeser
University of Wisconsin, Milwaukee

Brenda J. Child
University of Minnesota

R. David Edmunds
University of Texas at Dallas

Clara Sue Kidwell
University of Oklahoma

Tsianina K. Lomawaima
University of Arizona

MUSCOGEE
DAUGHTER

My Sojourn to the Miss America Pageant

SUSAN SUPERNAW   Foreword by Geary Hobson

University of Nebraska Press
Lincoln and London

© 2010 by the Board of Regents
of the University of Nebraska
All rights reserved. Manufactured
in the United States of America

⊚

*Library of Congress
Cataloging-in-Publication Data*
Supernaw, Susan, 1950–
Muscogee daughter: my sojourn
to the Miss America Pageant /
Susan Supernaw; foreword by
Geary Hobson.
p. cm. — (American Indian lives)
Includes bibliographical references.
ISBN 978-0-8032-2971-6 (cloth: alk. paper)
1. Supernaw, Susan, 1950– 2. Supernaw, Susan,
1950– —Childhood and youth. 3. Supernaw,
Susan, 1950– —Family. 4. Creek Indians—
Oklahoma—Biography. 5. Munsee Indians—
Oklahoma—Biography. 6. Indian women—
Oklahoma—Biography. 7. Indians of North
America—Ethnic identity—Case studies.
8. Indian scholars—United States—Biography.
9. Women scholars—United States—Biography.
10. Miss America Pageant—Biography. I. Title.
E99.C9S86 2010
976.6004'97385—dc22
[B]
2010004261

Set in Minion by Kim Essman.
Designed by Ashley Muehlbauer.

* * *

To my son Mekko Navarro—
this is your legacy.

CONTENTS

ILLUSTRATIONS

FOREWORD
The Power of a Smile
GEARY HOBSON

Susan Supernaw's memoir has been a long time finding its way into print. Written almost a decade ago, it won the 2003 First Book Award for prose in the annual competition sponsored by the Native Writers' Circle of the Americas for unpublished book-length manuscripts by American Indian authors. The book has followed a somewhat long and tortuous route since that time. I know a little about the manuscript's life history. Considering it all, I find it highly fitting that it is being published as part of the University of Nebraska Press's American Indian Lives series. The book clearly deserves a place with books about and by such strong-willed and charismatic Indian women as LaDonna Harris, Annie Wauneka, Alanis Obamsawin, Delphine Red Shirt, Esther Burnette Horne, and Virginia Driving Hawk Sneve, whose life stories have generated much student and general interest.

In almost every photograph of Susan Supernaw within, you will see her as a bright young girl, a vibrant teenager, and a hopeful young and beautiful woman, invariably with a smile "as big as all outdoors," as the expression goes in her home country of eastern Oklahoma. More than thirty years after the last events recorded in her life story, you will still see Susan Supernaw with that same characteristic smile, always more than merely lighting up the ordinary and the drab. With such an innate ability to grace and dazzle, how could she not have been a Miss Oklahoma and later a Miss America contestant?

Muscogee Daughter ends with the author still in her early twenties. This might lead the reader to wonder what kind of "life story" this actually is, since the story ends at a time when most of us are usually beginning our lives. However, a careful reading reveals that, regardless of how dazzling and stellar her participation in the beauty contests was at the time, along with the immensity of her experiences, and the richness of her growth and development in the limelight, came much personal physical pain and suffering, shattering family crises and poverty, and even some moments of racial prejudice at the Miss America pageant. All, however, is bolstered by the presence of a complex extended family that has its roots in the Muskogee (Creek), Munsee, Quapaw, Osage, and other tribes in the contiguous Tulsa area. So, yes, even though the book ends with the conclusion of the national beauty pageant, Susan Supernaw went on to become an expert computer systems analyst and a successful businesswoman in computer database programming, education and technology consulting, and networking, as well as further developing her skills as a writer and educator. While the present work was winning its First Book Award and making the rounds to various presses and editors, she wrote a novel entitled *A Wolf Named Coyote*, which I can easily envision will soon begin its journey to eventual publication as well.

Susan Supernaw's personal story is an inspiration, not only for young girls seeking fame and fortune through talent shows and beauty pageants but also for anyone who realizes that often a pleasant, outgoing, genuinely friendly disposition and personality—a smile—opens most doors of opportunity and, what is more, goes a long way toward keeping them open.

ACKNOWLEDGMENTS

In the American Indian world one can never say "thanks" enough. We are traditionally a generous people, and I learned the value of sharing with others at an early age. Oftentimes "thanks" came in the form of giving gifts, called "potlatch" by the Northwestern tribes and "giveaways" by Oklahoma Indians. Our generosity was so feared by non-Indians that giving things away was viewed as a type of insanity by the Europeans. Hence giveaways were out-lawed, and offenders suffered arrest. Imagine, arrested for giving things away to show your appreciation! Of course these days it's no longer considered illegal to give away your possessions, and the custom flourishes in many different tribes, but the reason always remains the same: to give thanks. When I was younger I'd sit in awe and watch Osage giveaways lasting all afternoon. No one can have a giveaway like an Osage, because when the Osage do something, they go all the way, no holding back. I couldn't imagine American Indian people with so much money. I always associated being American Indian with being poor. Of course that image would have died anyway, with the flashing lights of the casinos that blink on many reservations, including the Osage. However, here there are only words to express my thanks—no shawls or blankets, no groceries or horses.

I wish to first say *mvto* (pronounced *mado*, it means "thanks" in Mvskoke) to all the great people in the state of Oklahoma who helped me fulfill my dream. Besides all the people specifically mentioned in this book, there are several persons deserving additional recognition. My humblest gratitude, love, and thanks to my sister Kathy Supernaw, for showing me the love of a sister and helping me find order in the chaos. Aunt Sara Katherine (my dad's only sibling) is my only living relative from those old days, and she provided me with stories about my dad and mom, and my grandparents Charles and Carrie, along with some old pictures.

Another important "thanks" goes to Dee Stribling and his organization, In His Name Ministries. Although Dee recently passed on, his wife continues his work, offering assistance to women and children affected by domestic violence in Bethany, Oklahoma. If Dee hadn't compassionately picked me up off those deserted steps in front of Wheeling Avenue Church, well, I'm still not sure what might have happened. Yet in spite of Dee's assistance, and considerable time spent on the polished wooden pews of Christian churches, I've chosen to reflect on my past from the perspective of the Native American Church (NAC) and its teachings. Although I've experienced religion in a variety of cultural formats, the one with the most impact on my life has been the NAC. Throughout my life the NAC has continued to provide me with a link to our traditional leaders and ancient teachings since I was not raised in a traditional American Indian family. The NAC remains my primary tie to all my relatives, as well as to all those who have gone on. Kenneth Anquoe was instrumental in providing me with an important link to ancient teachings, those within the church as well as those of his tribe.

The controversy over the NAC during the 1960s and 1970s revolved around the use of peyote as a holy sacrament. The story of freedom from persecution and of the final recognition (with certain restrictions) of the Native American Church as a legitimate Native religion culminated only in 1992. This legendary fight for religious freedom is documented in a video called *The Peyote Road*, a 1993 Kifaru Production. My old friends Reuben Snake and Johnny Whitecloud, along with a host of others, give details in this video about the evolution of NAC ceremonies and the resulting legal persecution that led ultimately to the courts, resulting in the Indian Religious Freedom Act of 1992. The 1996 book *One Nation under God—the Triumph of the Native American Church* provides a more detailed account, compiled and edited by Huston Smith and Reuben Snake. Reuben died in 1993, and his church meeting filled the local gym.

Each officially recognized chapter of the NAC has several road-men, who are frequently traditional healers in their tribes. A roadman is roughly equivalent to a priest or minister—in essence a religious leader. To acquire the status of roadman one usually studies for many years, learning the duties of keeping the fire and hearth, perfecting the art of drumming, and memorizing numerous NAC songs in a variety of American Indian languages. The NAC is, after all, a pan-Indian religion crossing tribal bound-aries. Roadmen are responsible for overseeing every aspect of an NAC meeting, from its initial conception to extinguishing the fire, respectfully removing the sand altar, and dismantling the tipi. NAC meetings last all night and well into the next day. They are time consuming and costly and require detailed organiza-tion to obtain a meeting place, wood, food, and the holy peyote sacrament—referred to as "Medicine." Because of their complex-ity NAC meetings are not held on a regular basis, but rather by special request. Therefore a meeting always has a reason, and to have a meeting one must approach a roadman with tobacco to ask for help in sponsoring it. Howard Williams and Marcellus Williams were very important roadmen in my life. Their words, songs, and teachings will forever echo in my heart, especially when I hear the heartbeat of the earth as carried in the sounds of the water drum.

Not all tribes have official NAC chapters, and for reasons in-volving my employment with the government, I was required to obtain an official NAC membership card. I wish to thank Howard and Rosina Williams for providing me membership in the Caddo NAC chapter, since my tribe did not have a recognized chapter.

In addition to roadmen, traditional healers have helped me learn the specific beliefs of the Muscogee (Creek). Phillip Deere and Marcellus Williams performed traditional healings for me, in addition to the blessings I received in the NAC.

Thanks also go to the old Mel gang, especially Lynn Goodman, for his unconditional support. Jim Strain was the *Haymaker* newspaper editor and helped with the details of the Mel. Steve Bridwell, the *Haymaker* photographer, took pictures of the pageant and its contestants.

I offer my sincere appreciation to the Miss Oklahoma pageant personnel and to the Spencer Family, including Barrett, Gaye, Deidei, and Bonnie. Although Toni has passed away, she certainly faced a challenge in making a polished lady out of me, and she may not have been entirely successful. Bob McCormack was the official pageant photographer for many years. After his death in 2003 his son John gave the McFarlin Library at the University of Tulsa Bob's entire collection (over five tons of photographic negatives and five hundred cameras), gathered over his sixty-eight-year career. I wish to thank my alma mater Tulsa University and Marc Carlson, from the Special Collections at McFarlin Library, for giving me permission to use the pictures Bob took of me as a pageant contestant and throughout my year as Miss Oklahoma. The one picture Bob didn't take is the one of my father and me dancing together at my Oklahoma City powwow. I am grateful that Robin Kickingbird, from the *Oklahoman* (OPUBCO Communications Group), searched that paper's archives to find one taken in 1971 by its photographer. Joy Harjo, Minisa Crumbo Halsey, and Jane Ann Jayroe Peterson also gave me encouragement and support in my effort to publish my story.

Finally, I wish to thank the Wordcraft Circle of Native Writers and the Native Writer's Circle of the Americas for providing a support network for new writers like myself. Special thanks to Geary Hobson for his never-ending encouragement and for the time and trouble he took to comment constructively on my manuscript. When I needed to negotiate that huge hurdle between drafts by cutting out anecdotes and developing a stronger story line, I got editing assistance from Jessica Walker, an undergraduate senior from Oklahoma University working toward a career in publishing. Editors like her are a necessity to writers, and she has helped me further develop my craft.

In re-creating my past, I have used dialogue. These words are my best recollection of what was said at the time. All my experiences have been woven together, forming my personal star-burst pattern, to be viewed by all and understood by those who read between the stitches.

FAMILY GENEALOGY

In the world of the American Indian one is expected to give information about ancestry. A genealogy chart is included at the end of this section to provide a visual summary. Both my parents have passed away: Mom in 1984 and Dad in 1997. Rise Supernaw Proctor, the daughter of Bill Jr. and Irene Supernaw, is our family historian. She provided me with abundant information to help straighten out all those famous Supernaw stories of Northeastern Oklahoma. The original family name was the French word *suprenant*, meaning "surprising" or "amazing." This fact puts to rest all the stories about us earning our name by gnawing on bones to survive the harsh Northern winters (hence the name Supergnaw). The area south of Montreal was the original homeland of the Suprenants, and there are still Suprenants there to this day.

Isaiah Supernan, our first ancestor to show the name change, was born in 1817 in Quebec and died in Ottawa, Oklahoma, in 1894. Isaiah married Calista Robert, and they had seven children. John Webster Supernan (the youngest of seven) was born in 1862 in New York, and he married Sarah Wilson Sharpless from Kansas. Together they had five children: William J. Sr., Jesse A., Josephine E., Charles L., and Frank E. Most of the clan came to Oklahoma from Kansas during the early 1900s, although my grandfather Charles returned to attend high school at Haskell in 1918.[1]

My grandfather Charles (and his brothers and sisters) spelled their names "Supernaw." No one can say how the *n* became a *w*, although there are lots of stories about bad spellers and bad writing once they moved into Oklahoma. But that's how it all began, or so I'm told.

My paternal grandfather was Charles L. Supernaw, who was born on December 27, 1899, and died on July 4, 1956. For those interested in the ancestry of my second cousin, the country singer Doug Supernaw, his father is Irwin Ray Supernaw, the son of Jesse A. Supernaw and Rube Vera Grammer. Other famous family relations include John W. Supernaw's son, William (Bill) Sr., who married Maude (Tall Chief) Thompson, who was the last name-giver for the Quapaw tribe (from the Quapaw Tall Chiefs, not the Osage Tall Chiefs). Maude was the daughter of Louis Angel, better known as Kihekah Steh (Tall Chief, 1845–1918, and Wah Sis tah Claremore, Osage Indian). Kihekah Steh, the last hereditary Quapaw chief, was also the tribal *wapina* or medicine man, its spiritual leader and giver of names. William (Bill) Jr. married Irene McMurtrie, and they had four children: William III (Kugee), Carol Jean, Rise (Supernaw) Proctor, and Thomas. Kugee's business, Supernaw's Indian Store, made the Supernaw name famous in Oklahoma. His son Kywin used to play football for the Detroit Lions. Other Quapaw relatives and Kihekah Steh descendants include Lawrence Supernaw Jr. and Elnora Ann Supernaw. Their grandfather was William (Bill) Sr.

The maternal side of our "Supernaw" name begins with Sarah Wilson. Her parents were Anderson Wilson (born 1866, in Ohio) and Katy Ann Nathan (born 1868, in Wisconsin). Katy's parents were Nathan (no surname given, but he was a Wisconsin Munsee Indian) and Sabella Caleb (born 1817, in Canada). Anderson's parents were Joseph Wilson and "Cha Chah nah ha quais" or "Muck quah." Muck quah moved with the New York Indians to the Seneca Reservation in Southeast Kansas after the Civil War of 1860–65. Her name sounds amazingly like the word for "bear" in Ojibwe, and since our Munsee ancestors are listed on the Enrollment List of Chippewa and Delaware-Munsee living in Franklin County, Kansas, in 1900, it's not too hard to imagine one of them having an Ojibwe-sounding name, especially since the Munsees formerly lived on the Thames River in Kent County, Ontario, Canada. The original Munsee homelands were the upper Delaware valley in New Jersey, Pennsylvania, and New York. Pressures from white settlers forced them to leave their ancestral lands, and after a brief stay in Ohio they migrated to Canada around 1792 under the supervision of Moravian missionaries. The Munsee tribe was moved from Leavenworth, where their people had settled in 1837 among the Delaware. There they joined some migrant Ojibwas from Swan Creek and Black River, traveling eastward to lands reserved for them in Franklin County, Kansas. Some Ojibwa bands had already settled there under the leadership of "Esh-ton-o-quot" (Clear Sky).

✳ ✳ ✳

My dad's mother was Carrie Derrisaw, a Muscogee (Creek), born in Eufaula, Oklahoma, in 1903.[2] Her parents were William (Tuxey) Derrisaw and Polly Barnette.[3] Carrie and Charles married in 1921 and moved to Seminole, Oklahoma. They had two children: John (my dad), born in 1924, and Sara Katherine (Bourgeois), born in 1939.[4] They moved to Hominy from Seminole, Oklahoma, after Dad enlisted in 1942 and lived there until 1952. Then they bought a little house in Wynona, just north of Hominy, where they lived until Grandpa Charles Supernaw died in 1956 from a heart attack suffered when a fire started from stray fireworks on the Fourth of July, when Oklahoma is especially hot and dry. He and his family were trying to put the fire out by beating it with gunnysacks. He fell, and when Sara got to him he was gray and breathing his last. Grandma Carrie flagged down a passing car, which took them to the hospital, but by the time they got there he was dead.[5] After his death Grandma Carrie moved to Ardmore and lived with Dad's new family while Sara stayed an additional year so she could graduate from Wynona High School. In 1960 Grandma Carrie bought a little house in Tulsa so she and

Sara could live alone. Sara graduated from nursing school, got married, and moved to Texas in 1963. I had been isolated from Grandma Carrie for a few years, but we were reunited when she moved to Tulsa, because it was easy to get to her house.

Carrie's father was William (Willie) Derrisaw. He had four wives (serial monogamy) and ten children, only six of them surviving to adulthood. Willie was a farmer living in a little town named Fame, west of Eufaula, when he married Polly Barnette. They had two children, my grandmother Carrie and Lydia, who died as an infant. In 1907, when Carrie was only four years old, Polly died, probably from tuberculosis since there was a lot of it at that time. When Polly died, Willie married Polly's sister Susie.[6] Susie only lived eighteen months after their marriage, but she had a daughter named Judy. Susie also probably died from tuberculosis.

Carrie's Grandpa Barnette was a Baptist preacher and was more well-to-do than the Derrisaws. He preached in Mvskoke at a Muscogee (Creek) church in the country west of Dustin, Oklahoma. The Muscogee (Creek) sang in their language with no musical accompaniment. The women and children sat on one side of the room and the men on the other. One woman sang first, and then the others joined in. One man started singing first, and then the other men joined in. They also sang familiar church hymns in Mvskoke rather than English.

After the death of Susie, Willie married a white woman by the name of Mae, but she and their baby died during childbirth. Then he married Bessie, a marriage that lasted until she died in 1934. Bessie was the mother of his other children: Felix, Annie, Freland, Reo (also called Babe), Ben, and RosaAnna. Two died in childhood of the "summer complaint," which is known today as infantile diarrhea. Felix was two, and Annie was nine months old. Reo and Freland reached adulthood and married. Willie died on July 2, 1952, after a series of strokes and was buried in the family cemetery, deep in the overgrown countryside on his allotted land. His funeral was in Mvskoke since most of the Muscogee (Creek) in that area didn't or wouldn't speak English.

They sang in the traditional call-and-response style, where one person begins singing, and others join in.

After a minor stroke in 1969, Grandma Carrie received a pacemaker but had a major stroke in 1975. She was paralyzed on one side and couldn't speak. From that time on she wasn't sure who anyone was, mistaking her son (John) for her husband (Charles). While staying in a nursing home she developed breast cancer, which metastasized to her liver and caused her death.

When Grandma Carrie's half brother Freland married Lucille, an Osage, he completed the circle of Osage relatives, because there are Osage in-laws on both sides of my family (Muscogee and Munsee).

To complicate my genealogy there is even a Quapaw-Kiowa in-law connection back to Kenneth Anquoe, because his wife, Mary Helen Williams Bradshaw, was the daughter of Mary Thompson Williams (daughter of Maude Tall Chief Thompson Supernaw). Kenneth and Mary had one child, William Kenneth Anquoe. William Kenneth's great-grandmother Maude Tall Chief Thompson married a Supernaw, and Anita Anquoe (Kenneth's sister) married Melvin George, an Uchi Creek. So there's a Kiowa–Muscogee (Creek) connection. Confused? Well, so am I. But that's Oklahoma. You can't believe how many times I've asked my sister Kathy to explain to me once again why I'm not Quapaw, or at least Osage. Growing up we just recognized each other as family.

* * *

My mom's side is simple only because of a lack of information. Her family name was Cameron, and her dad, Stanley, had always farmed just north of Hominy, just as his father, Albert, had. The Camerons were originally from Scotland, but they blended in with the assortment of people living in the area. They were farmers and ranchers, self-sufficient folks. Grandpa died of prostate cancer in 1976. Grandma Cameron died in 1952 from breast cancer. Mom's maternal family name was Heacock, and they were of English origin. The Heacock family can be traced to Joseph H. Heacock (born May 31, 1860) and Lucy Annie Baer (a.k.a. Moore and Morse). The original Heacock (Jon Heacock) migrated to the United States from England aboard the immigration ship *Three Sisters*, in 1680. Upon arriving he settled in Pennsylvania, and some of his grandchildren moved to Iowa. Joseph H. Heacock moved from Iowa to Oklahoma as part of the infamous land rush. Shirley Heacock Bloodsworth helped me unravel our Heacock lineage.

Adopted relatives, Indian way, are a completely different matter. American Indians have always adopted outsiders, and individual tribes all have their own ceremonies, as well as traditions within the Native American Church. Adoption forges new responsibilities and kinship ties, uniting tribes in a unique fashion with a multiplicative effect. For example, when Uncle Marcellus Williams adopted my sister as niece, he inherited me too! I can't begin to list the relatives we have through him, because Marcellus called so many people of all religions his relatives. The same thing happened when Rosina Williams took my sister Kathy as a "friend." In Caddo ways a "friend" bond is stronger than the bond between sisters, and my sister now has obligations toward Rosina's children and grandchildren. Such an adoption meant that Kathy immediately inherited Rosina's immediate family, and I inherited them too. Rosina's husband, Howard, took a special interest in taking care of my son, Mekko, and me. I don't know all of my Caddo "friends," but I always get a warm reception when I visit, even from people I've never met before. The relatives I gained from being adopted by Kenneth Anquoe as a daughter include his brothers, Jack, Leonard, Gerald, and James (Ducky), and his sisters, Margerie, Mary Ann, and Anita and their families. This type of genealogy doesn't get any easier either, because the longer I stay in the church and go to meetings, the more relatives I accumulate. My family has grown so huge that it would be impossible to name all the members. The common phrase "we're all related" is truer than one might imagine in Oklahoma.

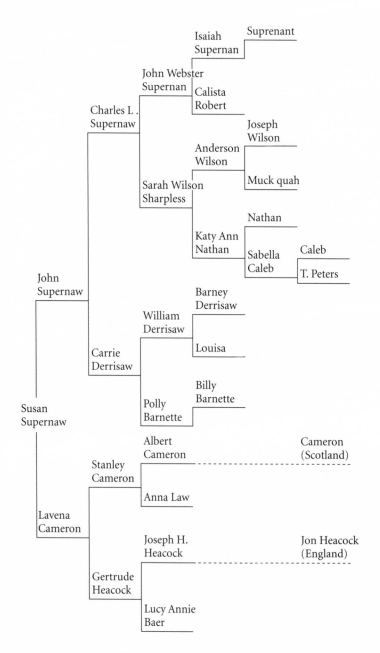

Susan Supernaw Family Genealogy Chart

MUSCOGEE DAUGHTER

1

Blessings Inside a Tipi

I gaze out the small window at the patchwork patterns of ground. I love flying in a plane, soaring above Tulsa like a hawk high in the Oklahoma sky. I'm coming home, and I know people will be waiting. Looking into my compact mirror I quickly comb my hair and then dust on some powder. I straighten my crown and re-anchor it with a few more bobby pins to prevent it from sliding in my fine, thin hair.

I finish my primping, and everyone is waiting for me. My body-guard offers his hand and helps me out of my seat. I straighten my dress and touch my crown to make sure it is still secure while my chaperone gathers my bags and takes my purse. I need both hands for greeting people. I wave at the people gathered outside and lead my entourage through the airport gate.

People line the halls as far as I can see. I smile and wave as everyone starts clapping. My ankles wobble, so I pause to accustom myself to high heels. Finally achieving balance, I begin my promenade through the terminal, waving, smiling, and blowing a few kisses to the soldiers dressed in uniform. With all this attention you might think I'm Miss America, but I'm not.

But I am Miss Oklahoma and a presidential scholar. I have two names: my birth name and my American Indian name, still unearned. I'll find out tonight if I have finally earned my Indian name.

"What's in a name?" I recall Shakespeare's claim: "That which we call a rose by any other name would smell as sweet."[1] I instantly disagree, remembering that the old ones taught us that there is power in a name. Only special people name children, and they take great care in finding the right name. Then there are names too sacred to be spoken often. My Indian name is not any of those. Yet it's not like my other nicknames: Jimmy, Bozo, Beef Noodle, and Super Sue.

I remember names kids chanted to me as a child, puns on my family name.[2] "Is Susie Super? Naw!" Each time they repeated it I vowed, "They'll eat those words." Now I notice some of them are here, fifteen years later, calling "Susie, Susie," and waving. I give them a thumbs-up. They are flattered by the special attention and return the gesture while cheering my name: "Susie, Susie." I laugh a little because I don't feel justified, I feel like a fraud. Everyone is so amazed at my achievements in mixing beauty with brains that no one suspects the awful truth: I am ashamed to go home; and when home, I am afraid to sleep. Yet I'm here because shame and fear serve as the catalysts in my life, forcing me to do things I never thought possible and to seek help from people I might never have known.

Standing in front of cheering fans feels so good that I stop at the door to imprint the moment in my memory. I wave and thank everyone, reach for my escort's arm, hurry into a familiar blue car.

My Kiowa mentor, Kenneth Anquoe, is driving, so I slide in the front seat.[3] I begin talking rapidly about my trip. Kenneth holds up his hand for silence and leans sideways to whisper in my ear, "We have planned a special meeting for you. It is time for thanks and your blessing." I sit speechless, trying to calm my thoughts and clear my mind. Why is he whispering when no one else is in the car? Have I earned my name?

We ride in a strange silence since Kenneth seems reluctant to talk. He puts his finger to his lips whenever I talk, so I distract myself by taking off my crown. We pull up next to a red brick house with a small tipi out back. He whispers, "It's time for you

to gather your personal strength. Now, go inside and change."
I grab my bag and head inside the house, kicking off my heels
and soon ruining my nylons. It's easier to change from elegant
to regular than it is to go from regular to elegant. It takes just a
few minutes to wash my face, comb back my hair, and change
clothes, but when I return outside no one is around. Wrapped
in my yellow shawl I walk a short distance downhill and stand
quietly beside the tipi, waiting for permission to enter. The flap
door opens slightly, and I bend down and slip quietly inside,
taking the first space I see.

Sitting cross-legged, I watch the flames feed at the split timbers,
providing energy for the fire, this tongue of God. The poles of
the tipi fade, darkened by the jumping flames in the center. The
rhythmic drumbeat echoes. In the west sits the roadman, the
leader of the meeting. Kenneth kneels, holding in one hand a
beaded wooden staff, a small bundle of fresh sage wrapped in
red yarn, and a fan of dark water-bird feathers wrapped in white
leather. With the other hand he shakes a gourd rattle. Beginning
the next set of songs he shakes his gourd faster to increase the
tempo. Following his lead, the drummer immediately adjusts
to the new rhythm, spraying drops of water off the vibrating
drum hide.

I hum along with a song that honors the creator. My thoughts,
like everyone else's, focus on the purpose of the meeting. We
are all one now in our minds and prayers. Our prayers circle
the tipi and then shoot up through the smoke hole at the top.
From there they go directly into the heavens, pushed east by the
drumbeat and carried to the stars by the piercing sound of the
eagle whistle, a polished wing bone with a hole drilled into its
large end, its marrow removed.

The song ends quickly, and a new one begins, a song asking
the creator to give us blessings. Tonight I will receive a blessing.
During this Native American Church (NAC) meeting the tipi
seems to expand, growing during the night with the power of
the medicine, songs, and prayers. The tipi will shrink again in the

morning light, but now my mind expands with it. The roadman finishes his song with a quivering of the gourd.

I don't recognize the next song, so I watch as pulsating flames lick the darkness. Grandfather Peyote Chief sits on his miniature Indian blanket in the center of the sand altar. My eyes gaze at the crescent-shaped mound of glowing coals that follows the curved lines of the sacred altar, and I feel contentment.[4] Outside I hear the eagle whistle blown by an elder to the four directions.

The fourth song, a water blessing song, reminds me that I need to get up after the water is brought inside in order to receive my blessing. After the sound of the rattle Kenneth sets aside his staff and bundle of sage and rests his water-bird fan on top of both.

Kenneth picks up an eagle-feather fan and his fringed cedar bag. He solemnly tosses holy cedar on the fire, and sparks dance in the air as Grandfather Cedar sizzles on the coals. When a purifying smoke rises, Kenneth prays in Kiowa. He fans the smoke in the four directions and then briefly holds the staff, sage, and fan in the cedar smoke so they too can be blessed.

He calls for midnight water with a nod to a woman who quietly leaves the tipi. She fills a hand-painted bucket with water that was cooling in the damp night air and waits quietly outside. The drummer swirls the water drum gently to dampen the stretched hide. Slowly a beat begins, changing tones as the drummer moves his thumb across the drum hide. The beat blends with the gourd and vibrates inside me. Sharing the oneness around me, I feel connected to all the people in the tipi. Although they pray for my happiness my heart still aches from hidden pain so great that my spirit remains wounded.

"Why has my life been filled with so much pain and suffering?" I ask the fire. A flaming timber explodes, causing the fire to cackle and burn brighter. I look into the glowing embers and behold a scene from long ago.

2

Jimmy

On the day I was born, November 11, 1950, a cold north wind made it feel like winter instead of fall. Gray skies and thunderhead clouds greeted our small wooden farmhouse at dawn. An old blanket was hung over a cracked window, and towels were pushed under the mismatched bottom of the door to help stop the chilly breezes. Concerned because her birthing contractions were two weeks early, my mom, Lavena Cameron, quietly gathered some clothes and personal belongings in a long bag made from an old, colorful Pendleton blanket.

After packing she turned her attention to her three young children. She said to the oldest, "Louise, help your sister get ready to go to Papaw's."[1]

"It's just across the way. We don't need no coats." Almost five, Louise picked a coat from the pile and yelled, "Judy, come here right now."

"I'm going to Tulsa, so you'll have to watch your sisters."

"I wanna come too. Mamaw don't need me."[2]

"Mamaw's been sick. Besides, I'm going to the hospital." Mom put her hands on her big stomach. Louise had seen that twice before, and each time a new sister had come into the family.

"What about Dad's new job?" Louise asked. He hadn't been around much the last couple of years because he'd been a student at Oklahoma University.

"He's been offered a part-time job, but it's not around here."

1. Lavena Cameron, Susie's mother, stands outside her parents' house north of Hominy, Oklahoma, in 1946. *Photographer unknown, from the Supernaw family album.*

Mom looked around to see if she'd forgotten anything and then picked up Kathy. She hurried, knowing Dad was warming up the car.

"Will that keep him from yelling when he drinks?"

Judy came running up. Louise tried to help Judy with her coat, but Judy grabbed the coat and tugged on it until her big sister let go of it and Judy fell backward on the floor. Shocked, Judy jumped up and began hitting Louise with her coat. Laughing, Louise used her right arm as a shield against Judy's assault. As they continued their fight with the coat Mom pulled a vest over Kathy's sweater and handed her a miniature pillow.

After Judy put on her coat Louise slipped on her jacket and tried to grab Judy's hand, but Judy pulled it away defiantly and ran outside. Louise ran after her while Mom closed the door. A sharp wind blasted their exposed faces with sleet as they crossed the road to Grandpa Stanley's house.

2. Susie's maternal grandparents, Gertrude Cameron, with her granddaughters Judy and C. Louise, and Stanley Cameron, standing with their horses during the summer of 1949. *Photographer unknown, from the Supernaw family album.*

The old farmhouse had a rusty screen porch, and a two-story barn stood behind the sagging clothesline strung between two cedar trees. A variety of sleeping flowers formed a neat border around the house, and a wisp of smoke rose from the chimney. Chasing each other the girls ran inside, slamming the door. Mom was greeted by Grandma Gertrude's fatigued smile and hug, while her loving arms reached for the infant Kathy. "Don't you worry none about us. Now get goin."

Mom waved goodbye. My dad, John Supernaw, was waiting anxiously in an old beige Ford. Mom threw her stuffed bag in the back and flopped into the front seat of the car, glad it was warm. The radio blared out a Hank Williams song, and she began singing along.[3] Dad joined in, and she smiled, thinking of better times.

Dad's family lived in Hominy, but they weren't from that area. Dad's mom, Carrie, a Muscogee (Creek), had been raised deep

3. Susie's paternal grandmother, Carrie Derrisaw (*right*), standing on the steps at Haskell High School in 1918. The girl on the left is unknown. *Photographer unknown, from the Sara Supernaw Bourgeois family album.*

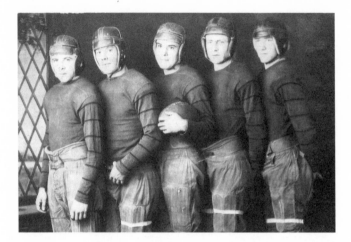

4. Susie's paternal grandfather, Charles Supernaw (*middle, holding a football*), with his Haskell football teammates in 1919. *Photographer unknown, from the Sara Supernaw Bourgeois family album.*

in the country west of Eufaula, on the former Muscogee (Creek) Reservation.[4] In the early days of Oklahoma statehood, American Indians were not allowed to go to school with white children, so Carrie went to Eufaula Indian Boarding School through the eighth grade, from 1908 to 1916.[5] She went to high school at Haskell in Lawrence, Kansas.

Of all the students she met at Haskell she chose Charles Supernaw, a Delaware Munsee football player from Kansas, as her boyfriend.

They married shortly after graduation from high school and settled in Seminole, Oklahoma, to be close to Carrie's family. Besides farming Charles worked seasonally in the oil fields with his brothers in Osage County, while Carrie tended the gardens and children at home.

Dad was fourteen years older than his sister, Sara. He liked to chase her around with his pet black snake, which he'd captured in the family garden but kept close by just to scare her. During the

5. Carrie Derrisaw Supernaw, holding her new baby, John Supernaw, with Sarah Wilson Supernaw, John's paternal grandmother, in 1924. *Photographer unknown, from the Sara Supernaw Bourgeois family album.*

6. Susie's father, John Supernaw, stands between his parents, Charles and Carrie, outside their home near Seminole, Oklahoma, in 1936. *Photographer unknown, from the Sara Supernaw Bourgeois family album.*

7. John Supernaw while visiting home on leave from his service in the U.S. Navy, 1943. *Photo by Charles Supernaw, from the Supernaw family album.*

summer he stayed with his uncle Jesse in Skiatook and worked with his dad, Charles, in the oil fields.

Grandma Carrie was devastated when her only son, my father, joined the U.S. Navy after graduating from high school in 1942 and working with his father over the summer.[6] He dreamed of being on an aircraft carrier and flying navy planes, but because he was an American Indian he knew he wasn't fighter pilot material. So he turned to his second love, radio communications, enlisting and attending NT School, a navy school for signalmen in San Diego, California.[7] He tried to be "Supe," just one of the guys, and worked his way through the ranks to become a signalman, first class.[8] He was assigned to several Pacific-based LSTs, including Flotilla 7, USS LST-466, and USS LST-474.[9] He also served on the USS LSM, Flotilla 13, and on the USS *Blatchford* (AP153).[10] In addition he served on various amphibious bases, where he was torpedoed at least twice. Dad was in combat in New Guinea, the Admiralties, and Hala Ma Hara in the Philippines, participating in over thirteen invasions. Besides receiving the Victory Medal and the Good Conduct Medal, he was awarded the Operational Star for Okinawa Gunto and the Asiatic-Pacific Campaign Medal with three stars.[11] He was discharged from Okinawa, Japan, in 1946.

His war adventures caused him to hate the Japanese, although not the Germans, but this wasn't because of Pearl Harbor or because he fought the Japanese in the Pacific. Dad hated the Japanese because so many people told him he looked Japanese. It grated on his nerves to hear his shipmates marvel at his similarly dark skin, straight black hair, and the small epicanthic fold over his brown eyes. The mere thought of any similarities between him and the enemy offended him. He was an American Indian, and any talk of similarities between him and the enemy would result in a bloody fistfight. Looking Japanese to others forced him to identify himself as an American Indian when he just wanted to be one of the guys.

Dad was especially thankful to come home alive and in one piece. When he returned he was a warrior, and warriors are highly respected in our Indian community. The warrior society from the old days now consisted of modern war veterans and their families.[12] Instead of making him wish to participate in traditional honors, however, his war experience left him sure that he wasn't going to do anything Indian because it was a white world, and he might as well act like a white man to live in it.

The Osage Reservation was dotted with families living among the Osages even though they were not Osage.[13] It was hard on Dad being a non-Osage Indian living among the Osage because even though he and the Osage knew he wasn't Osage, non-Indians didn't know the difference. Mom's mother, Gertrude, was English, and her father, Stanley, was Scottish. Both were clueless about the differences among tribes and thought of American Indians as lazy drunkards. So Dad experienced the worst of both worlds in discrimination.

Mom and Dad met because she worked as a secretary for a lawyer named Mr. Comer, who lived next door to Carrie and Charles. Mom had just graduated from Hominy High School and didn't feel the same way toward American Indians as most of the non-Indian population and was always nice to them. When Dad was discharged he moved to Hominy, but he wasn't planning on staying very long, because he wanted to use the GI bill to get an education.[14] He wanted to go to school at Oklahoma University and become a chemical engineer.

Although they met in town the Hominy airfield was where they really got to know each other through their common passion: flying. Ever since she was a child Mom had loved airplanes and constantly dreamed of flying. When her chores were completed she'd run north through the pastures beyond her family's farm to a small airfield nearby with a single runway. She sometimes worked at the airfield on weekends, at first cleaning, then keeping books and filing. Dad loved airplanes too and did some part-time maintenance on the radios and private planes while he dreamed of getting his pilot's license.

Dad joked about marrying Mom after the war, saying she couldn't run very fast and was easy to catch. She didn't mean to get pregnant, but since she didn't have access to birth control, it just happened. Having babies was part of the postwar celebration: lots of young women were getting married pregnant. Times were crazy, but at least he had married her, even if theirs was a shotgun wedding.

* * *

That was four years and three girls ago. No one then knew the gender of a child until its birth, but both Dad and Mom prayed that I'd be a boy, someone to carry on the family name. Clutching the door handle Mom cringed, feeling the familiar pain of contractions. She was concerned because she was scheduled to have a cesarean for this baby. But nothing was planned for a two-week-early arrival. The Tulsa hospital was still miles away, and the pains were starting to come closer and closer.

As they neared the northern city limits of Tulsa a single train whistle blasted through the stillness, and the crossing bars blocked the car's path. Dad turned right, desperately searching the buildings for signs of life. A small sign said "Hospital," with an arrow pointing toward a single-lane road with huge oaks lining both sides. The winding road led to a brick building with the words "Flower Hospital."[15] The on-duty nurse looked shocked as a disheveled man suddenly burst into her quiet world, shouting, "I need help!" More disturbing was that he was carrying a woman in labor.

"This is a private hospital."

Dad ignored her. Frustrated, he yelled to the nurse, "*Please* get the doctor on call."

The nurse understood unexpected deliveries. She reluctantly called the doctor, while Dad carried Mom down the hall to the first empty room. When the nurse arrived in the room my head was crowning. Much to her own surprise, the same nurse who had tried to refuse us help ended up delivering me. By the time the doctor arrived Dad had disappeared, and I was cradled in Mom's loving arms. Mom was having some internal bleeding and was weak. The doctor gave Mom data for a birth certificate and then said, "Go to your own doctor. You gave us quite a scare."[16]

A few hours later Dad returned, smelling of alcohol. Mom

greeted him and said, "The doctor said we should go on to Tulsa or Claremore IHS."

"I'll drop you off. I've gotta get back to school. I'm not about to be a farmer. I just don't have time for all these girls."

"My parents have always helped us take care of them. Your parents help too. Why leave your family?"

"I'm sure our parents will still help with the kids. Maybe we can leave them. I have to get an education, and now's the only chance I'll get."

Shocked, Mom couldn't focus on anything except his cold-hearted attitude toward his children. She could see no promising future unless she had a son. Dad dropped us off, promising to return the next weekend. During the quiet journey home Dad couldn't help being amused by one reoccurring thought: "Born on Veterans Day, should've been a boy. He would've made a glorious warrior." Instead I was just another mouth to feed.

When Dad returned the next week, Mom knew what to expect. While the girls slept a burning kerosene lamp blended with the morning light. Visiting for the weekend from Norman, Oklahoma, Dad coldly said, "We're leaving. I have to get back to school." Mom cried softly while Grandpa Stanley and Grandma Gertrude stared blankly. After several silent moments he continued, "We just need some help. Can you keep the newborn?"

Grandma was flattered that my middle name was hers, appreciating the family connection, but she was still recovering from a partial mastectomy.[17] She asked, "How long are you talkin' about? You know I'm sick."

"Just for a few months, 'til we get settled. We'll come back over Christmas break." Dad looked sincere.

"Well, if it's just gonna be a couple of months," she reluctantly agreed.

Mom hugged her and whispered, "Thanks, Mama." Grandma Gertrude patted her on the back while a single tear trickled down her cheek. "It's okay, child."

* * *

My parents left with three girls in tow. Mom brought the girls back home for Christmas, and although Dad came too, he spent most his time with his family in Wynona. Grandma Gertrude was getting sick again, but she hid it from everyone. Mom left again in January, and only a few days later Grandma's familiar cancer pains grew worse. During the day she'd lie on her rumpled bed with me beside her, piling old pillows around the edge so I wouldn't fall off. Together we watched the sun travel the skies from dawn to sunset. She spent most of her time sleeping, always near exhaustion, but when she woke she'd hold me as close as possible to her breast. It was her only breast, since the hospital doctor had taken the other one. She never really understood why. She only knew that she would rather die than return to that horrible hospital. There was no telling what part they might take next time. Somehow holding an infant made her feel whole again, like a complete woman. She smiled, fading in and out of sleep, relishing the warmth and the feel of my tiny body while our two hearts beat in unison.

When her tightened grip relaxed, Grandpa picked me up and changed my diaper. He placed me beside her again, giving me a bottle of milk or cold coffee. Grandpa was a man of the land, doing all the farm chores, and now had no one to help in the house. At least before, when Mom was around, he had extra help. Grandpa had no experience with infant care or child development. Once he tried to feed me some of Grandma's mush, but I spit it out. He thought I wasn't old enough to be eating, not that I didn't know how. Although he wasn't sure what to do, he was too proud to call Dad's parents for help. Lying there swaddled in blankets that smelled of her scent, I fell asleep beside Grandma Gertrude, only to wake and find her gone.

When Grandma Gertrude passed on, Mom immediately returned with my sisters. Grandpa said Grandma was happy because death had freed her from years of suffering. Mom might have been consoled about the loss of her mother, but she was aghast at her first sight of me. Having felt guilty for abandoning me in the first place, Mom now rushed me to the Indian Hospital. I remained there for three months while my tiny body tried to heal itself of rickets, scoliosis, and double pneumonia. Dad didn't stay around. When classes started in the fall he went back to school. Within a couple of years he had his son, Charles, named after his father, and that was all that mattered to him. It didn't even matter that my mom, even though they were still married, was not the boy's mother. While he was away from his family on the GI Bill he was evidently getting a lot more than an education.

✳ ✳ ✳

I slowly recovered and gained weight, eventually learned to walk. Although I had bad allergies and asthma, I grew strong from taking cod liver oil and eating lots of liver. I began running and playing with my sisters. Besides a little softball in the yard, one of my favorite games was Cowboys and Indians, but the way we played it the Indians won. Being the youngest I always ended up being the cowboy and got pretty good at dying when I was shot. When I wasn't a dying cowboy I was a secret superhero. I wore some old red tights with a blue T-shirt under my clothes. I'd wear an old pair of Mom's reading glasses and pretend I was like Clark Kent with his black-framed glasses, a superhero in disguise. After all I was a Supernaw, just a few letters away from Superman.[18] I convinced myself that someday I too would run faster than a speeding bullet and leap tall buildings with a single bound. After a while I figured out I wasn't going to be a superhero. The legend of Superman, like that of Santa Claus, died early in our family.

I felt bad about being so sick and always causing extra trouble for Mom, and the kids at church knew it. They teased me, saying, "You're not really one of the family, they adopted you." My eyes turned red as I fought back the tears. My family was all I had. One of the older kids said, "By your fourth birthday someone from the adoption place will visit, and if your parents don't want you, then they will take you back." Her ominous warning

8. *From left to right*: Judy, Kathy, Susie, and C. Louise Supernaw stand by the farmhouse in the fall of 1953. *Photo by Lavena Cameron, from the Supernaw family album.*

9. *From left to right*: Judy and Kathy stand with Susie before her boyish haircut in the fall of 1954. *Photo by Lavena Cameron, from the Supernaw family album.*

instantly improved my behavior immensely, while introducing a new fear in my heart. I could be taken away at any time, perhaps sold into slavery like Joseph in the Bible.[19]

I wanted to run and hide, but Louise, the almighty oldest, volunteered to help me with a disguise. "Since they'll be lookin' for a girl, I'll make you look like a boy." Out came the scissors, and soon all my hair was lying on the ground and my new look

was complete. Louise took me to the park and introduced me as
Jimmy, her baby brother. I liked being Jimmy. I played with the
other boys and found it more fun than girly games like paper
dolls. Mom was outraged when she saw me, and Louise really
got in trouble for cutting off my hair. I didn't think I looked
bad at all.

During the week of my fourth birthday, an elderly woman from
the church unexpectedly visited Mom on the farm. I thought she
had come to take me away, as predicted. I ran as fast as I could
across the road and into our two-story barn. Once inside I still
didn't feel safe enough, so I climbed up the ladder to the loft. I
looked down into the grain room, thinking it was a good hiding
place. I held out my arms and jumped down, sinking deep into
the grain. I moved some of the grain with my left arm before
glancing at a spot in front of me where the sun had leaked in.
I could see things moving in the grain, little heads and bodies
with lots of little legs. Corn beetles![20] I could feel them crawling
all over me. I started sobbing. Only after a flood of tears did I
convince myself that no one had ever died from the bite of a corn
beetle. But there was not just one beetle, there were thousands
of them, and I imagined their stinging bites turning poisonous
as they swarmed over my body.

I shook my head to get rid of the thought. I began to swim in
prefect breaststroke motions toward the side of the room. Each
stroke caused me to sink a little deeper into the grain, with those
creepy-crawly beetles getting closer to my face. By now I had the
dry taste of the corn in my mouth and corn dust up my nose.
I started sneezing and wheezing. The more I moved, the more
corn powder I stirred up, creating a noxious cloud around me.
My breaths became short and labored because of my asthma.
Finally touching the wall made me feel more comfortable.

I reached the lower portion of the door and tried to push it
open, but it was latched from the outside. Climbing to the top
of the grain didn't work because my movements cleared away

more grain, causing me to sink deeper. I was afraid I'd drown in that corn, and my thoughts turned to death.

I coughed between my sobs, wiping my eyes with my dirty sleeve. The shadows darkened as the hour grew late. I could barely see the other side of the room. I could hardly breathe, and it became difficult to keep my head out of the grain. Helplessness overwhelmed me as I wheezed and sobbed. I accepted my death and wondered if Grandma Gertrude was waiting for me in a cozy, warm haven, with fresh-churned butter and home-baked bread.

At first I felt surrounded in fog and closed my eyes to keep from being scared. I felt a faint breeze, so I opened one eye slightly and saw some of the fog clear to show a soft glowing light. I turned toward the light and opened both eyes widely, surprised to see a beautiful lady nearby. She was standing above the corn in a glow of soft yellowish light and wore a simple white dress with a nurse's hat. Her long black hair surrounded her peaceful smile, and I was overcome by a feeling of oneness. In her brown eyes I saw stars sparkling. It reminded me of the Muscogee creation story, when the earth mother throws water into the sky to create the stars. Suddenly I didn't feel alone, and I wasn't scared. Saying nothing she pulled a brown bottle out of her lower pocket. I thought of the bottles that the Indian Hospital gave me, filled with medicine. She smiled and returned the bottle to her pocket and then gestured with her lips to the east before slowing fading into the darkness. At first I thought I heard an eagle whistle blowing, but the more I strained to hear it, the more it sounded like a metal cowbell.

Hearing the outer barn door open, I started banging on the side wall because my mouth was too dry to yell. The door slowly opened. "Susie, how in the world did you get in here?" Grandpa extended his hand and pulled me out of the mass of grain. Grandpa and I had a special relationship, since he'd taken care of me since I was born. I knew he favored Judy for her spunk, but he always kept an extra eye out for me. I explained in gasp-

ing breaths what had happened. Calming me with a hug and pat
on the back, he said, "It's okay now. Nobody's gonna take you
away." Handing me the milk pail he added, "Catch your breath,
then get the milk." I wheezed while Grandpa made his special
mixture of feed for the cows, and then I started milking. When
the cows had been fed he looked at me seriously. "Susie, don't
tell no one about what happened."

"About hidin' and gettin' locked in?"

"Yeah. And about seeing the nurse."

"Was she a guardian angel or a spirit of the Corn Mother?"[21]

"I don't know about those things. I just don't want no one
to think you're crazy."

"Oh, okay." I never said anything else. Although nightmares
of biting bugs continued to haunt me, I never forgot the face of
the Beautiful Lady. I believed she was some sort of spirit guide
and wondered if I would ever see her again.

3

Bozo

Small farmhouses that had seen better days, dilapidated barns, and worn-out sheds dotted the landscape in our portion of Osage country. Lots of houses had no electricity, running water, or central gas heat. Growing up with these conditions made being poor seem normal, but in town the story was different.

It was hard not to notice the huge houses that looked like country clubs or hotels and knowing they were connected to the Osage Indian families with head rights (a method for measuring oil royalties).[1] The Osages weren't the only wealthy folks, as there were also plenty of white people who were well-to-do. They all lived on the "other side of Hominy." While they lived off what was under the land, on our side of Hominy we lived off the top of the land. We were farmers and knew the one basic principle of farming: the more you grew, the more you ate.

Dad got paid on Fridays and was supposed to give us some money for food, but he was never predictable. He always felt good with money in his pocket, so he'd stop by a bar on the way to our house, just to buy himself and his friends a drink. But he could never stop with one and often spent the entire evening in that smoke-filled bar, coming to visit with little or no money, or worse, not showing up at all. Mom always tried to put something on the table for us to eat on those Friday nights when he didn't come home. Mom fixed her famous bread soup: salted water with flour dumplings. Another Friday-night special, my personal favorite, was a ketchup sandwich. Occasionally there wasn't any bread or bread soup, and on those nights I drank "poor man's tea," which was hot water. Then I went to bed hungry and dreamed of warm houses and refrigerators packed full of delicious food.

✳ ✳ ✳

As for many American Indians of his generation Dad's self-image haunted him. The Bureau of Indian Affairs (BIA) and its schools caused plenty of inner conflict about being an American Indian, and both of his parents had attended BIA schools. But what is not generally understood is that ordinary white folks discriminated against Indians, especially on the reservation.[2] Dad attended school in Skiatook for a while when he lived with his uncle Jesse Supernaw and Jesse's son Irwin.[3] He hated it so much that he moved back to Seminole to go to high school. He only moved to Hominy to be with his mom and sister when he was discharged in 1946. After years of facing racial bias Dad would not speak his language or practice his cultural beliefs. He told us what he had been told countless times: "The only way to make it in this world is to forget about being Indian, marry a white person, and assimilate." This was the government's policy for dealing with the American Indian.[4]

Although Dad had fought in World War II, he was also a victim of another war, a war of cultural genocide initiated by the U.S. government against its Native populations.[5] That war left him between two worlds, so he drank in frustration and struck out in anger. He tried to be white, but non-Indians always pointed out that he was Indian. Somewhere along the way his values became distorted. He took his anger out on us, beating us physically. Maybe he hoped we'd run away so he wouldn't have to support us. Maybe the alcohol distorted his perception, causing violence to seem a normal way to feel alive. Instead of making me feel alive, his violence made me feel afraid. When I thought things couldn't get worse, he completely disappeared.

The town folks whispered that Dad was living with the moth-

10. Susie holds on tight while Judy takes her for a spin down the sidewalks of Hominy, 1956. *Photo by Lavena Cameron, from the Supernaw family album.*

er of his son, Charlie. After my parents divorced he moved to Holdenville with his new wife and son. When Grandpa Charles suddenly died of a heart attack, Grandma Carrie moved to live with Dad. I worried I'd never see her again. Only the animals on the farm provided any relief from my grief.

By this point Dad never came to visit, nor did he ever send any money. Things got worse for a couple of years, until a judge finally ordered Dad to give Mom child support checks. Even then he didn't always send the money, so Mom had to get a job.[6] Then and only then did our financial situation actually improve. But her getting a job meant we had to live in Tulsa during the week and come home on the weekends.

We shopped for clothes at the thrift store. Any clothes that needed sewing were stitched by hand since Mom didn't have a sewing machine. She only had one sewing pattern, and she made a special "small" version of it for me out of newspaper. After buying some calico material on sale she sewed us girls matching dresses for church.

Our church was located at the edge of town. I felt at home and liked the big warm rooms and indoor plumbing. But most of all I liked the food at the potluck lunch after services. One Sunday after the service I started thinking about the preacher's sermon on martyrs. He had poignantly asked how many of us would give our life for God. I'd never thought about it that way before. Church was more of a social event than a commitment for life. After several moments of quiet contemplation I decided I'd do whatever God asked, especially since He'd given me so much already. I felt a warm glowing light beside me, full of warmth and love, reminding me of the feeling I'd had when I saw the Beautiful Lady. I went forward the next week to affirm my faith and was baptized.

Before joining the church our family usually celebrated Christmas by drawing names. Mom gave each of us a quarter to buy a present for the sister whose name we drew. Everyone knew to get me a toy horse. We never really had those festive holiday meals we'd see in the magazines until those generous church folks helped us. Now Thanksgiving meant a big turkey with most of the trimmings, and Christmas meant a big ham and sometimes a little gift, when before it only meant vacation from school. I didn't mind being the church's charity project because the memory of hunger was too fresh.

Different people from the congregation often gave us clothing items. Being the youngest and smallest I received the clothes that no one else could wear or that no one else wanted. I didn't mind: I was just glad to get some new things to wear. The hardest things for me to wear were secondhand shoes. I've always had fat feet because of bunions. My sisters teased me: "You not only have yellow mouth, you've got 'moccasin feet.'"

Since moccasin feet were supposed to be flat feet, I'd hold up my pointed foot and say, "Silly billies, I don't have flat feet. Can't you see my beautiful arches?" Even Maria Tall Chief complimented me on my feet, which was, of course, the only time I ever received a compliment on my arches.[7] Leave it to a prima ballerina to notice. So officially my feet were not flat but fat. I spent many years forcing a wide foot into a narrow shoe, so most of the time my feet hurt. One year for Christmas I received two shoeboxes with strings laced across the top. I was the only one who didn't laugh. It became clear to me that moccasins were really the best because an outline of the foot is drawn on the leather to match the foot size. Homemade moccasins were the reason why I could run through the fields with fat feet chasing the cows and horses. Maybe I really did have "moccasin feet" after all.

*   *   *

On Saturday nights we often visited Jonesy, an old family friend who had a color TV. One night Mom saw the Lennon Sisters perform on *The Lawrence Welk Show*. That convinced her to make us into a family act. Mom sang soprano in the church choir and understood basic harmony and vocal arrangements. She taught Louise and Judy to sing first and second soprano parts, while Kathy and I, with lower voices, sang the alto parts. A song called "Whispering Hope" was supposed to be our big debut. Instead it was my biggest disaster. We wore blue dresses with a small lace yoke in the front. Another member of the congregation owned a beauty salon and volunteered to give matching haircuts and perms to the Supernaw Sisters. When it came time to perform, my sisters all looked great, with their matching hairstyles and dresses. Although my dress matched the others, however, my hair did not. My baby-fine, thin hair couldn't handle the chemicals, so the same perm that looked great on them burned my hair, breaking it off and frizzing what remained, turning it a funny orangey color. Hiding my hair under a red baseball cap in embarrassment, I was aghast when Mom said, "You *must* take off

11. Susie, still trying to control her Bozo curls, sits with C. Louise, Kathy, and Judy and plays with kittens outside their house, 1957. *Photo by Lavena Cameron, from the Supernaw family album.*

that awful hat. We're going to sing, you can't wear it. You must remove it. It doesn't matter how you look, it's how you sing."

Reluctantly I removed my cap only to discover that my hair had straightened a little at the top under the cap but had frizzed up around the bottom. I looked hideous! Mom dragged me next to the stage. My lower lip began to quiver as I frantically fought back tears. As we lined up to perform Judy saw me and laughed, "You look just like Bozo the Clown!"

"See, Mom. I told you so. I look horrible!" I began crying.

"Everyone be quiet. Now Judy, stop teasing Susie. Susie, you still have to sing, so stop crying. Now remember everyone, it's so important to do your best." Mom walked out on stage and sat at the piano while the Supernaw Sisters filed out in birth order.

There were gasps and snickers as I entered with red eyes and orange frizzed hair. As I stood in front of the microphone beside my three gorgeous sisters, my lip quivered, and tears started forming again in my eyes. My little hands tightened into fists.

The piano played the introduction, and my sisters began singing on cue. While the others sang in beautiful harmony I searched desperately for my note but couldn't find it! My mouth was open, but my voice froze. I panicked even after hearing my part coming from behind me. Mom was trying to help by singing my part. Her voice was the only one singing my part. I couldn't do anything but sniff while tears rolled down my cheeks. When they finish singing, during the applause, I bolted off the stage sobbing.

Although no one outside the family said anything to me, it was the last performance of the Supernaw Sisters. It was also the last time kids teased me by calling me Jimmy. They now had a new name for me . . . Bozo.

4

Horse Crazy

We had two sturdy horses that plowed our fields of alfalfa and corn. Sometimes Grandpa would ride them. I wasn't allowed to get close to them because I was too small, but I always imagined myself sitting proudly on their backs. When I was approaching six Grandpa received a two-year-old quarter horse/cow pony cross as a trade for work. She was named Dusty Rose and became Judy's horse. I wasn't allowed to ride her, but Judy let me take care of her, clean her feet, brush, and feed her. I was truly crazy about horses whether I got to ride them or not.

My real love affair with horses began a year later when Grandpa bought a small Shetland colt. Grandpa had noticed my love for horses. He often said I was "horse crazy" because at the sale barn I'd follow each one from its outside pen into the holding pen. I was Grandpa's sidekick, and no one minded as long as I stayed out of the way. Grandpa usually went to the sale barn to buy cattle. But I went there for the horses and the strawberry soda. One day I stayed inside the big barn of the auction house because the constant rain had created muddy pens. I watched a man lead in a baby Shetland so small that it was more the size of a large dog. I never took my eyes off his curly white coat until he was led out. I noticed Grandpa smiling and asked, "Why are you smilin' like that?"

"I just bought that big shaggy dog for five dollars," Grandpa said. "I figured ole Dusty needs a companion."

"You mean he's ours?" Grandpa nodded. "Wow! That's great!" I hugged him. "I didn't even know you were biddin'."

"That's 'cause you never took your eyes off him." Grandpa said.

I shrugged, a little embarrassed. "Then can I go look at him?" Grandpa nodded, so I ran out back to get a closer look. The colt stood in a back pen with a couple of skinny bay mares. I ran over with no regard to the mud splashing on me. I climbed up the side rails and peeked over the top for a closer look. He looked so tiny between the normal-sized mares. I watched him until Grandpa's truck drove up to the pen. Grandpa walked over, squatted down, put his arms around his tiny body, picked him up, and carried him over to our truck. I jumped in the front seat, and instead of putting the colt in the back of the truck, Grandpa put him in the front with me. When he stood on the floor his head rested on my lap, and I held him close. I heard someone say, "That colt is so small he could be used for fish bait."

I laughed and agreed. "Let's name him Fishbait. It sounds so cute."

Grandpa warned me, "A name is very important. You need to choose a good name, a name that represents the potential. Don't just pick a name 'cause it's cute."

"But he's just a Shetland pony," I whined. "He doesn't need a powerful name. Please."

"Well, he's gonna be your pony. I just wish you'd think about another name."

"Okay, I'll think about it," I said, even though I already knew what I wanted to name him.

Fishbait was about six months old and had plenty of time to grow. Even though I fed him extra handfuls of grain every day, he never got much taller, although he filled out some through the body. By the time he was old enough to ride I was nine, and my feet touched the ground when I sat on his small back.

When I rode him, I'd wrap my legs around his chest so they wouldn't drag on the ground. We had a small saddle, but I didn't

12. Susie sits on Fishbait in the back pasture at her grandfather's house in 1961. *From left to right*: Dusty Rose, Judy, Kathy, Fishbait, and Susie. *Photo by Lavena Cameron, from the Supernaw family album.*

want Fishbait to have to carry any extra weight, so I generally rode bareback. When I did use a saddle I had to pull the stirrups up as high as possible since his legs were so short.

Although my only experience with horses up to then had been just sitting on the back of Dusty, I wanted to train Fishbait. I checked out some books from our tiny school library, and our county extension agent found me a good guide to the basic schooling and training of horses.

After studying the basics I set out to put my new knowledge to use. The long lane east of the farmhouse looked excellent for my training needs. Grandpa gave me permission to use the area as long as I kept it clean so others could use it. I discovered several old fence poles and dragged them over to my new training lane. I paced off measured steps and adjusted the poles until each was the same distance from the last one. Finally I made a miniature jump by laying a pole across cinder blocks at the opposite end of the lane, between the training area and the exit. I felt the best way to motivate Fishbait to take the jump was to make him think he was heading back to join the other horses.

Soon Fishbait became quite good at pacing himself through the poles and could take the one-foot jump. I swung my leg over him, deciding to ride him over the poles and the jump. He stumbled over the poles, because my extra weight made a big difference, and wavered approaching the jump. I reined him straight into the jump, slapping his neck with the reins. Fishbait gathered himself to jump, so I leaned forward, unhooking my legs from around his body. At the last second the Shetland bailed out, and I sailed headfirst over the pole and landed on the not-so-soft ground, face down. My nose started to bleed. I wiped my bloodied nose with my arm and used the bottom of my T-shirt to wipe away my tears. Maybe Grandpa was right; perhaps I had given Fishbait a weak name. A really good name for a jumper would have been "Sputnik," after that Russian satellite put into orbit a couple of years ago.[1]

With our jumping career over I decided to train Fishbait to be a rodeo pony. I started using him to run barrels and practice my roping. The barrels were easy, but roping was harder. Still, learning to rope was fun, and I would race by fence posts, trying to rope them. Instead of holding the rope in my hand, I'd tie the end to the saddle horn, something I'd seen ropers do in rodeos. One day I actually roped a post and realized too late that ropers tied ropes around the saddle horn to rope moving calves, not strong fence posts. The rope tightened quickly and yanked the small Shetland back, breaking the saddle's cinch. Both saddle and rider went wildly flying toward the splintered fence post, while poor Fishbait was thrown to the ground, breathless. I knew then my rodeo career was also over.

Everyone laughed when I returned to the house with a bloody nose, covered with dirt and carrying a broken saddle. Grandpa took the saddle from me, saying, "Maybe you ought to hang around horses more so some horse sense will rub off on you." Nodding in agreement I realized I was good with books and school but definitely lacking in common sense. Grandpa worried about me so much that it was a miracle he ever let me ride again. But he loved me so much it was hard for him not to want to see me happy, and horses made me happy.

Soon after my roping disaster Grandpa traded a couple of calves and Fishbait for Nugget, a palomino quarter horse.

When Judy began riding Nugget I rode Dusty. Kathy was technically next in line, but riding wasn't that important to Kathy. So Dusty became my horse for the next couple of years.

I lived to ride, and riding a pony tall enough that my feet didn't drag the ground was the ultimate experience. Now that I had a real horse, I could ride with Judy. On weekends I hurried to complete my early-morning chores so I could play my favorite game. It wasn't a real game—it didn't even have a name—but its rules were simple: Judy would leave on horseback, and I'd track her. Not finding Judy by noon meant I'd do the dishes for her during the next week. If I did catch up with her she'd do the dishes for me.

One Saturday morning began like all the others: Judy left early, and Mom handed me a piece of cooked bacon scrunched in a slice of bread when I dropped off the eggs I'd gathered. I grabbed a plastic pair of sunglasses and put them on my head and hurried back outside, taking a big bite of my sandwich and stuffing the rest in my pocket. I opened the corral gate and whistled. Two horses came trotting up. Dusty led, followed by Cindy, our new white mare.

I went into the shed to get some grain and poured it into our wooden trough. Dusty nickered and began eating. Returning, I removed a well-used bridle from a big nail on the wall, hung it over my shoulder, and grabbed the rubber curry brush. The two horses were laying back their ears and nipping at each other, busy establishing a new hierarchy. Cindy seemed determined to be in charge while Nugget was away, but Dusty thought she should be in charge.

Quietly I slipped up beside Dusty and slipped a rope around

13. Susie takes one of the family horses, a palomino named Nugget, to the west pasture on the farm in 1962. *Photo by Lavena Cameron, from the Supernaw family album.*

her neck. I gently began brushing her in the manner that Grandpa had taught me. She turned her head and gave me a sniff but kept chewing, wanting to get her share of the grain. By the time the grain was gone I'd finished brushing Dusty, so I put my arm around her neck and pulled her head close to me, sliding my hand down her nose. With one fluid movement I slid the bridle over her nose and then the top of her head, carefully maneuvering her ears. She sighed deeply.

"Don't be so lazy," I told her. "You know the exercise will do you good." In horse language, when a horse sighs it doesn't want to do what you're asking it to do. I always talk back to horses, so they know I've heard them. Lowering her head Dusty sighed again, and I patted her on the neck. "Good girl."

Swinging one rein around her neck, I gathered the two reins at the top of her withers and swung one leg up and over her back. An old gate made of three strands of barbed wire opened to the side forty acres. I slid off, opened the gate, and led Dusty through. One more pasture to cross, and the tracking game would begin. Dusty trotted to the end of the field and stopped at the gate that led to a dirt road. This metal gate was easier to close because it swung on hinges.

Closing the gate I glanced at the ground to see the most recent tracks. "East, no problem." Leaping on her back in one movement, I lowered my sunglasses and gave Dusty a soft kick. She took off at a slow canter, while my eyes focused on the road ahead. When the fresh set of tracks turned off the road, I slowed Dusty to a walk. We went around some trees and into a back pasture behind a small pond. I saw something in the distance and pushed my cheap sunglasses up on my nose, shading my eyes. Yes, it was Judy! She wasn't expecting me yet and was letting Nugget graze.

I urged Dusty into a gallop through the open field. I loved the feeling of riding bareback. The wind was throwing my hair around, and Dusty was breathing in time with her stride. I leaned forward and urged Dusty to quicken her stride. Caught up in the moment I looked up to see Judy mounting Nugget to begin her escape. "Come on," I urged Dusty. She gave me the extra speed. We were flying until suddenly the ground gave way as Dusty's left hoof stepped in a rabbit hole. Her front leg buckled, causing her to fall forward. Dropping the reins I instinctively reached down and put my arms around her neck. I pressed my head against her and gripped tightly with my legs.

Momentum caused the seven-hundred-pound pony to flip through the air. I clung to her desperately, closing my eyes tight. I realized too late that she was going to land on her back, right on top of me. Suddenly my glasses shattered, causing several small jabs of pain before an excruciating feeling flashed through my body like a bolt of lightning. Then everything went black.

Light slowly filtered into the darkness. Everything was foggy. Focusing my eyes on an eerie twilight environment, I realized my new perspective was from the sky, and I witnessed a strange scene. After landing on her back Dusty rolled over onto her side, where she rested for a moment, gathering her strength before struggling to her feet. Judy squealed, seeing Dusty hit the ground, and reined Nugget in a tight turn toward us.

"I hope she didn't break a leg," Judy muttered as she rode, looking around and not seeing me. "Where's Susie? Susie, Susie!" Judy's hysterical shouting received no response. "Susie, Susie!" Riding toward Dusty she saw my twisted body on the grass. She quickly dismounted, dropped the reins, and moved closer. "Susie, are you okay? Can you get up?" Judy stopped short, gasping at my bloodied face. My sunglasses had shattered during the fall, cutting my face in several places, and each cut was now bleeding profusely. She squatted down and touched my shoulder—"Susie, Susie!"—but I didn't respond.

Examining me with her eyes she shivered at the sight of my twisted body, my neck, torso, and legs all going in different directions. Unconsciously her left hand moved over her mouth to cover her silent gasp while my bird's-eye view made me marvel at the weird geometrical pattern my body made. Judy quickly looked around for Nugget. Nervous from the excitement Nugget had run some distance before starting to graze. Dusty stood close to me with lowered head, as if she understood something was wrong. Judy walked slowly toward Dusty, talking quietly and holding her hand out as if she had some grain. "Easy girl, easy." Dusty sniffed at her hand. Judy patted Dusty on the neck while carefully reaching for the reins hanging from her bridle. With the hands of an expert she quickly felt the pony's legs. Dusty showed no pain.

"Feels solid," she said to herself, and then she led Dusty a short distance, carefully watching her move. She was looking for a limp, but her stride looked fine. Judy patted Dusty again and swiftly jumped on her back. In a moment she was off at a dead gallop. Judy rode to the road and turned toward our farm.

My body was lying in some tall weeds near a small pond with a few large oaks and cedars along its shoreline. More tall grass grew near the pond, and cattails flourished around and in the water. The area, filled with a mixture of brown and green, was disrupted by a late May wind rippling through the trees, rustling the leaves, and bringing in a fog.

I noticed a light glowing on the horizon and felt a slight breeze against my face. The fog disappeared slowly, revealing a sun growing larger and brighter, changing from a golden glow to a brilliant blue-white light. Then from the light walked a beautiful Indian woman, reminding me of the woman dressed as a nurse I had seen in my dream while locked the grain storage bin. Something about the woman was very comforting and strangely familiar. I wondered if she was a Corn Mother, since I'd first seen her above the corn. She was dressed in a white buckskin covered with turquoise star-burst beadwork patterns. Her leggings and moccasins were fully beaded with the same turquoise design. Her long black hair reached to her waist and hung loose. A single red-tail hawk feather was tied on the right side of her head. She cradled a small sickly bear cub in her left arm, and her right hand was resting on its back. The cub's skinny legs dangled lifelessly. It whimpered and tried to move but was so weak that it could only lift its head as she patted it gently. The cub closed its eyes and rested as its weary body went limp. She moved gracefully across the meadow. I followed her eyes as she turned her head and gazed to the east. Afraid she was leaving I ran over to her. Her face softened as she saw my fear and touched me gently.

"Part of you will die," she whispered softly.

"You mean I'm not dead already?" I was surprised.

"You're not dead, but your life will change."

"Why?"

"Because you are a warrior," she explained firmly.

"How can I be a warrior? I'm just a child, a girl child!" My spine pulsed with a cold current that caused goose bumps on my arms. It didn't make sense. Badger or Wolf clans usually protected others, not the Bear Clan.

"It is the spirit that makes a warrior." I realized that female bears can be quite formidable if challenged. Her voice interrupted my thinking. "You must fight yourself. It is a battle within your body." Her voice resonated in the air; the sound of her words stuck deep in my heart and vibrated slowly.

"Why?"

"To earn your name."

"I don't have any name to earn," I protested.

She hushed me by putting her finger to her lips. "Watch."

Then she turned to pick up the bear cub as it waddled over to her. It looked healthy now, its coat sleek and shiny, its eyes sparkling. I couldn't believe it was the same sickly bear cub she had held earlier. She patted it and whispered in its ear. The cub stood on all fours and ran a short distance before turning and facing me. Rising up on its hind legs it reached its paws to the sky then, giving a baby roar, began to wave. The cub lowered itself to all fours and started to dance. The cub danced a little shuffle and turned. It continued to dance by moving its whole body, doing rolls and flips, jumping, spinning, and twirling to a drumbeat that resonated in the skies. When the cub finished it turned and bowed low to me. As the cub rose from his bow I saw my features on its face!

"Am I the cub?"

"This bear cub is your totem. Your name is 'Ellia Ponna.' You are now Dancing Feet of the Bear People (*nokosalgi*)."[2]

5

A New Name

I woke up in the hospital. I looked at my swollen arm and saw a long silvery needle taped in it. The needle was connected to a thin hose that was attached to a bottle half filled with a clear liquid. The bottle was hanging from a metal pole at the side of my bed. The skin around the needle puncture was bruised and puffy, and my left hand was loosely tied at the wrist to one of the metal sides of the bed. I slowly moved each finger to touch my palm.

I started to sit up but couldn't move. My body was tied and pulled in different directions. Both my arms were fastened to the sides of the bed. My legs were in braces, and a foam collar was wrapped around my neck. I was in traction. The calm I had felt only moments before quickly dissolved. My face was wrapped in bandages. Moving my head made me feel as if thousands of pins were sticking in my face. I had been wearing sunglasses, and they had shattered, cutting my face. The prickling pain and bloodstained bandages horrified me as I imagined how my face would look covered with scars.

A nurse walked quietly into my room and checked the instruments, then looked at me. She took my right hand and squeezed it gently. "Welcome back, child. Why, you're darn lucky just to be alive. We were all so very worried about you."

"What happened?" I gripped her hand.

"You were in a riding accident." She patted my hand.

"Oh." I tried to remember the accident, but everything was blurry. "I can't remember."

"I'll tell the doctor you're awake, darlin', and then I'll be right back." On her way out she joked, "Now don't you go nowhere, you hear?"

I closed my eyes and tried to fight back tears. I didn't feel lucky at all and certainly didn't want to be in this world. I wanted to be with the Beautiful Lady in that brilliant green mountain meadow. I wanted to fly on the whistle of an eagle, float as a bubble down a rushing stream, and stretch myself to the wind so rain would fall through me. Instead I was a free-loving spirit trapped mercilessly in a useless body. Seeing death and experiencing its joy, I was no longer afraid to die, to cast away my worthless body. Unfortunately everyone seemed intent on saving that worthless body. It was only because they did not know the beauty in death.

The nurse returned and removed each hand from its strap. I squeezed her hand in appreciation. "I've sent word to your family. I'm sure someone will be here as soon as possible." She began to remove the bandages from my face. "Don't worry. The cuts on your face shouldn't leave lasting scars." I sighed in relief.

When the doctor arrived he put his stethoscope on my chest. "Now take a deep breath." Standing up he took the stethoscope out of his ears. Then he looked into each eye and examined my facial wounds. "You look better. Your face is healing nicely. It should be healed in another couple of weeks."

"What about my legs?" I asked, afraid of the answer.

"You've slightly fractured your lower back and are paralyzed from the waist down. We'll keep you immobilized for six weeks to see if it heals. The paralysis could be temporary; there's no way to tell right now. But you're young and healthy. We'll just have to wait and see." He continued to examine me by touching my legs, squeezing and massaging them while looking at my face. "Do you feel anything, anything at all?" he asked sternly.

I shook my head. "No."

He pulled a metal instrument from his pocket. Narrow and sharp, it looked like a huge needle on a handle. He moved to the end of the bed and took my left foot in his hand. He gently poked the bottom of my foot with the sharp instrument. "Can you feel that?" he asked, looking for some indication of pain or sensation.

Again I shook my head no then lowered my eyes. He went through the same procedure with the other foot. I shook my head one more time. With the examination finished he signaled to the nurse as he picked up my chart from the table, opened it, scribbled something on the top page, closed the folder, and handed it to the nurse. He left without saying good-bye. The nurse nodded a good-bye and followed him. I was alone again.

The realization of being paralyzed began to sink in. I felt alone, very alone. I started to think about my dream. At first all I could remember was feeling peace and joy. I felt such calmness that I didn't want to leave that feeling to come back to this life, not with all this pain. Lost in my own world I didn't notice Mom entering the room. "Susie, oh, my poor baby!" Surprised, I held out my arms, and she bent over and gave me a hug. "I've been worried sick."

"Mom, I'm so glad to see you. I feel so alone. So sad." After wiping a tear I reached for her hand.

She smiled. "I'm just glad to see you're better! Do you remember what happened?"

"Nothing after Dusty fell, but I had this crazy dream." She listened while I explained part of my dream. I didn't tell her about my new name. Yet whatever I said was enough to make her ask Philip Canard, a traditional healer (*vlecv*) she knew through Grandma Carrie, to help me. She had asked him to pray for me after the accident. Unlike her parents Mom respected American Indians and their beliefs. Living a simple life on the reservation, she went to school with many Osage children and thought herself no better than her classmates. She believed that what was inside a person was more important than the color of their skin or their religious or cultural beliefs. She found it fascinating that two cultures coexisted on the old brick Main Street in Hominy, and she knew that many more American Indian cultures existed in other parts of Oklahoma and America.

Philip came to visit the next day. He smiled and patted me on the shoulder. "Glad to see you feeling better." I relaxed at his gentle touch. "Your mom said you had a dream. Can you tell me about it?"

I retold most the dream.[1] When I paused he looked at me with knowing eyes and pressed me further. I fidgeted, unsure how to tell him about my Indian name, so I took a deep breath and blurted it out. "The lady told me my name was Ellia Ponna."[2]

"Do you know what that means?"

"She said it means Dancing Feet. Is a name the meaning of the words or the sounds making up the words?"

Philip raised his head and half closed his eyes. I felt he was trying to sense my feelings. "Both are important. The sounds making up words are as important as the meaning of those words."

"Even with names?"

"Especially with names."

He said it so calmly I wanted to scream at him but knew better than to be disrespectful. I took a deep breath to calm myself. "The difference in sounds between Ellia Ponna and Dancing Feet is important?"

"I'm saying your name is Ellia Ponna, not Dancing Feet." I shook my head in confusion. "It's not easy to understand the ways of the spirit world," he said.

I wanted to ask another question, but Philip held up his finger to indicate silence. I lay quietly while he prayed for me and soon fell asleep, dreaming about that beautiful mountain meadow and a dancing bear cub.

* * *

During his next visit Philip told Mom, "We'd like to have a prayer and healing meeting for Susie. She's gonna need a lot of extra help now." Mom nodded, but I interrupted.

"Thanks but no thanks. I'm okay, really." It was a nice idea, but I was ashamed to be seen by other people. My face had healed, but I was in this helpless condition and just wanted to be left alone. Mom didn't argue with me, but Philip did.

"Don't you care about earning an Indian name?"

"I want an Indian name. I just don't want that name." I avoided looking at him directly because he'd know I wasn't being totally honest. Quietly, in the manner of many Native medicine elders, Philip explained, "Your dream will give you power if you can fulfill it."

"Okay, but how can I become Dancing Feet if I can't walk?"

"Your spirit chose this path." Philip tapped my head. "Your spirit understands things your mind does not. Only by earning your name will your spirit and mind be one. The choice, of course, is yours." Philip grinned elusively.

I paused, thinking I never had a choice. The Beautiful Lady had said, "You are the bear cub." I hadn't argued with her then but accepted it, and wasn't I the one who had noticed my facial features on the bear cub? My spirit knew more than my mind was willing to acknowledge. I agreed to have the meeting, feeling honored but also scared.

A small private meeting was held quietly in the hospital room. My bed was by the window, close to Philip, and I could look out at the night skies. Philip softly blew a conch shell, chanted, and mixed some medicine. He took out a white reed and blew in the drink before handing it to me. I closed my eyes and drank in spite of its bitter taste. After hours of more praying and chanting he took out the tooth of a gar fish and scratched the bottoms of my feet. At midnight during a special prayer I realized that I wanted to earn my name. I vowed, "If I can use my legs again, I promise to fulfill my dream." I watched as Philip crushed some herbs and put them in a small leather pouch. Then he sprinkled them with tobacco. He also placed a small stone in the pouch before tying it shut. After blessing the pouch and singing four songs he moved beside me. I closed my eyes, and another man prayed and chanted while Philip moved his hand above my body. When the songs were finished Philip placed the small leather pouch in my hand. He closed my fingers around it, whispering that I should always keep it near. Holding it over my heart I prayed, "I'll always honor the power of the Creator and the path that was chosen for me. If I can use all of my body again, I will earn my name."[3] My eyes drooped, and my weary body finally slept.

When I woke only Philip and Mom were in the room. I shook Philip's hand, thanking him for the healing prayers and wishing him a good morning. He smiled and patted me on the head and walked out the room, talking with Mom. From the window I saw young boys chasing each other around outside, enjoying the morning coolness. I was jealous because they could run. A tear rolled down my cheek, and I brushed it away, hoping that no one had noticed.

* * *

I kept my small leather pouch nearby and held it frequently, always saying a short prayer. When I healed enough to sit up my daily ritual included pricking the bottoms of my feet with a hatpin. I figured since the medical doctor and the traditional healer had both poked my feet, it must be a good thing. I wasn't expecting anything, but this day I felt a distant sensation. Caught by surprise I carefully examined the hatpin in my hand then jabbed myself again. Delighted, I picked up my other foot and jabbed it with the pin several times. "Hey, I felt that!" I continued to prick my foot, shouting, "Yes, yes, I can feel that!" I picked up my foot and looked at it. My sole was bleeding, but I didn't care. I started rocking the upper part of my body, repeating, "I can feel it! I can feel it!"

* * *

My new journey was beginning, and my prayers had been answered. Maybe I really was going to have the chance to be Ellia Ponna. In a short time I started regaining muscle control in my legs and began walking, first with a walker, then crutches, then a cane. I still woke before dawn each day and performed my morning ritual of thanks, always with my small leather pouch. I took long slow walks but always stayed close to the house. I cherished the weekends at the farm because the land helped me feel the oneness of nature.

One weekend we didn't go to the farm because President John F. Kennedy had died.[4] I watched every minute of the crisis on TV and dozed on the floor instead of going to bed. I watched them capture Lee Harvey Oswald and watched Jack Ruby kill him. The Texas Book Depository was forever burned into my brain, as was Jackie Kennedy in her pink suit. I sobbed out loud when I saw the riderless horse with the boots backward in the stirrups, because President Kennedy had been my hero. He had made all of us want to be better than we were. He had wanted our country to be the first to go to the moon.[5]

✳ ✳ ✳

It was always special to welcome the rising sun with thanks and prayers from my personal place on our farm. Looking to the east I saw the morning sky in shades of pink. The early morning pink light quickly turned to gold, while the western gray sky faded to blue. The transition was quick but magnificent, and I offered a moment of thanks to the sun and creator of all things, to the universe, to God and Jesus, the four directions, the sky, the earth, the plants and animals, and all my relatives—known and unknown. Daybreak is the time for giving thanks and marveling at the awakening of a new day.

This particular morning I decided to face my fear and brought six sticks with me. I stopped at my personal spot and laid out four sticks, one in each direction. I placed my small leather pouch in the center of the directional sticks after touching it to my heart. Then I pushed one stick into the earth and pointed the other toward the sky. My small altar was complete. I offered some tobacco from my handsewn cloth pouch. Slowly I knelt down

on my hands and knees, facing east, and touched my forehead to
the earth, pausing while the energy of the earth tickled my entire
body. Leaning back and sitting on my knees, I folded my hands,
bowed my head, and began to pray. "I call for your help, Earth
Mother from the east, Corn Mother from the south, Water Spirit
in the west, and Master of Breath in the north. Help me to always
remember that we're all related, that all things are connected
through the creator and the energy of the universe. And help
me, please help me, overcome the fear in my heart." I touched
my forehead to the ground again, leaving it there while I felt the
energy of the earth gently flow into my trembling body.

Picking up my leather pouch and scattering the sticks, I felt
new strength and slowly walked toward the pasture. I tried to
calm my fear by speaking out loud: "Dusty was not to blame.
She tripped and fell, that's all. She didn't buck me off; she was
only doing what I'd asked her to do." The horses gathered for
their morning meal. I'd been out to see them a few times since
walking again, but when they clustered around me, instead of
lavishing affection on them, I was afraid. The horses sensed
my insecurity, and the more nervous they became, the more
intimidated I felt.

I slipped a halter on Dusty and brushed her while she chewed.
She looked and sniffed at me but kept eating. When the grain
was gone I led Dusty over to a fence post and tied her loosely. I
felt terrified; my hands shook uncontrollably, my muscles were
tensed, and my entire body felt rigid. Dusty looked at me and
sighed. "What? Are you really that lazy?" I suddenly blurted.
My voice broke the morning silence and sounded unnatural.
Dusty nuzzled me, looking for some hidden treat in my pocket.
I rubbed her neck, took the end of the lead strap, and looped it
through the side of her halter. Then I pulled the strap across her
nose and through the opposite side of her halter. Dusty threw
her head up in surprise, so I patted her neck, saying, "Easy, girl."
She settled down.

Instead of my old way of swinging a leg over and jumping on

her back in one move, I jumped up halfway, resting my stomach across her back, my legs dangling at her side. She turned her head around and gave me a quizzical look as she sniffed at my bottom. I'd never mounted her that way before. I collected my strength and slowly slid my right leg up and over her back. As I steadied myself Dusty turned again and sniffed at my knee. "I bet you're wondering why this is taking so long." Her ear twitched, listening intently as I continued. "Easy, girl."

She started walking so quickly I was caught off guard and wobbled a moment before regaining my balance. Dusty slowed for a moment then quickened her pace when she felt my knees weakly grip her sides. Approaching the gate I cautiously dismounted and slowly pushed it open. I noticed that the other horses had started walking toward us, ready to hit the back forty for the day. I quickly closed the gate and mounted her in the same awkward way I'd done before, but I did it a little faster this time.

Dusty started off with a fast walk, and when I pulled on the rein to slow her, her walk became frisky. She was ready to run, but I wasn't. The more she pranced, the more nervous I became; the more nervous I got, the more she pranced. I was beginning to doubt whether I ever could ride again. I paused, taking several deep breaths, and whispered, "It's now or never."

My left heel touched Dusty's side. She was waiting for such a signal and broke into a canter with the proper lead. The canter felt comfortable, like rocking in a fast rocking chair. Although Dusty began a little too fast for my comfort, I gently slowed her by saying, "Easy, girl." The first lap around the field was slow and well paced as I carefully watched the path for holes and rocks. Dusty was just warming up. As we rounded toward the gate she started to slow, but I reined her back to the path along the fence for another loop around the field.

This time she quickened her pace to a fast gallop. Dusty's breath was in time with her stride, and I synchronized my breathing with hers until I felt like part of her. Leaning forward I reached my arms down and slipped them around her neck as she moved faster. The cool wind was whirling around my face, and my body felt more alive than ever. As we neared the closed gate again I sat up, and Dusty slowed quickly. Her ears were perked up, and her nostrils were flaring. The other horses were prancing back and forth, feeling the energy of our run. As she slowed I threw my hands up, dropping the lead. The lead fell to the ground as Dusty stopped at the gate. I slid off and hugged her, thanking her for being gentle.

I felt eyes watching me. I looked around cautiously and saw Grandpa standing by the horse trough. He held his arm in the air to acknowledge my look. I should've known he'd be there watching me because he always kept a close eye on me around horses. Although the scene had caused him some anxiety, it had also brought him great joy. As gracefully as possible I crawled through the barbed-wire fence, leaving Dusty standing there, breathing hard. I saw a single tear trickle down his cheek. The expression on his face told me it was a tear of happiness.

When I got close to him we hugged in a tearful embrace. Usually he just gave me a short hug, but this embrace felt like it would never end. It took a few moments for Grandpa to realize how tight he was holding me, and as he released me from his embrace, I looked at him and knew something was wrong. "Susie, I'm really proud of you."

"Oh, Papaw. That means a lot."

"You're gettin' better, but I'm gettin' sick." His voice cracked, and his beaming face now grew somber. He took another deep breath. "I'm goin' to the hospital."

"I was in the hospital too, but I got better. You're gonna get better too." Sobbing, I buried my head in his chest. "Don't go. Don't go. I'll take care of you."

"I'm too sick." His long sigh ended with a cough.

I wanted to plead with him not to go, but he was sick. A couple of times before I'd thought he didn't look well, but I'd refused to acknowledge the truth because I'd been too concerned about myself. Now I felt guilty. "I'm so sorry. What can I do?"

"You've already done it. You're alive and well!" Grandpa considered himself responsible for the accident since he had bought the horses.

"Papaw, my accident wasn't your fault. It just happened— no, it was my fault. I just wasn't thinking. No horse sense, like you've always said."

Grandpa hugged me tightly, and I relaxed in his loving embrace. He took a deep breath, "You know, you can do somethin' for me."

"Anything."

"Will you stay true to your dream?"

I looked into his eyes, caught off guard by his question. Mom must have told him how important it was to me. "Of course, but why?"

Grandpa sighed while a tear rolled down his cheek. "'Cause I won't be comin' home."

6

Metamorphosis

Before dying of prostate cancer Grandpa suffered through his final days. I think he would have preferred to die at home, but there wasn't anyone to care for him the way he had cared for Grandma during her final days. I had to force myself to go inside the hospital because I really hated the overpowering aroma of disinfectants and the prevailing odor of death. Sitting beside his bed holding his hand I tried to control my feelings, but eventually tears came. Sometimes he knew I was there, because I could feel him squeezing my hand as if to comfort me in my time of sorrow. I knew he would be happy when he died because Grandma would be waiting for him, yet I didn't want to think of life without him. I prepared myself for the funeral by remembering that Grandpa wasn't Christian. Although he didn't believe in them, Grandma Carrie's stories said that the energy that was his spirit would journey along the Milky Way to join his wife and other spirits in becoming one with the source of all energy. I felt a strange calmness. It certainly seemed better than the consequences of not being Christian.

It didn't help the next day, because I couldn't help but cry at Grandpa's funeral. I always got in trouble for showing my emotions and crying. I had hoped for rain, but the day was clear and mild for early June, and a slight breeze danced through the trees. Before we left for his funeral Mom said, "We need the money, so I'm going to rent out the farmhouse." I was shell-shocked. I already missed Grandpa, but I was devastated by the thought of never returning to our farm. I couldn't quit thinking about abandoning our little farm and living forever in some city. The mere thought of always living in the city terrified me. Everyone else thought staying in Tulsa would be a good thing because they liked city life. Like my dad they were dazzled by the city's many bright lights, unlimited pleasures, and countless job opportunities. I sobbed all day, crying from anger, fear, and grief. Just as my dream had predicted, part of me died that day, and my life changed directions. The only thing that provided me any comfort was my small leather bag filled with herbs and a small dark stone.

*　*　*

We lived, with our meager budget, in a small rented house on the western edge of Tulsa. It was harder to be poor in the city because poor people were shunned and spat upon. In the country you worked in the fields or the gardens and earned food and respect.

The house we rented in town was an old wood frame structure with two ten-by-twelve-foot bedrooms and a small kitchen. It had a gas furnace in the floor, and the once-colorful linoleum was yellow with age and had many spots that never came clean no matter how many times I scrubbed it. The walls were covered with aged wallpaper curling up at the edges. The yard, mostly gravel, had a rusty blue swing set with two broken chains. One of the chains had a plastic seat hanging from it. I liked to stand on the faded red crossbar and watch the cars pass down the highway.

Dad started coming over again whenever his child support was due. He'd get drunk first and then threaten and hit Mom in the hope that she wouldn't try to force him to pay. He didn't want to waste his money on us because he needed it for his new family. He'd knock her down on the floor, and then he'd turn his rage on whoever else was there. Too often it was me. When I first got slapped and hit, I'd fall to the floor in hopes Dad would stop. I'd cover my head and cry out, "Don't hit me, please don't hurt me."

"Stand up. Look at me. Suck it up," he'd growl. Crying out in pain or begging him to stop only seemed to make him madder. Dad really hated it when I cried, and my tears always flowed too easily for him. Sometimes he'd grab and shake me, slapping my face. When I cried he'd say, "Don't be such a sissy, you gotta be tough!" Dad acted like he just wanted to make me tough, but it certainly didn't work because instead of learning strength I learned fear. Soon I started avoiding him and ran the other way when I saw him at the house.

Mom started dating Woody, a tall man with a horseshoe haircut who worked for the post office.[1] Once Dad came by when he was there, and although Mom never said what happened, Dad never came back. I thought that meant the end of the violence and was glad Woody was there to protect us.

Before long they got married. Woody seemed nice enough at first. We moved to his house and went to Rosicrucian meetings on Saturday nights because he was a member.[2] I enjoyed meeting the people who gathered, and in a strange way I understood the basic elements of their teachings. Unfortunately teachings of esoteric knowledge and humanism didn't help Woody enough, and he remained a living example of Dr. Jekyll and Mr. Hyde.[3] He was a kind Dr. Jekyll to everyone except his family. To us he was Mr. Hyde. Woody had been raised in poverty by an aunt who abused him as a child. As a result when he lost his temper he turned out to be more violent than Dad. Instead of escaping a violent situation we had just moved into another one. Woody would get drunk and beat us; he'd beat us sober if he got angry. He'd overturn the table if the stew had too many potatoes. He'd slap anyone who said anything he didn't like.

I thought he was crazy and was really scared of him. He was bigger than Dad, and his punches were a lot harder. I was sure he'd kill me with a good single blow. I used to just lay low when he got angry until he lined all of us up and threatened to shoot us with his shotgun. After that when he'd get mad we'd all hightail out of the house, shoes or not, any time of day or night. After I had to spend a day without a pair of shoes or a sweater, I learned to sleep in my clothes and keep slip-on shoes by the door.

Woody got frustrated because he couldn't control us girls, and he couldn't understand why we didn't respect him. So he beat us harder, calling us "damn Indians," while quoting the Bible about "fearing God and keeping his commandments." Once I joked about Woody comparing himself to "God" only to wake up in the hospital with a concussion. I didn't realize he'd been within hearing range. While I was in the hospital I had plenty of time to compare Woody and my father and the differences between the religions I'd been taught. The Native American Church taught that we should "honor and respect" God, while the Old Testament spoke of "fear and respect" for God. Both religions respected God, but the choice between honor and fear was an easy one. Comparing my dad with Woody was more difficult, although both seemed to have uncontrollable anger and rage. I was afraid of them both, but I still loved my dad.

Things were so violent at home that we begged Mom to get a divorce or just take us and leave, saying we didn't mind being poor again. Mom said that divorcing Woody would make him look bad to his friends at work. Although she was scared of Woody she encouraged us to do what we needed to do. She felt trapped because Woody had threatened her life if she tried to leave. He never said that to the rest of us. Kathy and I, the more mild-mannered sisters, endured Woody's abuse longer than Judy and Louise. Yet we too would soon be forced out of the house. It was a matter of survival, not choice.

Louise was never around much, but when she was she'd boss me around. She didn't like going to the farm or any local Indian dances and always had some excuse to stay in Tulsa. She reminded me of Lucy in the *Peanuts* cartoons, and I was surprised that I never had to pay for her advice.[4] I was jealous that she got to stay up late and talk into the night with Mom about "us kids."

Those late-night sessions gave her a sense that she was better than the rest of us and therefore entitled to more than her fair share. She always wanted to do less work or get that extra piece of pie because "she was the oldest." She made really good grades in school but suddenly got married at seventeen, escaping with her husband to a little town west of Tulsa. She had three kids and disappeared from my life while raising them.[5]

Judy, our wild and wacky sibling, was the only one to fight back when Woody would try to hit her. She would block his wild swings and dodge his violent punches. She even filed her fingernails to a point and used them against his brutal onslaughts. Her rebellion made him angrier, and I wanted to tell Woody that even Mom couldn't control Judy. Judy laughed when Mom spanked her, saying, "I know you want me to cry, but I won't give you the satisfaction." Mom told me that because of Judy's defiance she was never sure how to discipline Kathy and me.

Judy's exit remains etched deep in my mind. Woody was hanging around all day, drinking, when he stumbled into the front room, angry and cussing. Judy was ironing her clothes, and I watched in horror as he grabbed her and started violently shaking her. Quick as a cat she turned around with the hot iron in her hand and burned both his arms and one of his hands before he backed off. While he was busy loudly cussing in pain, Judy set the iron down on the ironing board, bolted into the other room to grab her purse, and quickly darted out the front door.[6]

Suddenly I realized that I was alone in the house with Woody, so I hurried out the back door and cautiously scaled the chain-link fence. Realizing I'd escaped unharmed I sat on a large sandstone rock and sobbed quietly. Feeling weak and helpless I envied Judy for what she had done. She was the only one who ever fought back. Why couldn't I do that? Maybe Dad was right, I was a sissy.

* * *

In between the violence Mom took me to doctors because even though I could walk (sometimes I even jogged when no one was watching), my back always ached. I prayed for help, holding the small leather pouch given to me at the hospital. But each doctor said the same thing: "You should be thankful just to walk again." They didn't understand my dream, my need to do more than walk so I could earn my name. I believed I could fulfill my dream if I kept trying. After each doctor's negative prognosis I'd ask Mom to take me to another doctor. I wanted to find someone who thought additional exercise would help strengthen my back. Finally Mom decided to take me to a chiropractor. I was ecstatic when he agreed that exercise might help me, and he became my favorite doctor. Between his frequent adjustments and my exercises, my back grew stronger.

I began a progressive series of exercises, always carrying my little leather pouch in my pocket. My slow jog became a run once my withered leg muscles regained their strength. As my leg muscles continued to grow stronger, my coordination improved, and I stumbled less. If exercise therapy got me started, then it was Kathy who kept me practicing. Since Kathy had taken some basic gymnastics classes in PE at school, I asked, "Will you teach me some basic stuff?"

"I know you're anxious to learn, but it's going to be really hard at first," she warned me.

I nodded my head. "I've got all the time in the world to practice."

"But can you be patient with yourself? Can you not get mad at yourself when you can't do something right?" Kathy grinned because she already knew the answer.

"Uh, well, sure, I suppose so." I really wasn't so sure about that. Patience has never been my strength. So I pressed my palms together and prayed, "God give me patience, and do it now!" We both laughed.

She was right. A simple forward roll was a huge obstacle, and my first attempts knocked the air out of me. Although it was weeks before I rolled without thumping my back on the ground, I tried not to get upset about my slow progress. When I could roll reasonably well I learned to stand on my head. To help strengthen my back muscles and spine I did a series of leg presses from a headstand. Moving my legs to different positions while in my headstand, I learned which muscles to move to maintain my balance.

Kathy, sensing my new strength, started teaching me harder things, including a round-off followed by a back handspring to a standing position. As part of my bending and stretching maneuvers she helped me to learn front and back walkovers. Mom saw my progress and tried to support my efforts by signing me up for a local dance class taught by Catherine Neff. I seemed to have natural flexibility and beautifully arched feet, but what I didn't have was the ability to be naturally graceful or maintain any sense of rhythm. My movements were clumsy, and I was usually half a beat off. Dancing was hard for me, and I envied Kathy's natural talent, secretly hoping someday I'd be good enough to dance with her. After a couple of classes everyone agreed I could quit dance lessons because I was so ungraceful and out of step. It embarrassed me to dance in class with other girls, but I hoped to take lessons again when I was more coordinated.

I watched Kathy try out for the cheerleading squad and was disappointed when she was not chosen. Regardless, Kathy always offered help to her baby sister. My desire to dance was genuine, but since dancing did not come naturally for me, Kathy suggested cheering. She asked our friend Reatha Compton to help me learn how to jump and cheer. I was honored because Reatha was a cheerleader at our school. Cheering seemed easier to me than dancing because the cheering movements were more precise and angled. I didn't need to be as graceful, and I didn't need much rhythm, except during the pom-pom routines.

Kathy and Reatha never discussed their strategies with me, but over time I began to understand what it took to be selected. There were the politics, judging by the student population, smiling, and stage presence. Reatha knew a high jump and some good tumbling moves were the best weapons a cheerleader could have during tryouts. Kathy was determined not to have me make the same mistakes she had. She wanted me to be better than she had been and wanted to help me learn from her mistakes. I never knew real work until I trained with my sister as a coach. My main reward for all my efforts was her proud smile. When Kathy smiled I knew it was for real, and that made all the hard work and pain worth it.

Tryouts for the school's cheerleading squad were held in early September, shortly after classes started. As all the girls ran out on the field, everyone began jumping and performing well-prac-ticed cartwheels and round-offs. I took three steps and threw a round-off, a backhand spring, and a nearly perfect back layout flip. My agility even startled me! I continued to jump up and down, keeping in competition with the others while searching the stands. Kathy and Reatha yelled and waved their fluffy pom-poms. Kathy wore a beaming smile that quickly evolved into a slight gasp and then joyous laughter as they announced the new cheerleading squad. I had made it.

I went to visit Dad and his family on holidays and during the summer. He wasn't violent when I was there, and I enjoyed seeing him relaxed. I liked all the food served, but it was never a comfortable feeling, since Dad's wife, Mary, never really accepted us girls as family. She was very protective of her son, Charlie, and it was made clear to me that he could do no wrong. Dad lavished Charlie with affection, and although he was only a "half brother" Charlie made life more miserable for me than all my sisters put together. He never had to do chores, and when he didn't do well in school his teacher was blamed. When he got caught stealing Dad blamed it on Charlie's friends, who were a bad influence. Unfortunately, when Charlie got into alcohol and drugs, well, Dad just looked the other way. Dad was good at only seeing what he wanted.

When Mary wasn't around I liked to wrestle with Charlie and rub his nose on the carpet, just to get out my frustrations. He'd hit me with his green stuffed snake. Eventually I had to quit wrestling him because even though I was two years older,

14. Susie cheers at a Tulsa Central football game in the fall of 1966. *Photo by Lavena Cameron, from the Supernaw family album.*

Charlie grew stronger than I was. Since Charlie never learned to play the piano, I played some church songs on their piano. My sisters could play a little, but I was the only one who kept practicing on the church's piano, and I got pretty good. Dad appreciated my music and cracked up one day when he saw me playing with my toes.

Dad's house was nice, and he was successful at his job.[7] I spent most of my visits in Dad's back office, where he had his ham radio.[8] At first I could only watch, but eventually he showed me how it worked. Each time I visited I learned more about the technology and science behind operating a ham radio. When he wanted me out of his office he'd put his fingers in the eye sockets of his human skull and his thumb in its jaw and make it talk. He claimed the skull was a souvenir from the war.[9] That scared me enough to get me to bail out while he laughed. I was fascinated as much with his electronics as I was with his hunting dogs.

Dad personally trained all his dogs, and I loved watching him work them. He always had at least two hunting dogs, a setter and a pointer, and he taught them to work as a team. I saw a gentler side when he was with his dogs. Once a year Dad would go quail hunting in western Oklahoma, and he'd let me go if Charlie didn't. I generally hunted with what Dad called a "woman's gun," a 20-gauge shotgun. I became a pretty good shot, and when I was able to meet his "challenge shot"—shooting a quail with a small .22 rifle—it was the only time I remember him saying he was proud of me. It was easy to clean the quail because I only had to remove a slug, not cut out all that shot.

When Dad moved east of Tulsa to Broken Arrow, Grandma Carrie bought a house and moved to Tulsa with her daughter, Sara. They had lived with Dad until then. After Sara got married and moved to Texas, I began visiting Grandma Carrie more because she was lonely. I took the bus to visit her little house off Yale, and she was always glad to see me. She wasn't ashamed to be American Indian, and sometimes she spoke her language, Mvskoke, and sang me songs.[10] I didn't understand much of

15. Susie practices the piano with her toes when no one is listening in the summer of 1965. *Photo taken by Lavena Cameron, from the Supernaw family album.*

our language, and instead of trying to learn it I asked her to tell me stories in English. The one phrase she never had to repeat because I learned it so quickly was "Hompkvs ce," which means "Let's eat!" I loved eating all kinds of her home cooking. I never wondered whether it was traditional Muscogee food; it was just Grandma Carrie's cooking. She made everything from scratch.[11] She said she'd cooked since she was old enough to look over the top of a wood stove. She always had a big garden and still canned vegetables using her old pressure cooker. She grew lots of cucumbers and made the best pickles: dill, kosher dill, sweet pickles, and chow-chow, which is a pickle relish. She made me blue dumplings when I bragged about eating Osage grape dumplings.[12] Both turned my teeth purple. My favorite was fried green tomatoes. When I told her that her traditionally soured sofkey was my least favorite, she said I was spoiled on white man's food.[13] Then she laughed and said she didn't care for sofkey either. I didn't realize she had gone to a lot of trouble to make it for me in the traditional way because I always wanted to try something different. Her homemade bread (*taklike*) was more like large fat biscuits than thin fry bread.

Sometimes I'd get to spend the night with Grandma. When she could get us a ride we'd go to stomp dances down by Duck Creek.[14] I liked that they danced counterclockwise, rather than the standard clockwise movement of powwows. It was at a stomp dance that I first saw Kenneth Anquoe and his brother Jack. Jack was one of the lead singers. I thought it was cool that a Kiowa man even wanted to learn our songs and was amazed he could sing them so well. I liked stomp dancing, so Grandma made sure I followed proper etiquette and joined the line after the adults.[15] She would visit with her friends and even talked one into teaching me how to shake shells.[16] I got the gist of it, but without a set of shells to practice with, my legs never got strong enough to last more than one song, not all night long. I'm sure I would have learned rhythm too if I had learned to shake shells well. Grandma explained the pivotal part Turtle played in our creation stories, sharing with me the symbolism of the stomp dance.[17]

After school was out for the summer I'd get to stay longer at Grandma's, so she could take me to our biggest celebration: busk (*Pusketv*), also called the Green Corn Dance.[18] The celebration lasted several days and marked our new year. We attended different activities, but I never fasted in preparation like many others did. I liked watching the women dance in their ribbon dresses and, of course, eating all the food. More important than eating was that the ceremonies gave me a chance to talk with some of the traditional healers who had gathered. I quickly learned to respect the fire and its symbolism.[19]

Marcellus Williams, a Muscogee (Creek) traditional healer and roadman, explained many traditional views, ideas, and beliefs.[20] He told me stories about our clans and their different roles in the ceremonies. He explained that originally those who helped with healing and sickness became members of the Bear Clan. Since I was Bear Clan I must not only protect bears but practice healing or growing herbs and medicine. I remembered my aunt Sara was a nurse, fulfilling her obligation as a member of the Bear Clan. Grandma always had a garden full of medicinal plants, as well as vegetables. I decided to grow healing plants.

Marcellus explained that the Muscogee concept of spirit (*puyvfekcv*) is not like the Christian spirit, which goes to heaven or hell.[21] At death a person's *puyvfekcv* travels to the skies, back to the original source in the Milky Way, and becomes part of the universal energy that is in everything (*Epohfvnkv*).[22] Since this energy permeates nature, all of nature and the universe must be respected. This energy is always flowing and changing, and it is our duty to live in harmony with it. Sharing this energy (love) with people and things (*vnokeckv*) is the first of four paths (or values) of our people.[23] Falling off this path means one is no longer living in harmony with nature. Marcellas emphasized the importance of the second path of humility and humbleness (*ekvncvpecetv*) because this value is not in sync with most of the non-Indian world.[24] Like many foreign terms that cannot be easily translated, *ekvncvpecetv* encompasses more than humility, including concepts like not acting or appearing more important than others and preferring cooperation to competition. Marcellas believed these first two paths are the hardest to walk, while compassion and empathy for others (*encaketv*) and strength in caring for oneself (*yiketv*) are easier paths once one has learned *vnokeckv* and *ekvncvpecetv*.[25] The four paths are not a simple set of behaviors because each path branches into several situations, each determining the way one is to interact with plant and animal life (depending on gender), as well as one's family, one's clan, one's tribal members, other tribes, the outside world, and the universe. These values merged with the teachings of the NAC, so it seemed natural to try to live by them.

Grandma introduced me to Phillip Deere because he also understood the traditional ways of our tribe and wanted to preserve our culture.[26] One night he pointed to the sky and asked me to identify the Big and Little Dippers. He explained that they were called canoes (or boats) by our ancestors, a big canoe and a little canoe.[27] He said they represent the prophecy telling of two canoes filled with people that will be separated during a storm. Someday, he warned me, I would have to choose which canoe to be in before the winds blew them apart. Then he pointed to Taurus and said, "Our legends call these stars a buffalo."

Phillip cautioned me about my schooling, advising me to never forget who I really was and to never abandon our distinct cultural beliefs because of my education. His parents had wanted him to learn Muscogee ways and language, rather than the ways of the white man at boarding school, so he had never completed grade school. But Phillip recognized the value of an education because of the discrimination he had received when trying to find a job without one. Phillip had seen many American Indians with education forget or give up their traditional ways, citing my father as an example. He explained that Muscogee beliefs are centered on the balance of male and female principles (also referred to as white stick and red stick principles). From our creation stories to our matrilineal culture women are equal to men, but with different responsibilities.[28] Besides cooking and raising children, they are responsible for teaching others, planting, mediation, counseling, and internal (within the tribe) politics. Because red blood symbolizes life, women are honored for their spiritual power especially during menstruation. Only by abandoning his culture could Dad abandon us. His excuse that he needed a son to carry on the family name was meaningless in our culture, since females, through the clans, carried on the family name. I assured Phillip I would work to help Indian people and stay true to our Native teachings.

Even though I didn't get to go to busk every summer, I never forgot it was "that time" and said my own prayers. When I couldn't attend traditional activities with Grandma I went to Native American Church meetings whenever possible. I tried to learn as much as I could each time, because I never knew when I'd get to another meeting. Marcellus taught me church songs so that I could sing along during meetings and would know what the words of the song meant. On the mornings after meetings I'd speak with traditional tribal elders from other tribes. One of them was Kenneth Anquoe, the man whose brother sang at our stomp dances.[29] Kenneth took a special interest in me and told me he knew about my Indian name. I felt a special connection with him. Sometimes I asked too many questions, but he was tolerant, understanding that I was trying to learn a lifetime of wisdom in a few hours. He advised me to slow down my thoughts and look inside for some of my answers.

Since NAC meetings lasted all night and through lunch the next day, attending a meeting took up the entire weekend. Kenneth often invited me to sit in the tipi after the services while the elders told stories. After I served the elders their ceremonial breakfast—coffee, cheese, and sweet rolls—Kenneth shared some of the things he'd learned from his traditional elders, as did Marcellus. I always enjoyed asking questions, but here, unlike in school, asking too many questions was disrespectful. So most of the time I just listened, restless from wanting to learn everything right away, realizing I was learning to be patient. Kenneth's own views had been taught to him by his grandfather, who had learned from his grandfather. The same was true for Marcellus. These ancient beliefs are based on who we truly are and the true nature of the universe.

Kenneth taught me that we choose our reality by believing in it. As Kenneth stretched his arms while shaking his hands to show that power is everywhere, he explained that a special power permeates the universe, a power that he called *dw dw*. I wondered if he was referring to a Kiowa concept similar to the Muscogee universal creator/spirit (*Epohfvnkv*), who exists as pure energy. All energy, whether static, dynamic, potential, or kinetic, is combined into a single sacred entity encompassing all laws that govern the universe. Maybe *dw dw* was an assistant like the Master of Breath, or a manifestation of one of the laws of the universe set down by our creator. Kenneth waited a moment before he explained that while an individual may have personal medicine or power, an entire clan or tribe can have its own medicine bundles or power. The Kiowa tribe has sacred medicine bundles called the "ten grandmothers." They are alive with power and are protected by special people because their existence benefits the entire tribe.

Marcellus emphasized that things are alive with the powerful energy of the creator *Epohfvnkv* (a name he whispered in respect), including the wind and the rain. It is in everything, not just things that you think are alive, like plants, animals, and people. Things like eagle feathers and buffalo robes retain much of this power. That's why they're used in healing ceremonies, because that special energy makes them sacred. "For the Muscogee there were sacred metal plates so filled with power that they would ring without being touched. They vibrated with special energy," Marcellus said. Marcellus and Kenneth understood unseen connections between energy and matter, similar to what quantum physicists are discovering at the atomic level.[30]

"So I have a part of that energy vibrating inside me, besides my spirit?"

"Yes, and it can vibrate faster." Kenneth smiled. Feeling a little silly I started shaking my body, a little at first, then faster and faster, until he laughed.

*   *   *

Kenneth explained about living a life that requires recognizing the interconnectedness of all things. He always reminded me, "Everyone, everything has a purpose in the universe. Because of that everyone, everything deserves respect."

"Do you mean everything is predestined, and we have no choice?"

"Having a purpose doesn't mean you can't choose your destiny. Everything chooses a path to follow. That path gives them purpose."

Before I could ask about the paths of photons in a double-slit experiment, Kenneth raised his finger for silence and continued: "Everyone is important in the church. Everyone, from youngest to oldest, has a special place in meetings, as well as in life."[31]

"Because we each have something to contribute?"

"In the church women are valued as the ones who nourish and sustain life like the earth, our Mother. You are givers of life, while men are the protectors of that life." Kenneth motioned toward the altar and then moved his hand to the food. "It takes both sexes working together to have a meeting." In school I had learned that separate roles meant unequal.[32] I liked the concept of men and women being treated as equals, but with different roles. It sounded just like our Muscogee elders talking.

"Children are the leaders of tomorrow," Kenneth said. "In the future, they will sit at tribal council meetings and parent the next generation. If not, who will tell our stories and sing our songs?"

"Okay. I thought you meant something more important."

"What is more important than preserving your culture? The depth of your wisdom is determined by your ability to understand the purpose of all things." Kenneth stopped and looked at me. "And to recognize the unseen relationship between all things."

✳ ✳ ✳

Returning home was always sad. I had to venture back into a world where I tolerated my violent reality by remembering the strength of my spirit. I prayed I could change my disconnected and violent existence into a life of oneness and harmony with all things. It proved a very difficult path for me to walk.

7

Sewer Rats

It was late summer before my sophomore year of high school, and I had cheerleading practice daily at Owen Park. Instead of going home after practice I started exploring the park, each day checking out another area. I started at the waterfall and followed its path to the pond. Walking around the pond I saw it drain into the ground and knew I had to see it up close. I looked around for a way to get into the ground, and finally I saw a storm drainage pipe. I slipped into the narrow access pipe, which opened into a larger drainage pipe that led to an area where the pond drained. I stood there for a while, letting the water splash on me. This underground fountain quickly became my favorite place to go on hot summer days. The large main pipe extended endlessly into darkness, with many smaller pipes draining in from the sides.

A few weeks later, while walking near the entrance of the drainage pipe, I saw Russ Holt, a boy I knew from school. We exchanged waves, and he walked toward the pipe entrance. I hurried to catch up to with him. "Have you ever been in there?" I asked.

"Of course," he said.

"Me too!" I said. "Are you going now?"

"You bet! Want to come along?"

"Sure!" I tried not to sound too eager. Russ was in a couple of my classes at school. I hadn't met many of the kids at school because I kept to myself, too ashamed to invite anyone home.

I liked his adventurous spirit, and his straight dark hair and puppy-dog eyes were cute.

We entered the pipe, and as it darkened Russ pulled out a flashlight and took the lead. I couldn't think of anything to say, and Russ didn't speak, so we traveled quietly through damp darkness. Finally I saw a faint light that became brighter and brighter. I knew the pipe was ending. "Gosh, Russ, where are we?"

"The Arkansas River."

"Wow, the Arkansas River! Are you kidding? That must be a couple of miles."

"More like 1.8 miles. Haven't you been this far before?"

"As a matter of fact, no. This is my first time." I blushed. We laughed. I ran around on the shore and splashed in the water while Russ skipped pebbles across the river. From then on I was hooked. I had never ventured too far in that direction because the pipe was so dark, and of course it had never occurred to me to bring a flashlight. That made all the difference.

Exploring the pipelines became a regular pastime for us. We hid a flashlight near the entrance, and I kept an extra pair of shoes nearby outside, since my feet always got wet. I didn't want any questions when I got home. The smallest mishap could mean the biggest bruise.

The two of us spent hours roaming through the pipe, putting colorful pieces of tape by the smaller incoming pipes as we explored them. "Russ, you have the map. Where do you think we are?"

"I think we're here," he said, pointing to the map.

"Oh, I thought we were here." I pointed to a different area. "I get so confused underground. I can't seem to keep my directions straight."

"I get disoriented too. That's why we're marking the pipes. Black electrical tape for north/south and the gray duct tape for east/west. Soon we'll have this whole area marked."

"Yeah, once it's marked, I won't be getting lost."

"Okay now, Susie, you surface and find the streets. Let's see where we're really at!" Russ boosted me into the pipe.

"I'm going, I'm going." I crawled out the narrow pipe and looked around for a street sign or two. I then backed carefully into the pipe on my stomach and slid down. Russ grabbed my legs and slowly lowered me. "Whew, looks like we're at Quannah and Archer."

"I see, here it is." Russ marked another X on our map. He was just a couple of blocks off."

Our map grew larger each time. We'd just finished mapping the area around Russ's house when he asked, "Where do you live?"

"Uh, west of here. And north."

"What neighborhood?"

"It's off Edison." I hated being so elusive, but I didn't want anyone to know where I lived, even someone as nice as Russ. "Why do you ask?"

"I wanted to put it on our map." As he held out the map I pointed to the general area.

"It's around here. Off Xenophen."

"Let's see now. We could take this pipe south until we hit this main pipe going east and west." I sighed in relief while Russ planned the route. "We'll have to explore a few more pipes before we can get there."

"That's fine. Exploring is the fun part." It was easy to show my enthusiasm.

"Yeah, and exploring underground is the most fun." We nodded together.

Soon Russ helped me discover how to get almost all the way to my house through those pipes. It wasn't easy, however, because the pipe that led to the surface was so narrow that I had to crawl rather than walk. Although I didn't like crawling, when I surfaced I found myself only three houses from our fenced-in backyard.

On the first Saturday after school had started, Russ really surprised me by showing up with a couple of his friends, Alan

Bowman and Ramon Garcia. I didn't mind the extra company and liked being the only girl around guys. I enjoyed the things guys did because they always seemed to get to do the fun stuff, like playing sports and exploring pipes. But a part of me was very aware that I was the only girl, and I relished the opportunity to have three cute guys around me on the weekends.

The news about the pipe soon spread around school, and more kids became interested in exploring. "We have to control all these kids. We don't want anyone to get hurt." Russ was concerned.

"Yeah, and we don't want our parents to find out," Alan said.

"Why don't we form a club?" Russ looked at the others.

"We can be the original founders," Alan said. I was thrilled because I'd never been part of any group since the short-lived Supernaw Sisters.

"Yeah, and everyone else has to be initiated," Ramon chimed in.

"Does everyone agree?" Russ asked, looking at us. Everyone was nodding and smiling at each other.

"Looks like we agree," Alan observed. We all nodded again: "Yeah." In true Tom Sawyer style we were going to form a secret society.

"What shall we call ourselves?" I asked, trying to think of a clever name.

"How about pipe rats?" Ramon suggested.

"Hey, that's pretty good. Storm pipe rats." I liked being called a rat.

"How about Sewer Rats?" Alan was great with names.

"Yeah, yeah." Everyone agreed. "Sewer Rats." We held out our right hands and stacked them on top of each other. We nodded while moving our hands up and down: one, two, three.

"Sewer Rats forever." We threw our hands in the air and laughed. While the guys were congratulating each other I asked, "Now what shall we call the new kids, the pledges?" They looked at me.

"Let's see. Sewer Rats. What's a baby sewer rat called?" Ramon asked.

"What are you before you're a sewer rat? A sewer mouse?" I shook my head—lousy name.

"Sewer rats, pipes, water, garbage, scum, dampness, dark, underground." Alan tried some free association.

"Wait, I've got it!" Russ was excited. "How about Pipe Scum?"

"Pipe Scum," we said, nodding to each other.

Russ deepened his voice to sound dramatic. "Then Pipe Scum it is." Again we held out our right hands and stacked them on top of each other. Together we nodded: one, two, three.

"Sewer Rats and Pipe Scum forever," we chanted and laughed some more.

With the hardest part over we made up some basic rules: "A Pipe Scum has to be escorted by a Sewer Rat at all times," and "Pipe Scum must keep fresh batteries in all flashlights." We also made a special initiation for Pipe Scum to become a Sewer Rat. Part of the rite was to travel the length of the pipe to the Arkansas River and back, alone. When the official rules were completed each of us invited one friend to join: Russ brought Brad, Ramon brought J.C., Alan asked Becky, and I asked Tommy Tate.

It was never quite the same after that because the number of Sewer Rats and Pipe Scum steadily grew until there always seemed to be a Sewer Rat in the pipes. I hardly ever got to walk the pipe alone anymore. Now when I went to the pipe, Tommy came too. At this point in my life Tommy and the original Sewer Rat crew were about the only guys I could talk to without feeling embarrassed. Tommy was more than ordinary Pipe Scum to me; he became my best friend.

8

Beef Noodle

I'd never seen such a collection of reading materials as I did at the Tulsa Library. Sometimes I spent hours reading papers and magazines from across the United States, other times reading a science fiction or historical novel, because there was still no improvement in my home life, and I spent as much time as possible away from home. It was hard not to get distracted and start thinking about my beautiful dream, but it was also frustrating because I didn't have the slightest idea how to earn the name given to me by the Beautiful Lady. More than once I wished I'd died in my accident. Eventually I'd snap out of my sorrow and go back to reading, hating myself for relapsing into the past. Still, it was easier to think about the old days than to face another new day in the city.

Even though I was never around horses anymore, I still read as many horse magazines as possible. But over the weeks I began to notice other types of magazines, the kind young women like to read. I had always felt comfortable being one of the guys, but now I was thinking more and more about being with one special guy. Woody's unpredictable fits of rage had already forced Kathy to leave home. She lived with Louise for a while and went to school in Sand Springs. I'd meet her in town whenever I could. It was always fun for me because we'd go on double dates together. I romanticized about someday falling in love. I dreamed my love would ride up to me on his pinto stallion and pull me up, and together we'd ride away.

One day while looking in the teen section I saw a copy of a magazine for teenagers. I'd never seen it before, but I figured it would be okay to read it, even though I was only sixteen. "I'm mature for my years," I rationalized, thinking the pictures might be too racy for me. But I enjoyed all of the color photos of pretty girls and the stories about guys and wondered if I would ever fall in love.

Near the back page I noticed an advertisement for a contest sponsored by a toothpaste company. There was an address to write for an application. In a moment of clear insanity I decided to enter my sister Kathy because she was so beautiful and had a perfect smile. I copied the information from the magazine and sent away for the application. I checked the mailbox daily for the next two weeks, and when the application arrived I carefully completed all the information, making up whatever I didn't know. There was only one problem: I needed a recent photo of her. That was a tough one and took some timing and planning. So I waited impatiently until one day when no one was home. Then I slipped into Mom's bedroom and checked under the bed, where she kept a brown shoebox filled with photos. After rummaging through countless pictures I found Kathy's recent school photo. It showed her beautiful smile. "Perfect!" I whispered. I took the picture and submitted it with the application, not considering the consequences.

I soon forgot about the contest because my mind was preoccupied with fear, and I had to be careful not to go home when Woody was there alone. I stayed at school as late as possible and came home only when I was sure Mom was there.

One night the light was on in the kitchen as I walked through the door. Mom turned and looked directly at me. Sitting at the kitchen table she asked, "Susie, do you know anything about this toothpaste contest?" A sheepish grin slid across my face. I hated not being able to keep a straight face, and I always looked guilty.

But this time I was really guilty, and I started to flush crimson. Mom knew instantly.

"How could you ever do such a thing?" she asked.

"I can't understand why you're so upset." I defended my actions. "It's not like I sent in a picture of her in a bathing suit," I added, hoping for a grin. Desperate, I blurted, "I entered her because I knew she could win. We all know Kathy has the prettiest smile around."

She wasn't satisfied and sat with a stoic expression, pondering her options. "You don't show respect for a person by going behind their backs and using their name."

"But she's so beautiful. I did it 'cause I knew she could win."

"Regardless of your intentions, it was wrong." Her verdict was final.

"Did she win?" I was hoping to change the subject, but it didn't work.

"She got an honorable mention, but that's not what's important. What's important is that you realize that you've done something very wrong." I bowed my head and nodded. She continued, "At the same time, I think it's time you focused on yourself instead of her."

"I learned my lesson, okay? What do you mean focus on myself?"

"Kathy knows how to be a young lady. All your sisters know how. Even Judy outgrew her tomboy stage with horses. It's time that you learned too."

"Do you mean like wearing makeup and polishing my nails?"

"Yes, and much more. I'm going to sign you up for a class. It will help you become a young lady."

"I'll do whatever they say." It didn't sound that bad either. I thought having your period made you a young lady, not how you dressed or acted.[1]

"We'll have to get you a new pair of shoes."

"Like dancing shoes?" I remembered my previous dance-lesson disaster.

"No. You're getting your first pair of heels."

Egads! Heels! I hid my terror. "Of course, anything it takes." Glancing over my shoulder as I went into the kitchen, I noticed that Mom had a slight grin on her face. Looking for something to eat, I found a piece of bread and some ketchup and made a ketchup sandwich. It was my comfort food now. Munching quietly I slipped out the back door. Hearing no one call my name, I whistled, feeling like I'd gotten off pretty easy. After that I attended my class at a local modeling school and forgot about the toothpaste contest rather quickly.[2] I was glad that now Mom could afford to buy me a few things since all my sisters were gone and she still had a good job.

Weeks later an unusual letter addressed to me arrived from the Tulsa State Fair Committee. I tore off the end of the envelope and looked inside, hoping perhaps I'd received some free tickets. I opened an official-looking letter, complete with letterhead and two signatures. Reading the first few lines I realized what had happened. The letter requested that I appear for interviews for the position of Tractor Queen at the 1967 Tulsa State Fair.[3] Mom had finally delivered her justice by entering me in a contest, but Tractor Queen? That evening when she returned home from work I showed Mom the letter.

"You must not only participate," she emphasized, "but do your best."

"Okay, I know, I know." Since Mom would settle for nothing less I agreed and secretly hoped this embarrassment would slip by, unnoticed by the kids at school. But the Tulsa newspapers made it impossible for that to happen.

There were procedures established for selecting the Tractor Queen, as every year there were several candidates.[4] According to the letter I had made the top five, and Mom acted a little bit proud. I could hear what my dad would have said: "You made

16. Susie poses on a tractor as the new Tractor Queen for the Tulsa State Fair in September 1967. *Photo copyright © 2009*, Tulsa World.

the top five? Must have only been five candidates!" Brushing aside a tear I wished I could make him love me.

Mom withdrew some of her precious savings and took me to buy a new dress and fancy shoes. I enjoyed the shopping trip with Mom. I tried on several dresses and modeled them for her, showing her I had learned to walk and turn. She seemed pleasantly surprised. After we found a suitable dress she took me to buy some shoes. I thanked my lucky stars they were flats. Although I could walk in heels, I was in no hurry to use my new skill.

I had a new outlook on the upcoming event. So what if the dress was for an interview? At least I had gotten a brand-new dress and shoes out of the experience, not to mention a chance to spend some quality time with Mom. After completing my outfit Mom took me to the beauty parlor for a new look to go with the new clothes. My long hair got a short styled haircut, but with no wild perm like before.

At the interview the panel was surprised to hear me say that I'd lived on a farm before and missed it terribly. Three judges smiled and wrote something down on the paper in front of them. When they finished asking their questions one man said, "Are there any questions you'd like to ask us?"

My confidence returned at the thought of the turnaround. After a deep breath I said, "Yes, I have a question. Aren't you going to ask me how to load a pig into a trailer?"

"Why is that important?" the elderly judge asked.

I squirmed. "That's a question only a real country person can answer." The judges laughed and whispered to each other. I held my breath in anticipation.

The youngest judge said, "Wait, I'm not from the country. So how *do* you load a pig?"

"Put a bucket over its head." All but one of the judges laughed as if they didn't believe it was true. The silent judge smiled broadly: I could tell *he* knew how to load a pig.

The youngest judge asked, "Any more questions before we finish?"

"Yes, I'd like to know if I get to change clothes and wear something more casual when I drive the tractor."

For some inexplicable reason all three of them laughed. After a few moments the roar of their laughter subsided as one of the judges wiped a tear from his eye, explaining, "You don't have to drive a tractor at all. You only have to smile and sit on a tractor for your picture. You'll also present the trophy to the winner of the tractor pull." Personally I was disappointed. I would rather have competed in the tractor pull than just stand there with a trophy.

That afternoon I found out that I'd won. I had my picture taken on all kinds of tractors, and it was more fun than I'd thought.

I was surprised to see myself in my straw hat, cutoff jeans, and white crop top on the cover of *Ranch and Farm World* and even more surprised to see a different picture on the "Program of Events" for the awards banquet of the Nationwide Junior Tractor Operators.[5] I sat at the head table, and the caterer served something I'd never eaten before, a luxurious taste that lingered in my mouth for days. I didn't know what it was called, but it consisted of pieces of tender beef covered in rich, creamy sauce served over a huge bed of fat egg noodles. Happily I slurped away, commenting, "Gosh, I really love these beef noodles."

As everyone laughed someone said, "That's beef stroganoff!"

"Well, it's become a new favorite for me."

✳ ✳ ✳

Seeing my picture in the Sunday paper, Mom cut it out and started a scrapbook for me. Grandma Carrie called to say I was well on my way to attracting a good Muscogee man, reminding me I still needed to learn how to make Indian bread. I heard her laugh and knew I wasn't even close to learning how to make any kind of bread. Grandma said she wanted me to keep her informed about what us young'uns were up to. She said something in Mvskoke that meant the children will lead their parents where they would not go on their own. I thought she was talking about Dad, but I wasn't sure.

The kids at school soon discovered my secret and started calling me "Beef Noodle," which was, I suppose, better than being called "Tractor Queen."

9

Susie Q

I attended different church services in Tulsa with various friends. After attending church with fellow Sewer Rat Tommy Tate for a year, I felt so at home that I transferred my membership from Osage Hills to Wheeling Avenue. Until then I hadn't even been aware that churches maintained membership rolls. It reminded me of American Indian tribes keeping track of their members. It was important for me to find a church to attend regularly since Native American Church meetings were seldom. I felt safe at the Wheeling Avenue church and became active in its youth group. Our youth director was a kind and gentle man named Dee Stribling. One of his many activities included recruiting for Phillips University, a small Christian college in northwest Oklahoma. He was a sympathetic listener, and I found myself opening up more about my problems at home. He always made time for me when I came to see him.

Since we started out just being friends and attending church together, I didn't think of Tommy as my boyfriend, but my thoughts changed the night he gave me a private nickname. At a football game in mid-November, Central was getting slaughtered by Bartlesville High School, 66–0. The wind was blowing sleet and rain sideways. The cheerleaders had put on their coats and were gathering under umbrellas on the sidelines. Even with my jacket on I stood shivering in the cold, so I kept jumping up and down, trying to stay warm. I heard those famous words usually spoken by Indian men of older times when they were courting. But this time the words were uttered by a younger, non-Indian voice.

"Want to share my blanket?" Standing under a drab green wool army blanket was Tommy. I walked over to him, and he raised his arm, opening the blanket. He wrapped his arm around me, pulling the blanket across my body with his other arm until I was completely enclosed. Soon I stopped shivering and became aware of his body next to mine. His curly blond hair was dripping water down his forehead. I noticed his muscular basketball-player build, and his musky smell lingered in my mind. In spite of the darkness I noticed his blue eyes. I'd never been close to Tommy like this.

Neither of us said anything as we watched the clock tick off the final seconds. For two intelligent people we were both totally speechless as we looked at each other and giggled from embarrassment. I had absolutely no idea what to say but managed to squeak, "Thanks for the cover from the cold and rain."

At first his words were rushed, but he slowed down as he spoke. "Do you, do you have a ride home? If not I could take you. I have my parents' car." I grinned at him, wanting to hug him for asking because I usually rode the bus to the games. Getting transportation to places was always a major task for me, so I was more than delighted to get a personal lift all the way home. Instead of hugging him or even saying anything reasonably intelligent, I blurted out, "Yes. I mean no! I mean okay." I always had some smart comeback for everything. Yet this shy young man in his honest sincerity left me babbling. Tommy looked directly into my eyes and then smiled from ear to ear. Thank goodness he didn't make any snide remarks about my answer. Instead he was rather reticent. He started to say something and then changed his mind. His silence made me extra alert, but I'm not sure why.

After we walked to his car he held the blanket over my head while I climbed inside the front seat. Once inside he started the car and let it idle. The windows were fogged over and icy. It would

be a few moments before we went anywhere. I watched him turn
on the radio, which was playing Creedence Clearwater Revival's
version of "Susie Q." Tommy started singing, holding his right
hand in a fist like a microphone. I soon joined in, leaning toward
him to share his pretend microphone. When the song ended we
both laughed at our silliness. With the sound of the disc jockey's
voice fading I smiled shyly at him and started shaking the water
out of my hair with my hands.

"Can you believe it? The sleet has partially frozen on my hair."
Unexpectedly Tommy leaned forward and touched my hair. For
the first time we gazed soulfully into each other's eyes. We were
both breathless and speechless.

When the windows cleared we drove away from the stadium
in a comfortable silence, listening to tunes on the radio, singing
along if a song came on that either one of us liked. When we
arrived at my house Tommy jumped out of the car, forgetting
his wet jacket as he ran to open my door. By then the rain had
stopped, but the wind was still blowing fiercely as he walked me
to the door with his hands in his pockets, pretending not to be
cold. He waited while I unlocked the door and pushed it open.
"I really had a good time, Susie Q," he stammered.

"Me too," I mumbled. "Good night." I slipped inside and
peeked out the side window. He smiled for a moment, and it
didn't look like he felt the wind at all. After that he always called
me Susie Q when we were alone.

✳ ✳ ✳

Going to Tommy's church was a natural part of our intimate
relationship. Sometimes we'd slip into the church when no one
was there and sit in the pews to pray. I wasn't sure of all the
things Tommy prayed about, but I always prayed that my home
life would become less violent. Earlier Mom had cautioned me
that things were becoming out of control at home and that she
feared for my safety. When she suggested I think about leaving
home like my sisters, it broke my heart. While I worried about

her safety, she worried about mine. Making plans to leave home was equivalent to giving up hope, so I prayed instead that I'd never have to leave. When the time came, unfortunately, I wasn't prepared for it.

One Friday night in early March I returned home from the library. Mom and Woody were in the middle of a huge fight in the kitchen, and he was choking her while she screamed. He paused for a moment when I entered. When I saw what he was doing I dropped my purse and coat. Running over to him I grabbed his arm and pulled violently until his grip around her neck loosened, and she fell to the floor. Turning, he swung at me, hitting me hard on the side of my face, next to my right eye. I fell back, dazed by the punch; my head hit the wall, and I winced in pain.

I opened my eyes in time to see him pick up a heavy brown Ovaltine jar off the kitchen counter and in a drunken rage swing it at me, hitting my raised arm before the jar glanced off the side of my nose. Blood started oozing down my face. I crumpled the rest of the way down to the floor, holding my nose and feeling excruciating pain. I glanced up and saw him lunge drunkenly at me. I instinctively rolled sideways and ducked, his grasping hands barely missing my neck. He stumbled into the wall and then fell to the floor. I staggered to my feet, leaning on the wall, and heard Mom scream, "RUN!" I didn't want to leave her and paused for a second, keeping my hands on the wall while my head stopped spinning. She yelled again, "RUN!" After gaining my balance I took a deep breath through my mouth and staggered out the door without stopping for my purse or coat.

Woody slowly staggered to his feet and followed me out the front door, screaming and shouting threats. The cool air was invigorating as I swayed into the neighbor's unfenced backyard, where I rested a few moments. The sound of his voice was getting louder, so I hurried toward the drainage pipe. I slipped several feet inside the pipe and lay there quietly, like a hunted animal. I shivered, hearing his drunken voice calling my name, feeling more alone than I had ever felt before. His angry voice came incredibly close. Just when I thought he was going to find me,

I heard a strange noise that sounded like a giggling child. The noise faded quickly, and Woody's angry voice slowly seemed to follow it. Everything became quiet. Too scared to move I lay there wondering what to do now that I couldn't go home. If the police found me they'd take me home.[1]

My head was still throbbing, and more blood was trickling out my nose and from the cut around my eye. I thought about Grandma Carrie's stories of the Little People, spirits that exist in plants and trees. Although they sometimes cause mischief, they also help lost or runaway children. After a silent prayer for help a song started playing in my mind. I was surprised it wasn't a church song or at least a Muscogee chant. "Left a good job in the city . . ." I started humming the tune of "Proud Mary," recently rerecorded by Ike and Tina Turner. There were stories about the domestic violence Tina had endured in the teen magazines. Thinking about Tina and her kids I decided my situation wasn't as serious as hers and then began softly singing the words of the song. After singing, "Rolling, rolling, rolling down the river," I realized I had to get down to the river.

Wiping the blood from my face with my sleeve I began to softly sing again, rising up to all fours and crawling deeper into the small pipe. I knew there was a flashlight at the end of it. I felt my way in the dark for the quarter-mile trip to the main drainage pipe. There was water in the pipe from the last rain, but it only formed a small stream and was not very deep, just cold.

Sliding into the larger pipe I crossed over to the regular entrance we used as Sewer Rats. It was dark, but I felt around, found a flashlight, and quickly clicked it on. The batteries were fresh, and the tunnel lit up with a glow that instantly made me feel warm and safe. It was the responsibility of the Pipe Scum to keep the flashlights stocked with new batteries, and they were evidently doing a good job. I started down the long path to the river, feeling assured that no one would find me in here or at the river. Being able to stand up and having light changed my experience. I wasn't scared anymore because I had escaped. Pain had numbed my swollen nose, but it still trickled blood. Then I began singing in a raspy voice: "Left a good job in the city, working for the man every night and day." I repeated the song until I reached the end at the river. Looking out I saw a deer glance at me before fleeing in the darkness and thanked my elder brother for watching out for me. Then I took a deep breath and jumped out.

My joy was short-lived as a wave of frigid air slammed against my damaged face and wet body, causing me to break out in a shiver. I folded my arms and jumped up and down to get warm. I searched the sky for Pleiades to gain comfort from the Seven Spirits, but the clouds obstructed my view. Where could I go? I first thought of going to Hominy, but that was over fifty miles away, and I didn't think I could make it that far without being seen. I thought of other relatives in Skiatook, but I couldn't make it to Skiatook without being seen either. Shivering and cold I looked toward Tulsa. Kenneth lived on the other side of town. I then thought about Tommy. His house was not too far, but I couldn't see his parents letting me stay there. My mind was racing down streets in town, through pictures of people's faces, trying to find an answer.

In desperation I cried out, "Now what?" My words echoed in the night air, and no sooner had I finished shouting them than a vivid picture came to my mind. It was a picture of my church, Wheeling Avenue. "Thanks," I whispered respectfully. It was only a few miles away, and if I ran I could stay warm. I hurried along the river toward town. I reached the church exhausted and collapsed on the front steps. It was almost 11:00 p.m. on Friday night. Everything was dark, even Dee's basement office. I huddled next to the door to keep warm and resigned myself to soft sobbing.

Dee had worked late that evening and was glad to be going home. He locked the basement door and walked toward his car. His eyes glanced at the front of the church as he opened the car door. He noticed something on the front steps and walked closer. Reaching down he put his hand gently on my shoulder. I lifted my head and looked up at him. The swelling of my nose had merged with the swelling around my eye, and my face had taken on a distorted appearance. I tried to talk but couldn't because my mouth was too dry. My words came out in raspy squeaks. Gently Dee covered my mouth with his right hand, not needing any words or explanations, having seen enough to guess what had happened. Taking me by the hands he helped me to my feet. I was still shaking when he put my arm around his shoulder and helped me walk to his car. He assured me, "Everything's going to be all right."

"Things will never be all right," I gasped.

"It's okay. You're safe now."

"Not if I go home. I can never go home again." I wiped my eyes with the bottom of my shirt.

"Don't worry. You won't have to go home."

"Where will I go?"

"I'm not sure, but for now you can come home with me." Dee smiled. "But first we go to the hospital."

I nodded my head in reluctant approval. "I don't have anything." He nodded and closed the car door.

"Don't worry. Tomorrow I'll go over to your house and pick some stuff up."

At the hospital Dee called his wife to let her know where he was and that he was bringing home company. By the time we got to Dee's house I'd fallen asleep.

Dee and his wife helped abused women and children as part of their ministry. I felt blessed to have found someone to help me. Now not only was I safe, but they understood my situation, so I didn't have to go into details about the violence that was already written all over my face. I stayed with Dee while I finished high school, and my home life was easier than I ever imagined it could be. They offered me comfort and security and allowed me to continue all my activities. Yet in spite of all their kind support I found myself worrying about Mom and feeling guilty about leaving home. I missed my mom and sisters and wished that our family could have been closer.

10

Super Sue

Studying for classes with Tommy made learning fun, and we studied together as much as possible. I thrived in his company but had to work extra hard just to keep up with him because he was always reading and learning more. He reminded me of my sister, helping me along when I was learning how to cheer. Tommy also helped me in my studies, always pushing me just a little. I couldn't let him see me falling behind, so I made it a point to study early every morning before classes and late into the evening until I fell asleep, often with my head on the book. I visualized the words seeping into my brain, learning through osmosis like Edgar Cayce.[1] It never worked as far as I could tell, because I had to reread everything several times. I even practiced memorizing things by writing them down.

I enjoyed studying quantum mechanics because the quantum world came closer to the more aesthetic traditional American Indian way of thinking than the fact-based Newtonian physics.[2] I enjoyed debating theories of multiple universes, a seamless whole, and the duality of nature and light with both Tommy and Kenneth Anquoe.[3] While Tommy detailed experiments for each theory Kenneth nodded with a knowing look, smiling. Quantum mechanics had many similarities to his American Indian beliefs, and he wasn't surprised that today's scientists agreed with his views.

"Do you understand what the scientists are saying? These

theories are explaining what we in the American Indian world know as 'everything is related,'" Kenneth said.

"Like a web of life?"[4]

"More like a 'seamless whole.'" Kenneth laughed.

He had used my words to get his point across, so I decided to use his: "Yeah, I know. We're all one."

We both laughed at the similarity between cultural and scientific theories. I didn't tell Kenneth that top physicists like Niels Bohr also referred to the insanity or unnaturalness of the quantum world.[5]

Besides discussing the quantum world with Tommy, I asked him to help me understand the standardized tests used for college admittance, since he always scored at the top in all areas. I wanted to learn his secrets for test taking, so I could score at the top with him. He was willing to share and never held back any information. We encouraged each other emotionally and challenged each other intellectually. During our senior year Tommy and I planned identical class schedules. We competed for the best score on all of our tests. It was exhilarating to compete on a friendly basis.

When I took the ACT it was early in the school year, on a crisp, clear, early fall Saturday morning.[6] Tommy and I had studied most of the summer for this big exam. As we walked into the room the teacher stopped writing on the board and turned around. "Please don't sit together," the teacher said with her mouth barely moving.

I laughed to myself, wondering if she thought we were going to cheat—unlikely, since Tommy and I were both straight-A students and taking honors classes. But as instructed, we took desks in the front of the room, three rows apart. As students filed into the room I noticed that the desks around Tommy and me filled up first. By the time the students were all seated it was eight o'clock, and the teacher began handing out the test booklets and pencils, giving two pencils to each student in case one broke during the test.

"Pencils can only be sharpened between tests," she explained. "No one is allowed to get up during the test, and there will be absolutely no talking!" She looked directly at me with a cutting stare.

As I broke the taped seal on my test booklet I looked over my left shoulder and smiled at Tommy. He flashed back a crooked half smile and then raised one eyebrow in his typical Mr. Spock imitation. He raised his right hand in the Vulcan hand greeting, his fingers split into equal pairs. Since I couldn't raise just one eyebrow, I hid one eye by placing my left hand over my left eyebrow to hold it in place so only my right eyebrow lifted. Then I returned the hand greeting, trying to stifle a giggle. This caused Tommy to laugh, which drew a stern look from the teacher. It was time to get serious.

I sat on the edge of my wooden chair like a finely bred racehorse nervously waiting in the starting gate. The test books were quickly thrown open, and I worked quietly and rapidly in the austere classroom. After each section I slyly scratched my chin on my left shoulder so I was able to quickly glance down at Tommy's answers. My eyes moved back and forth several times as I memorized the pattern of his marks and compared them to my own, trying to guess how far along he was in relation to my own progress. As he finished each section he too slyly glanced over toward me, trying to see what page I was on. As always we raced to see who could finish first.

Just to startle him I skipped ahead a few pages and started working. Out of the corner of my eye I waited for him to look my way. When he finally glanced at me, it was hard not to laugh. His face looked shocked as he noticed my progress by the page my test booklet was open to. He thumbed forward a couple of pages to get an idea where I was. After showing a desperate grin he shook his head and sighed deeply. Then he went back to the page where he was on the test and began reading again. As usual he was totally cool.

Finishing the difficult test first due to my trick, I quietly closed my booklet and gently laid down my number-two pencil, notic-ing that I had barely worn down the eraser. Tommy sighed. Then as if it were an afterthought I picked up the booklet and started paging through it, like I was reviewing my answers. I casually went back and completed the three pages I'd skipped. It was just a game for me, and I wanted to make it a challenge for my best friend, as I saw us as two yearling foals racing neck-and-neck through an open pasture on a brisk spring morning.

✳   ✳   ✳

I didn't spend all my time studying and cheering. I had a few friends, like Purna Gibson, Jan Coulter, Francis Evans, ReNee Works, and MaryJo Copeland. ReNee and MaryJo were African Americans, and I spent more time with them, dancing all night at slumber parties and going to church, than I did with my three Caucasian friends. They were proud of me for being a cheerleader and thought I added some color to the squad and joked that they wanted to teach me some rhythm. I think they were partially successful. Their parents never said I couldn't come over because I was Indian, like some of the cheerleaders' mothers did.

Jan and Francis were kind to me and invited me to their homes, where I learned about their lifestyle of debutante balls and girls' social clubs. They even offered to sponsor me for membership into their exclusive social club but knew I could never afford the dues. Still, it was nice to be asked, and I loved trying on their beautiful long formals.

Purna and I were senior cheerleaders, and Anne Barker was the head cheerleader. Purna, a fun-loving spirit with short frosted hair, always accepted me, while my relationship with Anne felt more like a competition. Purna encouraged me not to let oth-ers intimidate me and hurt my feelings. Being extra sensitive, it seemed I was always crying about something mean someone had said or done to me. I admired Purna's optimistic attitude, and she became a sister substitute, since Kathy and I were only talking occasionally on the phone.

My unspoken competition with Anne was insidious. Even though we were both cheerleaders and in the school's chorus, we kept a certain formality between us. Anne could sing and was tall and leggy, landing the part of Nellie Forbush, the female lead in our school's production of *South Pacific*.[7] I played Liat, a Vietnamese girl, the daughter of Bloody Mary and the lover of Lieutenant Cable. It was a very minor role, with a bit a typecasting, I'm sure. Anne, with perfect bleach-blond hair and blue eyes, was homecoming queen, head cheerleader, and a good dancer. I knew I could never really compete with all that. My only source of comfort was that she couldn't make straight As or tumble.

Our school also put on a yearly production called "Central Daze." Although it was basically a school talent show, it was a major production, and you had to audition for a part in it. There were singing groups, dancers, musicians, and comedy routines. The finale was an act by the Dazettes, a high-kicking Rockettes-style dance line of girls tapping in glittering outfits and high heels.[8] Purna encouraged me to try out for the dance line and helped me get a pair of tap shoes with heels. I was glad I knew how to walk in heels; now I only had to learn how to dance in them. Purna and I practiced together, and when we made the dance line after tryouts we attended classes together. Of course Anne was also a Dazette, and we'd each try to kick the highest. My main problem was that I was always at the end of the line because I was short, and when we broke into our star pinwheel pattern I had to cover the most ground. Instead of "step, kick" it was more like "jump, kick." I always managed to barely keep up. As if that wasn't enough I heard Anne was trying out for a solo dance in "Central Daze," so I also had to come up with an expanded floor exercise routine.[9] I didn't have the advantage of the special gymnastics mat floor, so I modified some of my tumbling stunts but kept my original choreography and music. Anne and I both got solo spots, but I never once thought about using this opportunity to earn my name.

✳ ✳ ✳

Weeks later I was asked to go see my counselor, Mr. Baer. Mr. Baer was a short, heavyset man with thinning gray hair and black glasses. I liked him and thought it was a good omen to have a counselor with a name similar to my clan name. Mr. Baer's office was piled high with college catalogs and career information. I maneuvered myself through the room to a couple of uncluttered chairs. His glasses were far down on his nose as he read an official-looking piece of paper. He glanced up at me.

"Go ahead and sit down, Susie. Get comfortable. I've something important to tell you." Placing the paper on his desk he took off his glasses, gently pinching and rubbing the bridge of his nose. "Have your ears been burning lately?" he quietly asked.

"No," I said, unsure of his meaning.

"Well, we've been talking about you, and sometimes they say that your ears burn when someone is talking about you." He continued. "A lot of people have been talking about you, and I was asked to fill out an application form with a recommendation letter on your behalf." I still had no idea what he was talking about. "Do you remember when you took the National Merit Qualifying exam?"[10]

I paused. "I don't remember my scores."

"Oh, I've got the scores right here. They were quite excellent and qualified you for a very special honor, one that has not been awarded to this school for some time."

"You mean it's a good thing?"

Mr. Baer's laughter became louder, and his whole body shook, especially his stomach, reminding me of a bear. "A very good thing. Folks at the national level like you very much and are extremely impressed with your academic achievements and your extracurricular activities. I emphasized the fact you are one of six cheerleaders on a squad that placed first in city and state competitions. And when I said you were also a cheerleading instructor for the National Cheerleading Association, and that last summer you taught boy-girl cheerleading stunts to college cheerleaders at the smu cheerleading clinic, that really snowed them!"[11]

I thought to myself, "Yeah, if only they knew I did all that stuff so I wouldn't have to go home, I bet they wouldn't be impressed at all."

Mr. Baer quickly added, "By the way, do you have any plans for the summer?"

"I was going to teach at the Oklahoma University summer cheerleading clinic for four weeks and another four weeks at Ole Miss."[12] I hadn't thought much about college, and there was no support from home for higher education, although my sister Kathy was going to college. Dee always encouraged me to attend college, any college. But without any financial support I didn't know how I could pay tuition. Mr. Baer's chuckle as I left his office made me wonder whether he was joking. I promptly forgot about what he had said until a couple of weeks later.

A hot and muggy afternoon in late May found me working in Mom's front yard, pulling little weeds from the freshly planted iris beds. I visited her more now, but only when Woody was gone. A man wearing a brown uniform hurriedly picked up a clipboard from the front seat of his Western Union truck.

"Does a Susan G. Supernaw live here? I have a telegram for her," he stated. I introduced myself by offering my hand. He looked surprised but shook my hand anyway. He held up the telegram and said, "Looks like an important one. Not everyone gets a telegram from the president of the United States!" I thought he was kidding.

"The president. Oh sure, I talk with him all the time." We both laughed. He handed me the clipboard and pen and pointed out where to sign for delivery. I waited until he drove down the street before opening the official-looking envelope with the seal of the president of the United States embossed in the upper left-hand corner.[13] I'd never received a telegram before, so I opened it slowly and began reading:

You have been chosen as one of this year's Presidential Scholars,
a group that represents the outstanding high school seniors in

*the country. I would like to congratulate you and invite you
to lunch with me at the White House on June 10th. Complete
details on your visit are being forwarded to you.*

Sincerely, Richard M. Nixon

I looked around, expecting to see someone who was not there.
I kept asking myself, "Who's playing this joke on me?" Then
I thought of what Mr. Baer had said to me about his recommendation letter. I folded the telegram and put it in my back
pocket. As I started up the steps to the porch I peeked behind
the bushes, hoping to see someone like a *Candid Camera* ambassador.[14] Nothing.

By the time Monday came I was starting to believe the telegram
was an elaborate joke because I hadn't heard anything else about
it. I was afraid to mention this to anyone. I went to school early
to talk to Mr. Baer. He motioned for me to sit.

"I told you, you wouldn't hear anything from *me*," he emphasized. "Did you get a telegram?"

"Yes, yesterday. Was it supposed to be from President Nixon?"
I asked.

"That makes sense. You're a presidential scholar, so why
shouldn't the president himself be the one to inform you? Now
that's class!" He leaned forward, chuckling to himself as I handed
him the telegram. He read it a couple of times, looked at me,
and then pointed to the phone. "Time to call the newspapers,"
he said winking at me.[15]

"I never applied for this. How did they select me?" I asked
anxiously.

"Don't you understand? You're a natural. You're a straight-A
student with a long list of activities."[16]

He switched the subject to something more interesting: money.
"Although the award itself is honorary, you have also been awarded
a four-year National Merit Scholarship to any university in the
United States. Santa Fe Railway will be your sponsor for the
scholarship. Next month when you go to Washington DC you'll

receive your presidential scholar's medallion and meet the president, the vice-president, and all your congressmen."[17]

"Sounds fantastic, but I'm not looking forward to meeting Vice-President Agnew. That man really irritates me," I confided.[18]

"Don't worry! He irritates a lot of people! Respect the position if you can't respect the man."

"I guess I can always cut his face out of the picture!" I joked.

I left to find Tommy. I couldn't wait to tell him the good news and share my happiness with him. Tommy had just been accepted to prestigious Princeton and would be moving east during the summer. I rushed to tell him. Holding the telegram to his face I said, "Look! Read this."

"Okay, let me see it." He read the telegram quickly. His reaction startled me as it was one of shock, not happiness.

"What's wrong, Tommy?"

"Nothing. Congratulations, Susie. This is really wonderful." He tried to smile, but I could see that his feelings were hurt.

"No, something's wrong. What is it?" As he pulled back from my embrace he looked away from me. I begged him, "Please tell me."

He was silent for a moment. "Why couldn't that happen to me, Susie Q? Maybe if I was an Indian too, it might have."

Never before had our different heritages surfaced in our relationship, but now they stood paramount. Tommy never inquired about the details of my personal life because he knew things were bad at home. Although I didn't talk about it, my Muscogee (Creek) heritage was a special source of personal pride in spite of the hippies, who made American Indians a fashion trend. The American Indian Movement, which encouraged American Indians to be activists for their treaty rights, had helped me realize how accepting I was of current prejudices and discrimination.[19]

Only MaryJo and ReNee asked about my American Indian ways. They instinctively understood the double life I led, temporarily leaving cultural values behind to blend in with the mainstream white world. I invited them to some summer dances, and they invited me to an overnight vigil when Martin Luther King Jr. died.[20] Why didn't I ever share my culture with Tommy? We had prayed together all night when Robert Kennedy was shot.[21] Perhaps I should have shared more, but I was so ashamed of my home life, and I had never separated being American Indian from my home life, even though I learned most of my cultural beliefs away from home. I was always reticent to give any personal details.

I gently hugged Tommy and rested my head on his chest. He sighed, brushing away a small tear. He cupped my face in his hands and kissed me gently. "Oh, Susie Q. I'm so sorry. I didn't mean what I just said. You're such a unique and wonderful person that you really do deserve this award. I could never do all the stuff you do."

We both understood why we couldn't share equal honors. We couldn't be considered equal because we weren't of the same race. The government had made sure of that by passing the Civil Rights Act of 1964, which separated us not just by race but also by gender.[22] Such a separation made him feel he had an unfair disadvantage and made me feel like I'd been given an unfair advantage. The competition was over, and regardless of his apology I felt that I hadn't won because I was better; I had won because I was Indian.

I called to tell Dad, hoping now he would be proud of me. He never said why he thought I had won or that he was proud of me. His only comment was that he hoped I was intelligent enough not to act like I was more intelligent than those people around me. He didn't sound like he was joking, so I assumed this was his advice. I wondered if this wasn't Dad's way of emphasizing that I should remain humble and true to the path *ekvncvpecetv*, by not making myself appear smarter or better than others. I began adjusting my English and conversation to better fit in with those around me.

Grandma Carrie was delighted with the news. She'd always

thought Dad was smart and told me I had inherited my book-learning skills from him. She opened up to me about some of the things that had happened since Dad left Mom. She said that if Mary had given birth to a girl instead of a boy, things would have been different. Dad only had one semester left to graduate as a chemical engineer from ou, but after Charlie was born Mary wouldn't let Dad go back to school for his last semester. Perhaps she was afraid he might stray. Carrie said not to be too hard on Dad because Mary did everything she could to keep him from us girls and to keep the child support payments away from us. She explained that every time Mary saw any of us girls or had to write a child support check to Mom, she was reminded of her sin and felt guilty. Because of her guilt she didn't want any of us around. Carrie also confided that Mary didn't like her or her daughter, Sara, either. She believed Mary didn't like being around Indians, maybe because she was afraid Dad would want to be Indian or maybe because she was prejudiced inside. So that was why Grandma had bought her own house. After our conversation I didn't feel so angry at Dad.

Several weeks later I learned that Grandma Carrie had suffered a stroke and been moved to a nursing home in Coweta. I cried as if she had died because I knew I'd never have the chance to go anywhere with her again. When I visited her at the nursing home she would only speak Mvskoke. I wished I had taken more time to learn our language so I could talk to her without a translator. Later they discovered she could understand some English; she just refused to speak it. Instead of feeling sad for her, I felt sad for me.

11

Tomorrow's Leader

Meeting the other presidential scholars was a shock for me because the stereotype of an egghead is a clumsy, unattractive person with thick glasses and no social skills or love life. Although that description may fit some intellectuals, it didn't fit the scholars I met. Not only did they enjoy school and find it easy (or an escape from reality like me), but they were also involved in many other activities. Besides being future scientists and mathematicians, they were athletes, artists, musicians, and writers.

Our government really "put on the ritz" for us. At all of our meetings we were called the "leaders of tomorrow," which happily reminded me of how roadmen talked. The Native American Church teaches that *all* youth are the leaders of tomorrow. I had been recognized by my elders as tomorrow's leader long before I became the first American Indian to be a presidential scholar. The thought kept me amused while listening to the speeches. Dinners and lunches were thrown in our honor with more different kinds of food than I knew existed. All those scrumptious new flavors alone were reward enough for me.

My mom came with me to DC, and we had a good time when I wasn't meeting important people or eating delicious food. We went for early-morning walks together since she didn't want me walking alone. When we went sightseeing I tried to lose her. Instead of waiting in line for the elevator to the top of the Washington Monument, I told her I'd meet her at the top and took off on the stairs.[1] Unfortunately she beat me to the top and was waiting when I arrived, breathless. I may have been tomorrow's leader, but I was also just a teenager, fresh out of high school, trying to have some fun in the nation's capital.

The culmination of activities was supposed to be lunch with President Richard Nixon. However, he was delayed on his return from Vietnam, and as a result Vice President Spiro Agnew presided over the presentation of the presidential scholarship medallions. I was disheartened, but regardless of my personal feelings it was a major press event. There were speeches that lasted for hours. The highlight came when each scholar was called to the stage to receive a personalized bronze medallion and a handshake from Vice President Agnew. In spite of my personal feelings I smiled for my picture anyway.

Afterward the press milled around with the politicians, talking with different presidential scholars. Bud Wilkinson, the Oklahoma University football coach when the Sooners won three National Football Championships, wanted to meet me because my name sounded familiar.[2] He walked over and offered his hand.

"Hi, I'm Bud Wilkinson," he warmly greeted me.

"Yes, I know. I'm Susie Supernaw," I said, shaking his hand.

"Yes, I know," he laughed. "Are you any relation to John Supernaw?"

"He's my father." I wondered how Bud knew Dad. Then I remembered that my dad had gone to the University of Oklahoma from 1948 to 1952.

"Well, I remember your Dad," he said. "Even though he didn't make the team, he sure did love football and had some good moves out there on the field."

The press noticed our conversation. At first just one camera panned to the scene, then another, and another. Suddenly a crowd of press agents gathered, some holding out microphones while others scribbled on paper. Bud asked, "Is there someone in particular that you'd like to meet but haven't?" "Yeah, I'd like to meet Shirley Chisholm," I said.[3] It was great meeting all the

Oklahoma delegates, but Shirley was the first black congress-woman, and I admired her.

"That can be arranged, I think. Tell me, have you seen the old SOB yet?" Bud's smile made me think he didn't know my lunch with Nixon had been postponed.

"Do you mean Nixon? No, I'm supposed to meet him tomor-row." Suddenly there was a roar of laughter from the entire crowd. I looked around at everyone, not knowing what was so funny. I saw Carl Albert walking toward me, giving a hand signal to the press that made them respectfully disperse.[4]

I looked back at Bud, who stifled a laugh and said with a straight face, "I meant the 'Old Senate Office Building.' I thought you might like a tour."[5] Realizing I'd made a major mistake, I still tried to act normal, hoping to hide my embarrassment.

"Sure, I'd love to see it." I started to walk toward the door, wanting to get away ASAP, when I heard a voice: "Wait a minute, Susie. Please, I want to talk to you." Oklahoma's Carl Albert, the current House majority leader and soon to be the Speaker of the House of Representatives, was shaking Bud's hand.

"May I talk to Susie alone for minute?" he asked. Bud nod-ded and left. "Susie, I want you to work for me here in DC, in my office." Carl, who was just about my height, wasted no time saying what was on his mind.

"All right, but why?" I wasn't sure why he'd want me to work in his office.

"Anyone who can call Nixon an SOB and get away with it *has* to work in my office!" He smiled, but he was serious.

* * *

All the presidential scholars gathered on the White House lawn the next day to greet the president. As President Nixon walked toward the White House from his helicopter, he stopped to speak with Carl, who was standing with Senate Majority Whip Edward Kennedy and Senate Minority Leader Everett Dirksen.[6] As Carl shook President Nixon's hand, he whispered something that caused all four men to turn and look directly at me. Then the president walked over and grabbed my hand. "You must be Carl Albert's little Indian friend and newest employee," he said in his low growling voice. I flushed and looked at the ground. "You look embarrassed," the president observed.

"Yes, but it's the kind of embarrassment one likes to have," I answered, trying to get up the nerve to say something clever. "Nice tan for so early in the year."

"Yours is much better. I bet you didn't get your complexion by playing golf," he teased. President Nixon turned around, looked at the students, and began speaking in a loud voice: "I want you to know that I am proud of all of this year's presidential scholars, for you are tomorrow's leaders." I laughed, trying to visualize him as a traditional elder. He rested his gaze back on me and grinned before he looked into the cameras and moved his hand in a motion that included the entire group. "Keep up the good work. I'm sorry I couldn't attend the presentation of the awards. I was late in returning from the Midway Conference with South Vietnamese President Nyugen Lee Thieu. I'm looking forward to lunch with everyone."[7] As he spoke I breathed a sigh of relief. He hadn't even mentioned the sob thing. Perhaps he didn't know. He'd been in Vietnam, and maybe he hadn't heard, just maybe.

*   *   *

The scholars gathered for lunch and sat at a long table. I arrived early and took a seat next to the head of the table. Everyone applauded when President Nixon entered the room. He sat down at the head of the table, right next to me. He smiled and said, "Hello Susie. That's your name, isn't it?"

"Yes, Mr. President. I'm Susie Supernaw." I flushed, surprised he remembered my name. The waiter came to take his order, but President Nixon motioned him to take my order first.

"May I take your order?"

"I'll have the luncheon steak and the bean soup."

"How would you like your steak cooked?" he asked.

"As rare as they'll let you serve it."

"I'll try to keep it on the plate," he joked, writing "Blue" on his pad. President Nixon signaled, and the waiter leaned toward him, listening closely with his eyes lowered. Looking at me he chuckled and quickly took the rest of the orders.

I decided to start a conversation with the president. "This is a new era for Indians. We take our traditional values and try to make them work in a contemporary way. We want to be in charge of our destiny."

"Are you referring to the Indian Civil Rights Act?"[8]

"Yes. As a result there is a revival of cultural awareness in my tribe, and pride in our heritage and language is being restored. But our indigenous religions need more help."

"What do you mean?"

"Many traditional Indian religious practices are in jeopardy. Eagle feathers are being confiscated by the FBI, and religious ceremonies are being busted by the FDA. Shouldn't we be allowed to practice our religion? Isn't religious freedom a right granted by the constitution?"[9]

"Yes, I agree. American Indians should be able to practice their indigenous religions."

Too soon our private conversation ended when a scholar asked loudly, "Mr. President, sir, when's it going to end, this war in Vietnam?

"I'd like to hear what you think."

Then everyone started voicing opinions about the war. When my turn came to speak I didn't hold back. I was against the war and told Mr. Nixon, "It's needlessly killing too many of our boys."

"There are always casualties in war."

"Those statistics so casually thrown about by the press are real people with real lives. Those are boys who have girlfriends and families waiting for them at home. May I tell you what some of those statistics mean to me?"

"Sure."

"Take Stan Wiles, for example. He was from back home. Everyone said he was the best hunter around, and because of his marksmanship skills Stan became a sharpshooter who led reconnaissance missions behind enemy lines. Stan went to Vietnam, then Cambodia, and then came home in a box. The boys who have returned are like Eddie Begay, who had a severe reaction to Agent Orange, or Bruce King, who came back addicted to heroin because it's so plentiful and cheap over there, or Edward Skeet, who's deaf in one ear due to battlefield noise." I stopped, realizing I'd gotten carried away. The president listened seriously and sat in complete silence.

Other scholars agreed and threw in their own stories of people they knew and how the war had affected them. The smell of lunch made the conversation stop.

The waiter began serving the food. When I removed the metal lid covering my plate I saw a raw steak in the middle of plate, surrounded by mashed potatoes and gravy, with a cup of bean soup on the side. Then everybody else saw the raw steak, and the group broke into laughter, with President Nixon laughing the hardest.

"Maybe I was wrong." I said, realizing that the joke was on me. "Ask the chef to go ahead and cook it. You know, run the cow by the proverbial campfire." Everyone laughed again, and this time I was laughing the hardest.

✳ ✳ ✳

Before I knew it I was moving to Washington DC. I had only lived outside Hominy and on the outskirts of Tulsa, so the nation's capital was unlike anything I'd ever imagined. I enrolled at George Washington University.[10] Although I shared a small apartment near the Capitol with another intern, it was much easier to study at school, so Noreen Balinski and Gayle Walch adopted me as their extra roommate. Noreen was from the Bronx and spoke with a strong, thick New York Jewish accent that took me a while to understand. She was truly a "big-city" girl. Gayle was from Denver and loved snow-skiing, along with other outdoor activities. I had a lot to learn from them, and I had things to teach them too, because neither had ever met an American Indian before. They both knew I was a presidential scholar and always asked me to help them study even though I wasn't taking their courses.

Even with a full schedule of classes, I also worked twenty hours a week. Each day after class I'd ride the bus to the Capitol and quickly gulp down my sandwich, so I could spend my extra time walking through its magnificent marble halls filled with history. It was exciting never knowing who might be seen or what historic room might be found. Sometimes I found someone to tell me a story about a room or stood in the rotunda and listened to people talk on the other side. Amazing discoveries like restaurants, banks, and small shops constantly reminded me I worked in a living national monument.

Carl had a large and highly personable staff. His offices were split between a reception area, with access to the majority of his staff, and Carl's office, with access to several private offices behind it. I worked in the offices behind Carl's office, sometimes reading newspapers and clipping out articles for Carl to read. One day I saw Carl quickly walking through. I started to talk to him but was quickly quieted by Pauline Girvin. I watched Carl leave through the back door. "Why'd he do that?" I asked.

"That means someone's in the main office that he doesn't want to see," Pauline explained. I quickly learned not to acknowledge Carl when he walked through and adopted a "speak only when spoken to" philosophy when I was working.

Most of Carl's staff had been with him a long time, some from when he was a congressman, before he became the big man from Bugtussle.[11] I liked Carl and knew a side of him most people didn't get to see, as he could be pretty down-home when he wasn't wearing one of his many political hats. Carl understood country life because Bugtussle, his home, was actually smaller than Hominy in size. When I got homesick Carl let me call home free, using the office phone, so Oklahoma didn't seem that far away. However, when I talked to my sister or mom they didn't care about what was posted in the *Federal Register* or how Carl was going to vote next on the floor. So my life seemed disconnected from theirs as I listened. One day, after hanging up from a call, I sat for a moment, still thinking about home. The phone rang, and without thinking I answered one of Carl's personal incoming calls. I used the standard phone greeting until I heard the words "the president."

"Hold on, please." I pushed the hold button and signaled to Pauline: "The president's on line two." She immediately grabbed the phone and started apologizing while I knocked on the door to signal to Carl as he picked up the phone. When I came out she looked rather pale.

"Please, Susie. Never put the president's office on hold. Do you understand?"

"Yes, it's a matter of respect." I apologized to Carl, but I never got to talk to the president again, to apologize to him personally. At least it wasn't as bad as the SOB incident.

Two pieces of new office technology intrigued me. The office had a signature machine that signed Carl's name on letters. Using an armlike holder for a pen, it automatically signed the preprogrammed name. I was really impressed until I saw the special typewriter I would use: an electric typewriter with a tape that fed into the machine. I would type something with the tape recorder on, and it would punch holes in the tape. I would proofread it and then retype it with any corrections. The final tape was used for the automatic typing of letters. I loved watching it type to the point where I had programmed a "stop," and then I added the name and address and pushed "go." Fascinated I watched it type the rest of the page. I rolled in the next page and pressed "go," and it started printing again. I thought that typewriter was more fascinating than all the dignitaries who passed through the office.

*   *   *

Being in Washington DC made the things that had happened over the last couple of years very disturbing to me. During the summer of 1969 our astronauts had walked on the moon, but the glory of fulfilling President Kennedy's challenge had been overshadowed by volatile and changing times.[12] Martin Luther King Jr. and Robert Kennedy had been assassinated the previous year, and the civil rights movement was now turning violent. In Oklahoma these events were having serious consequences: our high school gave us school IDs in the fall of 1969 to keep out anyone who wasn't a student for fear of riots and violence. But DC was the focal point for protests for the whole country. The tensions here were multiplied one thousand times. Fighting was everywhere in our nation, and minorities resorted to avid protests. The Black Panthers emerged with black armbands and fists.[13] Alcatraz was seized by a group of activist American Indians involved in a movement for restoration of traditional rights. The Vietnam War was in full swing, and more soldiers were needed.

The mandatory draft was replaced by a lottery in which every birthday of the year was reduced to numerical form.[14] One by one birth dates were selected, and a list was compiled. It was human bingo, and the prize was a one-way ticket to Vietnam.

I was against the war in principle, but I was never against our soldiers. They were fighting because they were good soldiers and following orders. Most of the boys I knew back home didn't want to be soldiers; they had been drafted.[15]

I was troubled about the war. Carl was clearly a hawk, so I never discussed my concerns about the war with him.[16] President Nixon called the antiwar students "bums blowing up campuses."[17]

Then the unthinkable happened. The news about the senseless killings at Kent State hit me hard.[18] All I knew was that four students were dead, and many others injured, because our own National Guard had fired at them. Although the Guard was supposed to be shooting at the protesters, some of the students who had died and even some of those who were injured weren't even protesting; they had been caught in the crossfire, as in some inner-city gangland war. If America was supposed to embrace freedom of speech and the right to protest for all of its citizens, why were the protestors being intimidated and persecuted? It reminded me of the persecution our elders in the Native American Church endured in their efforts to practice their religion.

My roommates convinced me to go with them to the anti-war rally.[19] By the time we got to the Ellipse protesters from all over the country were there.[20] I'd never seen so many people or buses in one place. The White House was protected by bumper-to-bumper buses, military guards armed with machine guns stationed between the buses and the White House. There were noisy chants, catchy slogans, and fiery speeches followed by more fiery speeches. It was a peaceful rally, and I felt new hope that perhaps the war might end since so many people were against it. Soon that new hope would vanish.

My enthusiasm was so great I called Pauline to tell her everything that had happened. As I talked Pauline was silent. Finally she spoke: "You should have told me before you went to the antiwar rally."

"But why? Did I do something wrong?" I asked innocently.

"You should not have gone to the protest. The protest was against the government, and the fact that you work for the government means that you can't protest against it."

"I guess I'll just have to keep my opinions to myself." This was going to be tougher than I thought. The protests over America's involvement in Vietnam had spread across the country, and rallies were being held everywhere, especially at colleges.

I caught a bad cold and was barely breathing when I saw my friends again at school.

"Hey, Susie, why don't you come with us?" Noreen asked hastily. "We're walking down to the Watergate Hotel. It's not far."[21]

"Okay, I'm not feeling good, but I could sure use some fresh air." Once outside I enjoyed the late spring day.

"What's going on at the Watergate?" I wanted to hear what was going to happen in light of the shootings at Kent State.

"Some students are getting involved in the protests over Kent State." I noticed that the number of students in the street increased steadily as we walked closer to Watergate. Most were coming from a main gathering that had been held on campus earlier. We stopped, falling further behind the main crowd.

"I'm pretty beat." Standing up on my toes I saw where the large loud crowd ended.

"Why don't you just stay here and watch?" Noreen suggested tentatively.

"I hate to leave you alone though, Susie, you look so pale," Gayle said. "Why don't I stay here with you? Noreen, you go on. Just stand toward the back, so we can see you in case we decide to join you in a few minutes."

I was resting against the wall when suddenly I heard Gayle gasp. I looked up to see a line of menacing police cars with lights flashing coming from each of the two side streets leading to the Watergate. From our viewpoint we saw a number of mounted police officers slowly begin moving toward the front of the hotel, while others moved their prancing horses toward its sides.

"Let's get out of here!" Gayle said, quickly grabbing my arm, trying to get back to the dorm.

"What's going on?" I asked, wanting to rest a bit more.

"They're closing in on the protesters," Gayle replied without looking back. She held my arm tightly and started walking faster, pulling me along. "Don't turn around," she warned. "Just keep walking like you don't know what's going on behind you."

We continued in spite of the sight of riot-control policemen in full battle gear. Some held highly trained police dogs on thick leather leashes. The line of closely spaced riot police slowly moved down the street, while police cars blocked off all streets around the hotel. Mounted police guarded the sidewalks in front. The students, realizing they had nowhere to run, began to confront the riot police who were blocking their retreat. I heard loud shouting then saw someone throw a rock. Suddenly the riot police began fighting the students brutally, hand-to-hand, and small clouds billowed up as tear gas was fired into the crowd.[22]

Terrified students ran screaming as they tried to escape the brutal police. A desperate charge for escape in our direction broke the line of riot police. Those who resisted were beaten. Several students pursued by the police headed in our direction, so we ran into the first dorm we came to. I stopped at the back stairs, gasping, and signaled Gayle to go on to the second floor. "I'll catch up in a minute." She ran on. I leaned against a window, wheezing. I saw several students run inside, followed closely by two policemen. I heard several small explosions as more policemen wearing gas masks ran into the building, shooting several canisters of tear gas, trying to smoke us out.

With my eyes burning and tearing, and feeling sick to my stomach, I opened the window to throw up. A policeman wearing a gas mask came at me. He brandished his club, so I raised my hands, wheezing. He turned me around and gave me a kick on my bottom, and I hurried outside. I started to sit down on the curb to catch my breath but was thrown hastily into a waiting police wagon. In the dim light of the paddy wagon I cautiously glanced around at the other people. They all looked like students; some, judging by their profuse bleeding, had been beaten rather roughly.

I was especially concerned about a guy who was bleeding heavily from his nose. I moved close to him and placed his head in my lap. I started praying, realizing that I hadn't been praying regularly. I hadn't been watching the sunrise in the mornings. I never went for morning walks, and I'd forgotten about the oneness of all things. I was forgetting my cultural values, just like Phillip Deere had warned. I held the stranger's nose while pressing a little more firmly on his upper gum, silently praying he'd recover from this brutal attack. I also prayed that I could recover from my lost connection with the universe.

The vehicle started with a lurch, and we continued to travel in silence except for a few hushed whispers and muffled groans from the injured. The door slowly opened. "Get out, one at a time, or I'll come in there and drag you out!" The students closest to the door stepped out and began to form an informal line.

"This man needs help." I sat holding his head.

"Oh, don't worry, we'll help him," an officer said, laughing hauntingly. He reached inside and grabbed the man's feet, dragging him to the door as if he were a sack of potatoes. The officer standing next to him leaned over and heaved the limp body over his shoulder. As I crawled out the officer hit me in the chest and grabbed my arms, pulling my hands behind me. He slapped on a pair of handcuffs and adjusted them extra tight.

Instead of receiving any medical treatment the students were removed from the cells one by one and taken to be booked. I was led down the hall into a room where several officers sat at small desks, interrogating students. The room was cluttered with file cabinets, a copy machine, and a large blackboard on one wall. My booking officer was short in stature, but heavyset and muscular. He wasn't rude like the others but was visibly irritated. "So, what's your story?"

"I was brought here, but I didn't do anything wrong."

"You're saying you weren't protesting?" He didn't seem surprised.

"Yes," I said quietly. "I was in the dorm lobby when the police came in and forcibly removed me," I cautiously explained. I paused while he wrote on his notepad. "I work at the Capitol in the afternoon and go to school in the mornings. As a matter of fact I should be at work now." I stopped to choose my words carefully. "Would it be possible for me to call work and let them know I'm not going to make it in today? They really get mad, and I could get fired if I just don't show up."

Reluctantly the officer reached toward the phone. "Here's the number," I said, quickly picking up a pen and writing on a scrap of paper. "If you can't get by the receptionist, just give me the phone."

"Why? Who am I calling, the president?" The officer laughed.

"No, just the Speaker of the House," I replied quietly but confidently.[23] He looked sternly at me, evaluating my story.

"You work for *who*?" The officer's voice rose sharply.

"The Speaker of the House." I held back a smile as he quickly hung up the phone.

"Look, obviously you were brought here by mistake. When the police followed the protestors into the dorm, there was no way for them to separate the protestors from the good students. I won't book you with any charges, and you're free to go."

The next day many cases of police brutality were filed against the DC police as a result of the incident at the Watergate Hotel. Because of the unprovoked attack on many of the students in their dorms, our school closed its doors, and classes were cancelled for the remainder of the school year, which was only a couple of weeks.[24] Students were sent home with pass/fail grades and could take finals in the fall when classes began, if they wanted. Since the dorms were closing, and I was totally confused, I wanted to go home. I called work and then called my sister Kathy in Oklahoma. I thought for another moment and decided to call Tommy, my best high school friend. I wanted to visit him at Princeton before I went home.[25]

12

Coming Home

Filled with both joy and apprehension I stopped by Princeton to see Tommy before I left the East and its hectic "business-only" style. After spending several months apart with occasional letters and even fewer phone calls, I needed to know how he felt. Unsure of what I was going to do I desperately needed to talk to him to help me sort things out.

I arrived at Newark, a short ride from Union Station.[1] Union Station was the not just the busiest travel hub I'd ever visited but the smelliest. I could really tell that I was still a "country kid" even after the months spent in this congested land of endless cityscapes because I was still overwhelmed by the multitude of people everywhere. I considered myself lucky to have Tommy waiting for me, a familiar face in the crowd. After a warm welcome hug and kiss we stood gazing into each other's eyes for what seemed like an eternity.

"I'm so glad to see you, Susie Q!" Tommy sighed. "It's been too long."

"I missed you too," I blurted out as my voice cracked from weariness. Seeing him again was overwhelming because he felt so much like home. Pressed against his chest I felt my heart race, although my body relaxed in his arms. The strength and love of his spirit were so intense that I felt uncomfortable, although I wasn't sure why. "Uh, I have to go to the bathroom," I said, dancing around to ease my nervousness.

"Okay, I'll wait for your luggage."

"I brought the plaid brown suitcase and an old blue suitcase." I awkwardly turned around, searching for a restroom sign, and headed off. Tommy waited as the luggage from the belly of the bus was emptied. When I returned he held my suitcases, and we made our way through the crowd to his car, hidden among a mass of others. Even though it wasn't really that bad, I began ranting and raving about the terrible ride I'd had. It was mostly just to ease my tensions, but he listened intently.

Tommy pointed to his car as we neared it. After loading my suitcases into the trunk he opened the passenger side door and waited while I got in. He bowed, closing the door, encouraging my laughter. Tommy never tried to hide his feelings around me. That's what I really liked about him: there were no little white lies, tricks, or disguises. He was always just himself, so adorably honest.

"Where would you like to stay?" He hesitated before continuing. "You could stay in a hotel here, but it's a little expensive. My roommate's out of town this weekend. You could stay with me." He forgot to mention that he had bribed his roommate to leave town. I could sense it though; his eyes held expectations.

"Your place is fine," I said. Tommy wasn't just any guy; he was my best friend and boyfriend from home too. "Besides, I didn't come all the way to Princeton to stay in a hotel!" He smiled sheepishly. Once on the campus grounds he talked about life at Princeton. We stood alone in one of the grand hallways, its large plate-glass windows overlooking the perfectly manicured grounds, when he turned to me.

"Why don't you apply to Princeton? It's not just a boys' school anymore. They've admitted their first class of girls. You know they can't turn you down."[2]

"Why?" I was surprised and flattered.

"Because they'd never have the nerve to turn down a presidential scholar, even if she is an Indian." His face was bursting with pride, and I realized he was trying to smooth over any hard feelings I might still have regarding his "why couldn't that happen to me" comment during our senior year. There was some truth to his thinking; I felt a lot of confusion over minority preference.

"Don't be silly. I can't get into Princeton."

"Any place that would accept me has to accept you." He squeezed my hand gently.

"Then this isn't about us trying to compete with each other?"

"No, not at all."

"So you don't have any ulterior motives?"

"Oh, who am I kidding? I miss you so much I'd do anything to keep you here." He took me in his arms and kissed me.

At first his kiss was soft, but as I relaxed into his arms our kiss became passionate. The months we had been apart faded quickly, and I got lost in the moment. Now I was really confused. Our meeting was more intense than I had anticipated. My body still ached for his touch as he melted me with his kiss.

I didn't really know what I wanted, except I had a mission to fulfill. When I thought of marriage my mind replayed my dad's voice, echoing in my subconscious: "You don't have to be smart to get married and have kids. As a matter of fact it's better if you're not." I didn't know how to quiet his voice.

We spent the next two days together, and Tommy was at his best. He fit into the Northeastern lifestyle much more easily than I did. We talked about being together again and our future. He wanted to stay in the East, even after college. He wanted me to stay too and suggested that we get married. I lost myself in his beautiful dream, enjoying every sight, sound, and taste, but I knew my destiny was in Oklahoma, not at Princeton.

Tommy took me to the bus station early in the morning and hugged me tightly. Then I looked directly into his bright blue eyes, which matched his shirt. There was so much I wanted to say but couldn't. "I'll miss you."

He smiled. "Tell me now: are you going to go to Princeton

as my friend, or are you going to marry me? Please, say you'll be my Susie Q."

"Maybe I'll apply to Princeton." Feeling extremely uneasy I said, "Even if I'm accepted, I don't think I could come here." I hated being so honest, but I didn't want to lead him on. The day was already gray with an approaching rainstorm, but after what I said his eyes fell into his heart, and it became just a bit darker around us.

"Why?" He froze.

"It's not about you. It's about me. I just don't know what I want right now. Please understand."

"Sure." Tommy forced a small weak smile before he grabbed me and kissed me longingly, knowing he might never see me again. I felt his lips quiver and his body shake.

"I can always change my mind!" I pulled away from his kiss. "You know I always do." I faked a smile, trying to cheer him up, but he didn't respond. I took an index card out of my purse and handed it to him. I had written a poem on it the night before, knowing I would have trouble saying the right words. "Here, I wrote this for you."

> *When I part from you friend, I grieve not,*
> *For that which I love most in you—*
> *is clearest in your absence.*
> *Let there be no purpose in our love*
> *except the deepening of the spirit.*
> *For love that seeks only to reveal its own mystery*
> *is not love but an illusion.*
> *When I part from you friend, grieve not,*
> *My best was yours.*
> *You will always be a part of me.*

Tommy mouthed the words as he read them. I felt guilty, confused, and scared. I wasn't just leaving my friend; I was running away from love. I really didn't know why. Not knowing why is what hurt the most, for both of us.

His eyes scanned the card a couple of times while another tear fell and slowly rolled down his pale cheek. He did not wipe it away but stood there in his brown raincoat with his back to me. The bus left. He never turned around to look, so I didn't get to wave goodbye. I knew I wouldn't see him again for a long time, and by then our high school romance would just be a memory. The sky darkened and cried for me.

The soft rain lured me to sleep, and I dreamed of sitting inside a tipi. Kenneth was speaking: "We choose how to view reality."

"How do we do that?"

"We personalize it. We limit the amount of data we use in order to create our personal reality."

"That sounds just like my dad."

"Everyone does it. When parts of our reality overlap with other realities, they don't always match."

I dreamed about my dad and how good he was at creating his own world where he wasn't responsible for us girls. Then I dreamed about my mom who was good at blaming herself for any abuse she received rather than admitting it was her husband's problem. Then I dreamed about the parts of reality I was ignoring so I could live my life now. Since all my traditional ways and habits had disappeared during my stay in Washington DC, I realized I'd given up my tribalism, my unique oneness with all things. I sat down on the dirty concrete and cried, missing the coolness of sitting on grass.

Then I was standing in a chemistry lab, and Kenneth was wearing a white lab coat and sitting by a Bunsen burner, its flame turned low.[3] I said, "Since all things are possible in the quantum world, then by our actions (and deliberate observations) we choose which path we take through many quantum worlds. Would you agree?"

"I agree that all things are possible and that we choose our path." Kenneth and quantum physicists agreed on some basic points about choice and destiny.

"I'm afraid I'll never earn my name. I don't know what to do."

"Didn't you say that all things are possible in the quantum world?" I nodded. Smiling, he said, "Then remember, never say never. There is always that possibility, no matter how minuscule." Kenneth chuckled. "Anything can happen, and there are other worlds besides this one for them to happen in."

* * *

I felt sunlight on my face and opened my eyes to see the familiar landscape of southwestern Missouri. I thought about seeing my family and friends. With a feeling of being lost still hanging over me I wished for a personal Native American Church ceremony. I decided to sponsor a meeting after arriving home. While I day-dreamed in one part of the country my dreams were becoming reality in another.

Kenneth had been thinking a lot about me and had talked with Kathy about having a meeting to welcome me home properly, cleansing and blessing me. "We want to have a special meeting for Susie when she gets back from Washington DC."

"That's like what we do for returning soldiers," Kathy said. "I'm sure she'll need it." She tucked her hair behind her ear and pushed her chair back from the wooden table. "I'll stop by the store for some groceries." She made special notes to get a cof-feepot and a painted water bucket.

Jack, Kenneth's brother, came in from the car. "I'll get a couple of guys to help gather and split wood."

"Who's gonna put up the tipi?" Kathy asked Jack.

"Guess me and the boys can do that too. When's Susies due?"

"I'm picking her up tonight at seven."

Kenneth turned to Jack and asked, "Can you help round up a few singers?"

"No problem!" Jack said enthusiastically as he walked out the door.

* * *

My body was jarred when the bus stopped suddenly before entering the Tulsa bus station. I didn't see Kathy until I went inside. She hugged me. "They're having a meeting for you tonight. We're going over to Kenneth's. Dinner is ready."

I was dumbfounded. How did they know I wanted to have a meeting? I didn't bother to ask any questions, and we chatted only briefly. We'd talk much more later, but this moment was for reflection. It was time to calm my mind and gather my personal strength.

By the time we arrived the men had already eaten and were outside. Some of the women were sitting at the table, eating and feeding the children. After all of the "welcome homes" and "good to see yous," I sat down and ate quickly. After dinner I put on my shawl and went outside and gave silent thanks just to be home.

Everyone gathered outside the tipi, lined up in the same general order in which they had been sitting inside. Kenneth led the group in a huge circle around the tipi as a way of helping us to clear our minds. Then each person kneeled down and entered the tipi. After everyone was settled Kenneth stood up and announced the purpose of the meeting. Jack sat to the left of the tipi door so he could bring in the extra wood and adjust the flaps at the top of the tipi so the smoke would always ventilate upward.

My meeting began with a long prayer in Kiowa. Kenneth sang four songs that called to the spirit for its blessings. At first I sat comfortably on my knees, and I prayed for a blessing from the spirits. A light engulfed the entire bed of coals, and a small shadow slowly formed in the middle. A human silhouette began walking toward me. I could make out some features of a young woman. Looking directly at me she waved. It looked like me, but was it? Was it my sister? "Maybe it's Ellia Ponna," I jested, recalling my Indian name.

My eyes watered as I searched the fire for answers. The figure seemed like me, but it didn't look exactly like me. She floated across a stage in a blue chiffon gown that glittered gold in the overhead lights. Her long dark hair was fluffed and curled like that of a groomed poodle. Her shoes shimmered silver in the glow of the footlights, while cameras flashed and people cheered. She briskly walked away. As the lights faded around her I saw the faces of the crowd. Slowly I realized they were my old friends from high school, the Sewer Rats. The picture zoomed back slowly. They were part of a larger crowd, a roaring crowd on its feet in excitement. Everywhere people of all ages, sizes, and shapes clapped and cheered loudly.

I shook my head in disbelief as the picture faded. For a moment I was lifted upward with the drumbeat, and my vibrating spirit was tempted to follow the rhythm into the skies. Instead of flying I went inward, searching my heart, only to find loneliness. My spirit felt empty when the singing stopped. I hadn't succeeded in earning my Indian name. I hadn't been able to enjoy the life and job I'd been given. I couldn't love my high school sweetheart. I felt like a failure in everything.

Kenneth stood and motioned for me to stand. I moved in front of the fire with my hands held out, palms up. Kenneth threw cedar on the fire and waited for smoke to form. With his eagle feather he fanned the smoke from the fire over my body, patting my hands firmly. After fanning me four times he shook my hand before handing me the cedar bag and eagle feather. I reached into the cedar bag, searching for the right words. Throwing small handfuls of cedar in the four directions, I patiently waited while they popped and sizzled. When a huge puff of smoke gathered and burst upward, I fanned and patted myself four times. I lowered my head and began to pray.

"Thank you, dear heavenly father, for giving us this sacred altar and its holy elders. Thank you for my sister and all the other women who brought this special food. Thank you for all the caring people with their families who came to sing and pray for me on this special occasion. Thank you for this holy sacrament and its blessings, for our songs and our way of worship. Thank you for our ancestors who gave us this religion, and be with our religious leaders now, as they suffer religious persecution from our government. Give them the strength to endure. Bless President Nixon and the legislators in the Congress of the United States, and help them find the insight and wisdom to grant us Indian people the right to continue our worship in this sacred manner without persecution. Please protect our soldiers in Vietnam, and help ensure their safe return. Have mercy on the sick, elderly, homeless, poor, and lonely, especially our veterans, and those in hospitals and old folks' homes, and help them find happiness instead of loneliness. Bless my family and my relatives, and give me strength and wisdom. Please help those I've forgotten to mention, and thank you for everything that's been offered to me by the outside world. In your holy name, amen."

Some of the men acknowledged my prayer by saying "A-Ho," an Indian version of "Amen" and "Thanks" combined. I turned and shook Kenneth's hand, returning his beaded bag and eagle feather. I sat down and continued praying silently during the meeting.

After the morning water and meal were served I was still unsure of what to do. As I left the tipi I shook each person's hand and smiled. Each person contributed to my calm, and I felt closer to each than I had the night before. "Good morning," was all I said. Things always seemed different after a meeting. Peace flooded over me.

I knew I would stay in Oklahoma, but I wondered about the person in the blue gown. What did it mean? I had no clever new ideas except to go to college. The only college I knew much about was Phillips University.[4]

13

Scorpio Sue

Once again Dee proved to be a worthy rescuer, but this time he was helping me get into college. Although it had been a while since I'd seen him last, I saw his familiar station wagon in the restaurant parking lot. Inside I easily recognized him, sitting at a table sipping some coffee. I had already started walking toward him when he saw me and waved: "Susie." I gave a half wave. He stood up, and we hugged. While greeting me Dee pulled out my chair, and I sat down, putting the strap of my purse over the back of the chair. Then he looked at me.

"I need some help getting into college."

"What? *You* need help getting into college." He laughed.

"I don't want to go back to DC, but I do want to go to school this fall. Can you help me get into Phillips University really quick?"

"I'm sure they can offer you a good financial package." Dee nodded. "An academic scholarship for starts. After all you *are* a presidential scholar. And doesn't your National Merit Scholarship apply to any school?"

"Sure. But . . ."

"You can get a work-study job to help with your personal expenses. You can type, can't you?"

"Ninety words a minute," I bragged.

"Then there should be no problem. If you want to go to Phillips, I'll make sure you can afford it!"

"Sold. Where do I sign?" Dee reached into his briefcase and pulled out some papers. I completed the applications and left, hoping that I'd made the right decision. I'd find out soon enough.

✳ ✳ ✳

Standing outside the girls' light-colored brick dorm, Clay Hall, facing a new campus and lots of strangers, I started to doubt my decision. I saw two girls walking toward me from the dorm. I recognized one as a high school friend. She waved.

"Susie. Susie." Judi Coleman was my size, with poodle-like blond hair.

"Hey, Judi! I didn't know you go to school here. Dee said my roommate would meet me inside Clay Hall. Do you know who that is?"

"Sure do. Me. I'm going to be one of your roommates this semester." She hugged me.

"And who's this?" I motioned toward the girl with long auburn hair and hazel eyes.

"This is Lynda Fialkowski. She's our other roommate." Lynda shook my hand and then gave me a hug. She wore a metal and leather brace on her lower left leg, an unfortunate souvenir from a childhood bout with polio.

"Hi, Susie. Glad to meet you. Welcome to Phillips."

I turned to Judi and asked, "What's it like going to a college that has fewer students than our high school?"

"It's really fun. You get to know everybody."

"And everybody's business, I bet." I planned to keep a low profile, maybe make a couple of Bs, and not try out for cheerleader.

"You're already pretty famous around here, you know." Lynda smiled.

"I had no idea!" I was shocked.

"Well, there was an article about you attending Phillips in the local paper."[1] Judi giggled.

"Oh no! What did it say?"

"Let's see. That you are a presidential scholar, class valedictorian, cheerleader with a straight-A average, and intern for Carl Albert, or something like that."

"Nothing about Tractor Queen?"

Judi and Lynda looked at each other and laughed. "No," Judi said, finally catching her breath. "I don't think so."

I sighed in relief. "That's good."

"But all the girls are jealous, and all the guys want to meet you," Lynda said.

"Well, for starters, let's meet some guys!"

I looked at their smiles, and Lynda said, "We'll go this afternoon when they have football practice."

"And Susie," Judi said, "they're called the Mel."

We went inside the dorm, and they showed me around. Our conversation shifted to information. There were so many rules, I would probably break one sooner or later. Our first-floor room had only one window, which faced the east. Excited I asked, "Can I have the area next to the window for my bed? It faces east, and I can watch the sun rise." I could also look out the window through the bushes at the manicured lawn and watch the moon and stars at night.

"I don't care. I don't want any sun in my eyes in the morning," Lynda said.

"Me neither. Sure, go ahead and take the window."

I smiled and said, "Thanks." I was glad they were so nice and hoped it didn't have to do with that silly article in the paper.

Later in the afternoon we walked across campus and joined two other girls standing along the sidelines at football practice. Lynda introduced me to Vicki Dayton. "Now, who are these guys? What exactly is Mel?" I asked.

"Mel began as an unofficial organization built around 'the dirty dozen,' a group of guys in the north wing of Earl Buttes Dorm," Vicki said, waving to someone on the field.

"The guys loved football but hated fraternity pledging and initiation. So they formed their own group," Lynda said, also watching the field. I decided to hold my questions until the play was over or there was a time-out. I watched for a few minutes.

"What does 'Mel' mean?" I asked Vicki. I wondered if they had made the name up, like we did with the Sewer Rats.

"The word 'Mel' came from a Bill Cosby recording about a sportscaster and superstar athlete named Mel who did shaving commercials."[2] Vicki imitated shaving her face, cutting it, and then continuing to shave. "I just love this stuff." I laughed at her impersonation of Cosby.

"Let me get this straight. Although Mel began as a rebellion against social organizations, they participate in campus activities as a social organization nonetheless."

"That about sums it up," Vicki said.

"Cool," I said as the guys came to the sidelines for a break. The first guys I recognized were Curtis Fisher and Johnny Wolf. Both had gone to Sand Springs High School with my sister Kathy, and both had played on its state champion football team. Curtis had been my double-date boyfriend when Kathy and I went out, and Johnny was a fellow tribesman. They both gave me a hug.

Rod Phillips, a musician and friend of Dee's whom I had met earlier, gave me a hug, whispering, "Glad to see you again." He later became my boyfriend. Then I saw Bill Wolfe and Lee Semones, two guys who had played football at my high school. I wondered if Phillips appreciated the football talent that played on their field. Lee had always been nice to me, so I gave him a hug in spite of his shyness. "Good to see you here," Lee said. Bill hugged me and said, "I was surprised to hear you were coming here. Didn't you like Washington?"

"No, not when they have to close school to prevent any antiwar protests."

"Wow. Here, the draft lottery is our main concern. Some of us might not be here for long since the lottery is later this month. Anyway, let me introduce you to some of the guys."

Several girlfriends of Mel guys arrived with water. There were more Mel introductions: a musician and artist known as the Grog (a.k.a. Lynn Goodman); Jim Strain, the editor of the school newspaper; Brad Broadfoot, a varsity tennis player. Then there were so many more names and faces I gave up trying to remember them all. Here were some of the hunkiest guys I'd ever seen; I hardly could have imagined that they would become a major influence on my life. The Mel ruled the football field as they did all sports at the intramural games. I finally could cheer for a winning football team.[3]

The semester floated by with plenty of activities. I loved getting up at dawn and giving my traditional morning thanks before my run around the university golf course. One day I saw Johnny, and we ran together. We both missed our traditional foods and ceremonies and sometimes felt a little lonely without our tribal network. Just talking about our feelings helped us feel better. We decided to form the first Indian club at Phillips even though there were only five Indians there. Since being Indian was an important part of our identities, each of us held a position of leadership in the club, although we didn't restrict membership to Indians.[4] We had our tribal differences, but we were a closeknit group with lots of connections in the Indian world.

Unlike the Mel the members of the Indian Club wanted it to be a real campus organization, so we put on a schoolwide American Indian Awareness conference. We didn't have a budget and worked for donations through our own personal connections. Among the five of us we managed to schedule volunteer speakers for a week, to get a traditional feast donated, and to arrange a powwow.[5] The kids at Phillips had never been exposed to Indian culture so thoroughly, so we saw this as an opportunity to sock it to them. Some of the attendees (both faculty and students) experienced a bit of culture shock and resentment, but most sincerely enjoyed the experience. They especially enjoyed learning about all the different foods and how they're connected to the different local tribes. Not long after our Indian Club eventually was offered campus recognition as an official campus-sponsored club.

While I was busy getting the Indian Club recognized, Mel tried to remain an "unclub." They had no charter, no dues, no officers, no faculty sponsors, no initiations, and no membership roll. No one could join Mel. Individuals were simply absorbed into the group through the camaraderie of competing together or simply hanging out. Mel meetings occurred whenever someone said, "Let's have a meeting!" All the guys were notified, and whoever was available came as soon as possible. This type of nonconformity was viewed rather harshly by some faculty and students. The year before a petition had been submitted to the Inter-Club Council (icc) trying either to force Mel to become an official organization or to bar them from participating in campus activities and competition. After a lengthy and heated discussion the icc had voted that no action be taken. One faculty member, the anthropology professor Robert Rhoades, considered the Mel a unique phenomena, and at least two of his Mel students (Curtis Fisher and Lee Semones) wrote research papers analyzing it.

After one spring evening of playing pool and drinking a couple of beers I went back to the dorm room.[6] I was sleeping soundly and didn't hear the phone ring, but my roommate did and handed it to me.

"Hi, Susie. Sorry to bother you so late, but we were having a Mel meeting," Rod explained. "We'd like to nominate you as our representative in the Miss Phillips pageant this year."

Mel was technically viewed as an independent group. Because Miss Phillips and the Miss Phillips pageant represented the entire campus community, not just organized groups, the Student Senate had ruled that even independents could sponsor a contestant. Therefore Mel was allowed to nominate girls to participate as contestants in the pageant. Last year their contestant, Mary Pat Hurlihy, had won not only the Miss Phillips pageant but the chance to compete in the Miss Oklahoma pageant.

I faltered at Rod's words. All I could think to say was, "Well, I guess, okay. It'll be my first time. I've never done this kind of thing before." I was not thinking clearly, and I'm sure my roommates couldn't help but wonder what I was talking about.

"Okay, then. We'll submit your name and the entry fee." These words were followed by the click of the phone being disconnected. Finally I could get some sleep. Since I was so drowsy when we spoke I remembered very little of the conversation the following morning and thought nothing of it until I read in the school newspaper the next week that I was Mel's entry for the Miss Phillips pageant.

I called Rod to make sure this wasn't some kind of joke. He reminded me of our conversation. "Okay. I'll do it," I said, "but I'm going to need some serious help."

"That's what we're here for."

I asked both roommates for help. Since I didn't have anything but jeans, Judi (who was my size) volunteered to loan me some of her nicer things. Experienced in tumbling, Lynda volunteered to help me train by being my spotter. Sally Sanders, our PE teacher, helped me choreograph my dance, and Rod helped me with my music. The best choice for fixing my hair and putting on my stage makeup was the expert Kathy. I asked for her help during the pageant, but not before making her swear not to tell Mom.

I was amazed that there were so many people willing to help me. Others provided the expertise, and I provided the sweat. Every day for three weeks I skipped some classes to work out in the gym for several hours. Then I'd meet Rod at the music building. While I rehearsed my piano part Rod wrote an arrangement for a string quartet. My song sounded like classical music and fit perfectly with my floor-exercise routine. I cherished this song because it had so much of me in it. It was my first attempt at classical-sounding music with no lyrics. I added some secret words anyway, just to make it easier to dance. Certain moves and strings of tumbling went with certain lyrics, giving me another clever way to try and stay in time with the beat. It was easier to map the routine in my brain if I could mix music and lyrics with body movements.

Rehearsals began, and all sixteen contestants had their pictures taken by Steve Bridwell, a student photographer for the newspaper and the pageant program booklet.

Rod and the Grog wrote the musical score for the pageant, as they had in previous years, so I saw them at every rehearsal. It made me feel good to have friends around, because I'd never

17. Susie poses for her picture in the Miss Phillips University pageant booklet, 1971. *Photo by Steve Bridwell,* Haymaker *staff photographer, 1970–71.*

even seen a beauty pageant before, much less participated in one. The Mel guys had participated in previous pageants and knew what to do and expect.

I knew about the Miss America pageant but couldn't tell you how it was different from the Miss Universe pageant or even a state pageant.[7] To me pageants were all Hollywood, a far-off world of shiny rhinestone crowns worn by tall beautiful women.

Too soon Phyllis George, the current Miss America, was arriving, Jane Ann Jayroe was practicing with Rod to emcee the pageant, and the judges were conducting the interviews.[8] Everyone was excited because Jane Ann was there, since she was famous throughout all Oklahoma for being Miss America. Seeing her onstage made everything seem glamorous. The next days were filled with meetings, receptions, interviews, and our final dress rehearsal. Kathy and Judi assembled my clothes while the judges interviewed me. The large drafty dressing room backstage had a mirror and small area for each girl. Each mirror was decorated with an artistic rendering of our astrological sign, cut from construction paper, taped to the top. Mine read, "Scorpio Sue." I really liked my scorpion picture, so I carefully removed it and placed it in my pageant booklet to preserve the memory.

Everyone began the process of getting ready, each of us confined to a small space in front of our mirror. Hair was combed, ratted, and sprayed. A cloud of mist rose from the many aerosol cans. Body makeup was applied over various body parts such as my legs and arms, parts that I never imagined needed makeup. Time passed quickly, and soon the announcement came, "Five minutes until show time," followed by the sounds of exhaling and the zipping of dresses. Makeup was rechecked, and the piles of already coiffured hair were sprayed once more. Kathy added a quick curling-iron touch to my hair before I left for the introduction of contestants.

The evening progressed quickly. There were five major changes of clothes: for the evening gown, swimsuit, and talent competitions, as well as for the opening introductions and the finale. I only had one gown, so I wore it for opening introductions, the evening gown competition, and the finale. Some contestants wore a different gown for each, but I was just glad to round up enough stuff to get by.

My talent segment went well; I spun high, jumped, and tumbled. Then between the different dance steps something very strange happened to me. While I was performing a jazzy move an image of the bear cub dancing flashed into my head. My move looked like one of his moves. For a brief moment I felt like I was finally dancing part of his dance. My next tumbling string needed my mind back in this reality, so I focused and took three steps, did a round-off and a back handspring, and finished by floating from my back layout flip to land in a split. Graceful landing, full splits, and both arms up. The crowd reminded me I was on stage by a roar of screams and applause. I breathed a sigh of relief and smiled. I had survived.

After the finale, the top five finalists were announced. Rod repeated my name twice before I stepped forward. Since I wasn't expecting to be one of the finalists I wasn't listening very closely. Now that I was a finalist I would be asked the BIG question. The BIG question is the one asked the five finalists on stage so the judges can make their final decision. The moment is especially tense because everyone is listening, the press is waiting to mis-quote you, and your answer might well decide whether you or Ms. Perfect, on your right, is going to win.

I was a little concerned because I'd never thought about hav-ing to speak intelligently on stage. Still I felt confident that I could, if given the right opportunity. Then the spotlight was on me, and my throat became dry as an Oklahoma August. I forced a swallow as the audience became shades of gray behind the bright stage lights.

"Why have you chosen anthropology as a major?" My mind darted around, accessing several bits of info. Should I say, "It beats political science?" Or maybe I could try, "Because I really had a good Intro to Anthropology teacher." I could confess, "It's the

only way I could get college credit for learning about Indians!"
Wait, I thought. I'll get philosophical. Now what would I write
on one of Rhoades's anthro tests? Let's see.[9]

"Anthropology is the study of man, both past and present.
Only by studying our past can we hope to make a better future
for ourselves and our children. Only through understanding the
differences among cultures can we learn to live with our differences. Living in harmony, together, regardless of race or religion,
is our only hope for world peace." The words flowed effortlessly
out of my mouth, and as soon as I finished speaking the crowd
began to applaud. Bob Rhoades, my anthro professor, was one
of the first to stand and applaud. I blushed, feeling that perhaps
my answer was pretty good, but I couldn't believe I had made
the "world peace" comment. Had I written the words, I would
have erased them. Not everyone wanted world peace; after all, we
were still at war in Southeast Asia. Someone might think I was
antigovernment, and I certainly didn't want to go there again.
As the other contestants answered their questions, I realized the
questions resembled the type of conversation one has in a social
setting rather than in a classroom.

The judges scribbled quickly on pieces of paper that were
gathered by the head judge, who tallied the scores and handed
the results in an envelope to Rod. When Rod opened the envelope
he scratched his ear before starting to read the names.

"That's the sign," Brad whispered in the back corner, as he
told me later. "We asked Rod for a sign if Susie won. And that's
the sign."

"No, you're kidding," Curtis said. "He wouldn't do that."

"Sure he would. Listen."

Rod read off each name until there were only two of us left. I
was standing at center stage with Nancy Fisher, a tall, beautiful
brunette with long hair.

"First runner-up," said Rod, "is Nancy Fisher, which means
that the new Miss Phillips is Susie Supernaw."

I remember hearing my name called out, so I started to walk

forward, but Nancy stepped in front of me. "I'm first," she said, stepping gracefully forward.

I stood for a moment with my mouth open. Something about being named "Miss PU" made me laugh to myself. I thought of the saying, "If a skunk went to college they would call it PU (phew)!" So I was Miss PU. The official Phillips team mascot was the Haymakers; its unofficial one was a skunk named Stinky. The roar from the crowd brought me back to the stage.

People in the audience were clapping wildly, and the judges were smiling at me. I looked around at the other contestants, and they were smiling too—well, most of them were. A couple of the girls hated losing to me, and I overheard one say, "It's so dehumanizing to be beaten by an Indian!" Her words stung my ears and hurt me inside.

I felt bad that she took this personally and rationalized that these girls just took the pageant and the whole concept of "beauty queen" too seriously. Pageants aren't objective, like running a race. I didn't see myself as better than these girls, even though I had no idea how we had been judged. I didn't mean to cause any of them shame. I was well aware that some of them didn't care for me and tried to remember what Kenneth said whenever I felt bad about something someone said about me: "If someone doesn't like you and you have done nothing to them, then it is their problem, not yours." Phillip explained the same phenomenon by simply saying, "We see in others what we dislike about ourselves."

Alone on stage I turned around and held up my arms in the air, smiling my biggest and waving with both hands. Three spotlights centered on me and darkened the faces of the crowd until I could barely see the stage in front of me. It was mildly distracting, and my main fear was falling off the edge of the stage. Mary Pat Hurlihy, last year's winner, walked over to me with the crown. Mel had won again, for the second year in a row. Surely this would enforce the significance and influence of the original dirty dozen and their dream of creating the ultimate unclub. For some reason I didn't understand, the validity of a men's fraternity or club was determined by the women who were willing to hang out with its members. Mel guys seemed to have lots of beautiful girls hanging around.

Mary Pat held a small crown with rhinestones that shone beautifully. She tried to pin it on my head, but it didn't fit: the bottom of the crown was flat, made for a bouffant hairdo. My hair, however, was pulled back, and I didn't have enough hair piled on top to anchor the crown. My sister, who saw what was happening, ran to the dressing room and brought out several large hairpins and clips. With the extra reinforcements the crown managed to stay in place for the next thirty minutes, which was long enough. The worst was over, or so I thought.

The crown was wobbly. I had been bending my knees the entire time I was being "crowned," and now they had frozen. I slowly straightened myself, my knees screaming in pain. It was difficult to move with the crown, which felt like a book balanced on my head. Roses were handed to me as I turned toward the small runway and bravely walked to the end. Everywhere I looked people were standing and clapping.

I acknowledged the crowd, waving vigorously. After bathing in the crowd's affection and the warmth of the spotlights, I cautiously walked to the center of the stage, careful to keep my head level. Mary Pat walked gracefully to the top of the staircase at the back of the stage and stood on a small platform beside my throne, an overstuffed chair. I wasn't worried about walking up the stairs, but I should have been! I had never walked *up* steps in a long dress before. I had only practiced walking *down* stairs at rehearsals, so this was very different.

When you walk down stairs in a long dress, it naturally flows behind you. To take a clean step down you need only to make sure you land soundly, toe then heel. Placing your toe first keeps you from falling on your dress, especially if you give a little kick, using your toe to push your dress away from your foot. This action gives you a clear place to step. When you walk up stairs, however, gravity plays havoc with the "kick with your toe" approach. The gown is moving down, the stairs are increasing in height, and your feet get tangled in between. The resulting tangled feet are not a pretty sight. The good part of falling *up* stairs, of course, is that you don't have a long way to fall.

That night only two steps tangled my feet in my gown, and I fell. Fortunately one hand was free, and it stopped my fall before I totally crashed. But the sudden movement caused my crown to fall from my head. I grabbed it and looked helplessly around the stage.

Phyllis was watching from a few feet away as I struggled with my gown. Getting my attention she motioned to me, extending her arm down in front of her gown. Then she grabbed her gown with her hand and pulled it a few inches off the floor. Buh.[10] Of course! Forget physics! I reached down for my dress in the exact way Phyllis had just showed me. With my dress successfully off the stairs my feet were free to move once more. I finally made it to my throne at the summit of the stairs. Maneuvering up those steps was the hardest thing I experienced that night, but once I made it to the top the view was great.

People rushed around the platform, climbing the steps quickly, covering the area like an army of ants. Everyone wanted to touch me, hug me, kiss me, or shake my hand, as if by touching me they would receive part of the magic. Then the press cleared the crowd off the steps, so the picture taking could begin. When the official pictures were finished, I floated down the stairs into the waiting crowd. Talking with people and smiling for photos came naturally, but signing my autograph in pageant books felt weird. I was astonished not only by the number of people around me but also by the different kinds: it was their enthusiasm and hard work that had made the pageant seem like magic.

People were still buzzing around me like drones around a queen. Invitations for appearances were being offered all at once. It was all quite new to me, being asked to speak at luncheons, museum openings, open houses, being invited to be a guest at powwows.[11] I felt needed, wanted, and suddenly popular!

Eventually things settled down, and I asked to be left alone. I

18. Susie sits atop a small platform crowded with people waiting to congratulate her on being crowned Miss Phillips University, 1971. *Photo by Steve
Bridwell,* Haymaker *staff photographer, 1970–71.*

sat in the empty, quiet dressing room for several minutes, contemplating the evening, hearing only the faint buzzing of the many lights surrounding the makeup mirrors. For a moment, behind my reflection, I thought I saw my bear cub smiling. "Why am I sitting here?" I thought. "I need some fresh air. I need to see the sky and the stars and feel the night breeze." Still mesmerized by the evening's turn of events, I quickly changed into my best jeans and T-shirt, carefully hanging up my dress. After covering my formal with a plastic bag I flung it and my other clothes over my shoulder and picked up three small bags. Like a pack mule I plodded outside and headed toward the car. It had all happened so fast that I hadn't taken time to think about the implications of being Miss Phillips. I had never considered winning.

The silence of the night was overwhelming compared to the noise of the pageant. The stars were shining like afterimages of camera flashes, and the night air was calm like the cool waters of a mountain lake. The previous commotion seemed more like a dream. I drove back to the dorm in a trance and went to sleep without unpacking the car.

By the time I woke the next morning Kathy was gone, and one of my roommates had left the Enid newspaper on my desk. It had my picture on the front with information about the pageant. My first thought was that I should call Mom, but I decided to wait, not knowing how to explain it. A couple of days later I found a note with three ominous words: "Your mother called." Apparently Mom had been overwhelmed by phone calls the past couple of days. People were asking all kinds of questions about me, and she wasn't sure why, because she didn't even know I'd been in a pageant. She'd learned from a neighbor that my picture was in the *Enid Morning News.*[12] It would be another couple of days before the Tulsa papers picked up the story. When she saw my picture she laughed, seeing that the *Tulsa Tribune* had used an old picture of me that it had run when I was featured as a Little League baseball coach.[13] It was hardly a beauty shot. The photo in the *Tulsa World* a day later was from the presidential scholar article, but at least my hair was combed.[14] Only the Enid paper and one from Oklahoma City used pictures from the pageant.[15]

"Mom, hi. Now before you say anything let me explain about last Saturday." I began a condensed version.

She remained quiet then finally spoke. "When I got the first call about a beauty pageant I thought they were talking about Kathy. She was homecoming queen a couple of years ago and seemed a more likely candidate than you."[16] All my sisters were attractive and had lots of curves like Mom. I'd been a sickly kid named Jimmy, a skinny tomboy named Bozo, a walking reference book with bird legs called Super Sue.

"Don't worry," I laughed. "It's hard for me to believe it, and I was there!"

I could tell by her silence that she was still stunned, although bits of pride lingered in her words: "My skinny tomboy is a beauty queen. Who would ever believe it? Miracles never cease, I guess."

I felt guilty for not having told her about the pageant. "I honestly didn't believe I stood a chance of winning." She sensed my remorse but remained silent. "But the important thing is I'm coming to Tulsa in June for the Miss Oklahoma pageant. Can I see you then?" Although we talked on the phone each week it had been a several months since we were together.

"Of course! I'd love to see you. You can stop by the house. Things have gotten better here since you left, and all your stuff is still here."

"Sure, and there will be a ton of rehearsals that the mothers can get permission to attend."

"Why don't you think about using this opportunity to earn your name?"

"Huh? Oh yeah, right." I didn't want to even think about that just yet. "Good-bye. Love you." I hung up quickly before she could say more.

I waited a couple of weeks before I made the next call. Kathy did not sound surprised to hear from me; she was concerned I hadn't called sooner. School would be out soon, and the Miss

Oklahoma pageant was the first week in June. There were a ton of things to do, so we had to get started. Kathy was so good at taking care of me and helping me be my best that she became my chaperone at pageant events. A beauty queen cannot be seen alone and must always be accompanied by a chaperone.[17]

Yet Kathy was a more than just a chaperone. She was only thirteen months older than I, and we looked similar, were about the same height, and had the same hair color and smile. I knew if Kathy was going to be with me, then not only would we make a good impression, and not only would I look my best, but there would also be some time for relaxing and partying. Not something you can always expect from the usual chaperone, who might be thirty years your senior!

Everyone loved seeing us together because we were almost like one of those sets of twins from the Doublemint "double your pleasure" commercials. When people spoke to us they talked to her, thinking she was the beauty queen.[18] We looked alike enough in the face, but a viewer had only had to drop his or her eyes to know which Supernaw it was. Surprisingly, though, not many folks seemed to catch on to what I called the "chest test." It never failed to identify me. Maybe my family shouldn't have called me Jimmy when I was young. Never underestimate the power of a name.

I wore a little makeup on a daily basis, but stage and photography makeup was different. I never put on enough rouge and lipstick, and I always used too much light makeup to hide the dark circles under my eyes, caused by allergies. Color cameras are highly sensitive instruments, and any light color is extremely highlighted. The result, when I did my own stage makeup, was a white-eyed masked face with no mouth. My hair was another real disaster. My dark hair is baby fine and thin. My solution was always just to pull it back in a ponytail. However, even I realized that this style was totally unsuitable for public appearances. Kathy was going to have to give me some serious lessons and a good haircut, so I could maintain an acceptable look when she wasn't around.

I liked the photo sessions because they gave me a chance to "ham it up" and to revel in that part of being a beauty queen. I had no trouble smiling for the camera, and it seemed I was as popular as Santa Claus: everyone wanted to have their picture taken with me. Closeups were easiest; the hardest were the full body shots, as I was never too sure what to do with my body in the photos, especially my hands. They always felt awkward and ugly, making me unusually tense.

My other problem was my posture. I was quite comfortable in the slumped-over, shoulders-forward posture. It was part of my casual country style. Cheering or on stage, dancing or moving, I tended to move more fluidly and hold myself more upright, but whenever I sat down I'd always slump. To me slumping was part of relaxing, and it became the hardest habit I had to change. So I made it into a routine. I'd take a deep breath and throw my shoulders back, tossing my hair. Then I'd smile my "plastic smile."[19]

Besides finishing my finals I spent the rest of my time getting my clothes together, practicing my dance, making a new tape of my music, finding suitcases, and getting extra makeup for the Miss Oklahoma pageant. I even spent a lot of time trying to find a blue dress that looked just like the one I was wearing in the scene I saw in the flames at my church meeting last year. Finding that perfect dress was a good sign, and I used most of the money the guys at Phillips had raised for me to buy it.

Kathy kept a list of things: what to wear for each event, which shoes matched the evening gown and swimsuit, casual clothes to wear for rehearsals, dresses for the three interviews, matching hair clips, bracelets, necklaces, rings, purses, shoes, and of course nylons. The list was quite detailed, full of items I'd never imagined. I was glad Kathy knew about color coordinating and accessorizing.

Once her list was complete she unleashed me on a treasure hunt. After we'd managed to borrow or buy everything on the list, I breathed a sigh of relief and felt warm inside. Once again I saw people pulling together to help me and was humbled.

14

Superstar Supernaw

The activities around the Miss Oklahoma pageant were quite different from those around the Miss Phillips pageant. Although the Miss Phillips pageant did feature an appearance by the current Miss America, Phyllis George, and was emceed by the former Miss America Jane Ann Jayroe, the difference between the two pageants was not just in size and grandeur, but in professionalism. At the state level pageants have much more than the entertainment provided by the contestants; they have professional musicians, dancers, and a variety of celebrity entertainers and emcees. The contestants at the Miss Oklahoma pageant arrived at least a week before it began, since pageants consist primarily of rehearsals. These rehearsals weren't just for the contestants, but for the supporting stage staff, orchestra, and visiting guest stars as well.

I enjoyed going to the rehearsals. They seemed familiar after high school musicals and plays. You came to a rehearsal with your lines memorized and your staging perfected. The rehearsal helped you get in sync with those you had to perform with onstage. I was really glad that I'd been practicing dancing and staying on the beat, since most of the routines incorporated a little dancing and lots of graceful arm movements. When the contestants were required to sing as a group I could fake it by just moving my lips. Sometimes I just sang extra softly. It's easier to fake being a singer than being a dancer.

After rehearsal I visited with Mom.

"Have you seen Margaret Collier? She went to Central."

"Yeah, I've seen her. She's Miss Tulsa." I laughed, remembering that she'd been a drum majorette and that, for some unspoken reason, drum majorettes didn't hang with the cheerleaders. "Sure, I remember Maggie. She'd twirl anything: two batons, knives, even fire! Then she'd throw them high into the air and spin around three times before catching them behind her back." Maggie had once called me "Supersquaw," and I wasn't sure if she meant it in a good way.

"Did you know her first runner-up was a cheerleader from Central?"

"No, who was it?"

"Anne Barker."

I smiled, somehow feeling vindicated.

* * *

Upon arriving at the hotel I was told to be at a press conference at the Four Hills Country Club, near the swimming pool. I was also asked to wear my swimsuit. I'd never been to a press conference in a swimsuit before. If I'd thought logically I would have selected my competition swimsuit, a beautiful one-piece bright yellow suit. The only other swimsuit I had with me was a fluorescent orange bikini I used for water-skiing. In a moment of clear insanity I decided to wear the orange one with a pair of matching flip-flops, saving my nice one for the stage.

I drove to the country club in my trusty gold Ford Pinto, wearing only a big fluffy towel and that little two-piece swimsuit. I was waved through the security gate and felt like a true celebrity. Not just any celebrity, but the girl in that 1950s song "Itsy Bitsy Teeny Weeny Yellow Polka-Dot Bikini." After finding the pool-area parking I wrapped the towel around myself and headed for the group of people gathering near the pool. I sat down on one of the white lounge chairs.

The media people were already waiting for the opportunity to interview and photograph the contestants. I noticed a couple of other girls walking to the swimming pool in beautiful one-piece swimsuits complete with nylons and four-inch heels, their hair and makeup immaculate. They looked like they had stepped out of a modeling magazine, and I looked like I was ready to go water-skiing and picnicking with cold beer and grilled hot dogs.

Realizing I'd made a big mistake, I took a deep breath and gathered my nerve. Bravely I stood up, unfastened my towel, and tossed it over my left shoulder. I approached the small group and introduced myself as they discussed possible photo backgrounds. The other girls were in beautiful swimsuits, and everyone wanted to use the swimming pool for our picture.

Not paying attention to the other girls, I waded into the water until it was about chest deep, glad to cover some of my brown skin. As I turned around I noticed that the other three magazine-perfect girls were sitting at the side of the pool, being proper as ever. They removed their color-matched shoes and put their perfectly manicured feet, nylons included, into the cool water.

The photographer Don Hamilton commented, "It's really great that you're willing to get wet. I've never met a beauty contestant willing to get her hair and body wet for a picture."

"Watch this." I acted like I was in control, but my legs were shaking underwater. Feeling like a fool for not knowing how to dress properly, I moved toward the shallow end of the pool, where the water was about three feet deep. Leaning forward I dunked my long black hair into the water. Then in a smooth, swift single movement, doing my best imitation of Rita Hayworth's hair flip in *Gilda*, I stood up and flung my hair over to my back.[1] Don was impressed. He immediately held up his camera to frame the picture and asked me to move to my right. After several dunks and many photos, he had his picture. My long hair spraying water in all directions provided him the perfect picture for the Sunday newspaper.[2]

I laughed when I first saw the picture. I was at the center of the color picture, the three gorgeous contestants smiling in the

19. Susie wears her best swimsuit at her second pool press conference for the Miss Oklahoma pageant in June 1971. *Photo by Bob McCormack, permission obtained from Bob McCormack photographic studio archive (2008.049), Department of Special Collections and University Archives, McFarlin Library, University of Tulsa, Tulsa OK.*

background. Before I had my first interview I already had my first official press picture, a full page in the *Tulsa World*. Still I was embarrassed to have been photographed wearing that little bikini and wished I'd been in deeper water. I'm a quick learner, though, and I vowed to wear only my best swimsuit, nylons, and heels to any future pool press conferences. That lesson paid off, because during the pageant there was another pool press conference, and I was ready.[3]

The pageant contestants were sorted into two groups of seventeen girls, for a total of thirty-four. I was in group two. We followed a simple rotation system. On the first night group one had the talent competition, while group two had the swimsuit competition. On the next night group two did talent, while group one did swimsuit. The show's format was the same regardless of which group was competing, so each night the group songs and dances were the same. On the final night ten contestants would be selected to compete in all categories.

Most of the girls there were serious about competing. Many of them had been in the Miss Oklahoma pageant before and were coming back for another chance at the crown. I didn't know enough about pageants to take them seriously. I wanted only to do my best and not embarrass myself or those who supported me. Whenever I got nervous I remembered the image of the young woman in the blue dress, wondering if she represented a future me.

One of the people I met during rehearsals was Gaye Spencer, a young professional dancer. Although I didn't know it at the time she had been around pageants and contestants most of her life because her mom, Toni Spencer, worked for the pageant. We joked a lot and danced around backstage during rehearsal breaks. I loved watching her dance and made mental notes of her style in an effort to improve my own dancing. I knew enough dancing to know good moves when I saw them, and I thought she danced even better than Kathy, although it was a close contest. Certainly her long legs made her look graceful.

Everything about the pageant was a new experience for both my mom and me. My mom's official pass allowed her to watch all of the rehearsals, observe everything, and relish each moment. We sat together during a short break while Judy Adams, the current Miss Oklahoma, practiced for her evening performance, playing the violin. Her crowd-pleasing song was "The Hot Canary." I saw Mom smile as she quietly hummed the tune along with Judy.

"I like your playing better," I whispered, gently squeezing her arm. "And you have perfect pitch, which is so important for the violin." That made her laugh, remembering the years she'd tried to teach me the violin, not understanding that I really couldn't tell I was playing off pitch.

"Well, I never played in front of so many people."

"I still like your playing better!" It was hard for Mom to take a compliment. She participated in all the activities arranged for the contestants' mothers. All of them, from socials and teas to press conferences, were new to her, and she was always nice to everyone. I overhead one of the contestants remark, "Susie's mom stands awkwardly and doesn't know which fork to eat with." I felt offended because Mom and I were alike; I just hid my ignorance better. I fumed quietly, listening to the contestant whine, knowing she thought Mom and I did not belong at the pageant.

I tried not to let her words bother me, but they cut deep. Still, I decided her comments deserved no acknowledgment at all. Other than some contestants and their mothers, the pageant people and stage crew were nice to us. Many of the other contestants' mothers would argue with the stage director and crew on where their daughters were standing, the lighting, who was standing next to whom. The entire stage crew loved my mom because she never gave them her opinion; she just watched quietly. They appreciated her for not being a stage mom.

There were three nights of competition. Getting through the first one would be the hardest. Kathy fixed my hair in the afternoon and sprayed it so much that it would hold through most of the pageant. When I arrived at the convention center I arranged my clothes and accessories in order of use. There would be a few quick changes. I retouched the makeup Kathy had put on my face and resisted the temptation to add more white under my eyes. Tension grew steadily as the contestants hurried to finish getting ready before show time.

I received a whole bunch of telegrams that made me feel great. They were from a unique collection of people: the judges of the Miss Phillips pageant, Phillips students, the Mel guys, the Indian Club, Tommy, and even Carl Albert. I picked up the next telegram, and my spirit bolted when I read Kenneth's words.

"Superstar Supernaw, do you think you're what they say you are?" The words almost matched the beginning of the song "Jesus Christ, Superstar," from the musical of the same name. What was Kenneth saying? Did he mean I was making my own reality or that I was letting others make it for me, or did this have to do with my Indian name? Superstar Supernaw. I liked that, but it lacked something. Kenneth was always stopping me and making me think about the nature of things, but I'd have to ponder the real meaning of his words later. I'm sure he would have said, "Now is exactly the time you need to do it." But I chose to ignore his imagined advice.

Finally it was time to get backstage and line up. The introduction of candidates was our first appearance on stage, and each contestant walked up to the microphone and said her name. When it was my turn I stepped on the stage and stood in the spotlights. I said my name and heard a tremendous amount of noise from my right. I looked over, and there were a bunch of the Sewer Rats, yelling and cheering. I couldn't help but smile. I heard other familiar voices coming through a small megaphone: they belonged to my fellow cheerleader Purna Gibson and Carole Nasworthy, our staff cheerleading sponsor from high school. Beside them sat Nola Jane Shelton with a pom-pom. I smiled at them and raised my eyebrows. They cheered louder.

Competition would be easier with my own personal cheerleaders. I didn't realize that my old high school buddies would be reading about me in the paper, much less attend the pageant as a group. It warmed my heart. The first night was my swimsuit competition, and I was glad to get it over. I felt uncomfortable in high heels, nylons, and a swimsuit, walking down a runway in front of too many people to count. I relaxed as we lined up on stage at the end of the evening, glad the night's competition had ended without any embarrassing moments.

I wasn't listening when a contestant nudged me. "It's you, Susie," she said with a big smile. "You won!" She pushed me forward.

"The winner of tonight's swimsuit competition is Miss Phillips," the voice repeated. I heard some hoots and whistles from the Sewer Rats and blushed. The rest of the audience applauded as I stepped forward to the emcee. He was holding a trophy.

"Ladies and gentlemen, the winner of tonight's swimsuit competition, Susie Supernaw, Miss Phillips University," he proclaimed, waving his hand over his head and toward mine. The spotlight found me walking, and when I reached him he smiled and gave me a little hug. Then he handed me the trophy and whispered, "Stand right here while I announce the other winner."

He proclaimed the name on the next index card in his hand. "The winner of tonight's talent competition is Leisa Johnson, Miss Norman!" A cute blond with perfect curls and big brown eyes stepped forward in her shimmering gown for her award. He whispered to her, and she turned and stood next to me. I looked at her out of the corner of my eye. She was about five-feet-six-inches tall, and I was glad she was standing next to me since the other girls were taller than both of us. The crowd broke into more applause, and cameras flashed as the audience cheered. Slowly the shouts quieted.

I stood big-eyed, frozen like a deer in headlights. I believed swimsuit was my worst competition. Always self-conscious about my body, I thought it was a fluke when I won the swimsuit competition at the Miss Phillips pageant. Some women like to flaunt their bodies, but I had never been comfortable with mine, especially compared to my sisters. Now that the swimsuit competition was over I pulled myself together and talked with the Sewer Rats.

After they congratulated me Russ took my arm, leaned forward, and gently whispered in my ear. "Do you remember when you used to have a crush on me?"

"Why yes, of course." I was surprised because I had never said anything to him and didn't know that he was aware of my feelings. But I've never been good at hiding my feelings.

He blushed. "I didn't want anyone to know that I knew such a skinny, awkward girl." He paused from his confession. "I just wanted to say I'm sorry that I ever felt that way about you. You've always been a truly neat person. I can't believe I ever denied being your close friend."

"Well," I interrupted, placing my finger on his lips before he could say more. "At least now you won't have to deny it anymore." We both laughed, I hugged him and gave him a kiss on the cheek. I was secretly glad that he'd apologized and wished I had the nerve to give him at least one good kiss on the lips for being so adorably honest. Of all people, I understood. My self-image had been established when I was a skinny, awkward kid called Bozo.

The next morning the picture of the two winners appeared on the front page of the morning paper.[4] The evening paper featured my picture in a swimsuit.[5] Most pageant contestants are tall, over five-foot-eight. Unlike the movies, where a camera can make a small frame look normal, the stage is for the long-legged, and I was only five-foot-three. Even in four-inch heels I just couldn't match the look of those long-legged beauties. Yet for my size I had a good shape. Although I never got the huge bustline characteristic of my sisters, I did end up with enough cleavage to turn a few heads. Years of exercising had molded my tiny body into solid muscle.

The next night was filled with more competition. I was glad to get my talent performance over, but I felt concerned. Although I'd felt the presence of my bear cub during my dancing, he'd stood off to the side, just staring. He hadn't danced with me. Although I'd danced my best, I now worried that I'd done something horribly wrong. But so much was happening that I didn't have time to worry for very long.

The third day brought my private interview with the judges. "There's a rumor going around that you were once Tractor Queen. Is that true? I don't see it anywhere here on your resume."

"So you found the skeleton in my closet! I was hoping you wouldn't find out." They were amused by my surprise.

"You should've listed it. It shows prior experience in beauty contests."

"I would hardly consider Tractor Queen a real contest. It was a lesson in humility," I replied seriously, although the judges thought this was funny, and everyone laughed. "Do you really think being Tractor Queen qualifies me for being Miss Oklahoma?" I heard them laugh again. I really enjoyed making people laugh.

The first judge said, "Seriously, it shows you have had experience with judges and interviews, with photographers and with the press."

"Experience with the press," I exclaimed gleefully. "I'll tell you about my experience with the press, and it doesn't have anything to do with being Tractor Queen. It's about the time I called President Nixon an SOB and got my first job offer!" I was shining now, talking in full confidence. It was fun to laugh at my previous mistake.

However, the next question silenced me temporarily, centering on the "short and skinny" statement I'd made to the press earlier, after the first round, when I won the swimsuit competition for my group.[6] While I felt my words were true, I regretted having said them, not realizing the quote would end up in the newspaper. I was about to regret these words even more, because now the judge wanted to know what I thought about winning the swimsuit competition.

"I guess the bottom line is, the more you go in, the less you have to come out." A couple of the judges tried to hide a smile, while others burst into boisterous laughter. Oh no, I'd blurted out something silly again. "Please let me explain!" I begged him.

"Not on your life!" he responded through laughter. "I wouldn't touch that statement with a ten-foot pole."

Still trying to explain I said, "I only meant that if you're small and have a small waistline, then you don't need an extra-large bust to look good."

The judge raised his eyebrow as if he were going to dispute what I'd said.

I felt defensive, so I stammered, "Don't get me wrong! I'm not saying Dolly Parton doesn't look good."[7]

I stopped talking because the roar of their laughter was too loud for my words to be heard. I joined in their laughter and blushed brightly. I couldn't wait to get out of that room.

Winning Miss Congeniality was a personal victory for me because this is the only award determined by the contestants themselves. Given to the girl who has been the most fun and a friend to all, the award traditionally goes to a girl who is not going to win because if she were a real competitor, she wouldn't be viewed as so friendly. I'd tried to help the girls have fun and get them to work together. We'd sing songs and act silly, often imitating popular people like Phyllis George, the current Miss America.

I could dismiss winning the swimsuit competition as another fluke, but being selected by my fellow contestants was an honor. It didn't matter that I wasn't going to win the pageant. Those two awards ensured that I had represented my family, the guys in Mel, my college, and my tribe well.

Jane Ann Jayroe, the former Miss America who had been the mistress of ceremonies at the Phillips University pageant, had encouraged me to get a dress that didn't look like a wedding gown and a swimsuit without a front panel.[8] She'd explained that at the Miss Oklahoma pageant she wouldn't be able to be friendly, since other contestants would view any attention as an unfair advantage. So this time she whispered her encouragement when she presented me with a trophy at a luncheon press conference on Saturday before the evening's final competition. My picture was in the paper that night.[9]

That evening I made the top ten and competed in every category in front of cameras and a live audience.[10] I did my best throughout the night, inspired by the fact I'd won Miss Congeniality that afternoon. At the end of the competition I was concerned that I hadn't seen my bear cub, realizing I'd forgotten to focus on the cub or on earning my name while I was dancing. Although I was disappointed with myself, I was glad to have survived another evening without any obvious blunders.

The competition neared the finale. Ten contestants were narrowed to five, and I was still standing. That meant it was time for the BIG question on stage. My question was almost the same as the one in the Miss Phillips pageant: "Since anthropologists study the American Indian, why are you studying anthropology?"

I really wanted to say, "To study the white man," but I knew this was not a joking matter. I decided to use an answer not quite as academic sounding as the one I'd used in the Miss Phillips pageant and without the comment about world peace. "Anthropology can offer hope to mankind by allowing us to study ourselves. By learning from the past we can better meet the challenges of the future." I hoped that wasn't an antigovernment statement, since I didn't mention peace. It was hard to think of something to say that didn't offend someone. For example, although I respected the women's lib movement, just being in the pageant (not to mention winning the swimsuit competition) made me a target.[11] It seemed like no matter what I did or said, I ended up offending someone. During the applause time slowed, and the scene blurred. I saw a bright light to the side of the stage and caught a glimpse of the Beautiful Lady. I stood in a trance, oblivious of the other contestants' answers, until the light faded. Winning didn't matter; my spirit guide approved.

The judges' opinion was handed to the emcee in an envelope,

20. Susie poses with her crown, robe, roses, and trophies after she is crowned Miss Oklahoma in June 1971. *Photo by Bob McCormack, permission obtained from Bob McCormack photographic studio archive (2008.049), Department of Special Collections and University Archives, McFarlin Library, University of Tulsa, Tulsa OK.*

and then the countdown began: five, four . . . I remained standing in shock. Three of us were left, staring anxiously at each other, the excitement rising.

"The second runner-up is . . . Miss Norman, Leisa Johnson." Leisa stepped forward to accept her trophy. There were cheers and energetic applause. "The first runner-up is . . . Miss Oklahoma University, Jan Ameringer." Jan waved and joined Leisa with her trophy, while the applause continued. "Ladies and gentlemen, the new Miss Oklahoma 1971 is Miss Phillips, Susan Supernaw. Ladies and gentlemen, here she is . . . Miss Oklahoma 1971, Susie Supernaw." He made a grand gesture with his arm, and the spotlights focused on me.

I stood startled for a moment, while hundreds of flashbulbs went off at once. I cautiously stepped forward, and the crowd rose to its feet, cheering and whistling. The Sewer Rats were going crazy. Purna and Carol were jumping up and down, hugging each other, while Nola Jane Shelton shook her red and white pom-pom. I graciously accepted my roses and waved, thinking how far I'd come since my stage catastrophe that started my Bozo days.

I kneeled as the outgoing Miss Oklahoma, Judy Adams, placed the crown on my head and put in several pins. The crown wobbled again. "Oh, why is my hair so flat?" I whispered. "I can never get one of these to stay on."

15

The Barefoot Queen

The first official Miss Oklahoma appearance was a Kiwanis Club reception. This was an opportunity to meet all the people associated with the Miss Oklahoma pageant, since the Kiwanis Club was a cosponsor.[1] Everyone gathered at a five-star restaurant at the top of a tall building in Tulsa, waiting with anticipation to meet the newly crowned Miss Oklahoma.

Meanwhile Toni Spencer was talking to me: she never left my side after the pageant. Toni was the executive director of the pageant, but she took on extra responsibilities for me. Right now she had a hundred things to say to me and was trying to say them all in only a few minutes.

"I'll be in charge of your life for the next year."

"Like a manager or agent?" I felt important, like some sort of movie star.

"I'll do more than just book your appearances. I'll help you get some dance and runway training. I'll groom you and educate you in the Miss Oklahoma and Miss America culture."[2]

"Wow. That sounds like a lot of work, but I'm ready. When do we start?"

"Right now, with your first appearance." She moved back a couple of steps and inspected me from top to bottom, like my sister Kathy always did. Her eyebrows rose when she saw my bare feet. "Where are your shoes?" She glanced around and saw them on the floor, where I had kicked them off after the press left. I hurried over and picked them up. "Don't lose those," she said, waiting for me to put them on. Then she led me backstage to a dressing room. She proceeded to stick more bobby pins in my crown and noticed immediately that my hairstyle was not well suited for wearing crowns. As she worked on anchoring she offered her first advice.

"You'll need to get a small hairpiece. You can sew it to the inside of the crown. That way when you need to wear your crown, you'll just have to pin in your hairpiece."

"Wow, my first hairpiece." I silently hoped it wouldn't be too expensive.

When Toni finished my crown felt secure. "Now move your head back and forth." Toni stepped back and watched as I moved my head. "It looks secure, but how does it feel?" She looked at me for an answer.

"It feels great. Best crown fitting I've had." I laughed. "You're much better at this than all those beauty queens who do it on stage." Toni smiled and turned me around, examining me closely. She stepped forward and straightened my banner.

"You'll want to take good care of this banner, because you'll be wearing it all year." She stood back and checked me again. The she took me by the arm. "It's time to go. Your limo is waiting."

I giggled to myself. "My limo?"

An usher dressed in a black tuxedo and patent leather shoes cautiously opened the back door of the convention center, and I saw an official pageant limousine waiting there. Rain had fallen for several hours during the evening, and by now the streets were starting to flood, the wind blasting the rain in a thousand directions. The limo's chauffeur jumped out and opened the car door. Taking this as my cue I made a dash for it. I had only taken a couple steps before my banner fell around my feet, but I didn't notice until I took my next giant running step. I heard a loud tearing sound before I started falling to the ground. With my feet tangled in my banner I landed in a huge puddle of water hands first, tearing my dress and my banner. Rain washed away a couple of frustrated tears as Toni came running. After untangling my feet I stood up slowly, while Toni reached down to retrieve my banner and put it back up over my shoulder.

Once my banner was in place I lunged into the backseat of the limo, head first. Unfortunately I wasn't really accustomed to wearing a crown and forgot to lower my head. My crown hit the top of the door, and I heard a cracking sound. Since the crown was securely fastened to my head, my body stopped its forward momentum as my head jolted back. I fell out of the limo and hit the edge of the curb. Water flooded above my ankles while I sat there for a moment, my head spinning and my pride severely injured. Toni helped me get slowly to my feet. She'd been right behind me and almost caught me, but everything had happened so fast. With my left hand holding my crown on my head, I slowly backed into the car, swinging my head extra low. Toni climbed in after me, picking up the pieces of crown that had broken off, hoping it could be repaired.

The news traveled fast, and by the time we arrived at the reception everyone knew what had happened. Thank goodness the press wasn't there. Toni and I stopped by the bathroom to clean me up as much as possible. Soaking wet, and looking more like a drowned rat than a beauty queen, I gathered myself together, took a deep breath, and entered the room with my head held high, the broken part of the crown hidden in the back. Charlie Welch, the president of the Kiwanis Club, stood by the door and was the first to greet me. He extended his hand in greeting and started to chant: "Susie fell down and broke her crown, and Toni came running after." I stood there totally embarrassed, unsure of what to do.

Toni laughed. "You're right! It's going to be a long year!"[3] Everyone laughed, especially me. I sure had a lot to learn about being a beauty queen.

Charlie escorted me into the room and introduced me. He whispered, "Give these folks a typical Indian greeting." I took a deep breath and said, "*Hesci.* Charlie told me to give you a typical Indian greeting, but I didn't know whether he meant a typical greeting like the one the Wampanoag Indians gave the Pilgrims at Plymouth Rock—or a typical greeting like the one the Lakota and Cheyenne Indians gave Custer at Little Big Horn. So I just greeted you in my language."[4] As Charlie blushed and the group laughed, I forgot about my wet hair and smiled, something I could never have done as Bozo.

* * *

Toni had been the executive director of the Miss Oklahoma pageant since 1964 and had been involved with the pageant when Beth Meyerson was Miss America.[5] Toni, who had lived in New York at the time, kept records on each contestant and on the winners. Whenever Toni gave me a fact I knew she had the statistics to back it up.

I asked her, "I never understood why I won the swimsuit competition in both pageants. Can you explain it to me?"

Toni said, "I know exactly why, and it has little to do with your body."

Joking, I said, "You mean it wasn't so I could get revenge on my sisters?"

"Not at all. It has more to do with how much the judges liked you in your interviews."

"That doesn't make any sense to me."

"Both the swimsuit and the evening gown competitions are areas where the judges can stack points for their favorite contestant."

"Stack points?" I made a curvy motion with my hands.

"Each judge wants to make sure their favorite candidate makes the top ten."

"Then what happens?"

"Once contestants are in the top ten, all the slates are wiped clean, theoretically. But each judge still has their favorite candidate."

"So that's how it's done. It's all been a mystery to me." I raised my eyebrows, and Toni chuckled.

"Over 95 percent of all Miss Oklahomas won the swimsuit or evening gown competition for their group. Miss Norman won evening gown the first night."

"And she was second runner-up. The first runner-up was Miss ou, who won talent the first night." It was starting to make sense to me.

"Talent's judged differently, but it's normal to have the top contestants winning the first night."

"Okay, so the judges liked me, not my body." That was easy enough to accept. I wished Toni had explained that to me before I told the press I was short and skinny.

✳ ✳ ✳

Toni took the pieces of my crown to a jeweler in hopes it could be repaired. Although the jeweler glued a few of the broken pieces of the crown together, the damaged side never looked quite right, so I made sure it always faced the back. I still had trouble wearing it. I didn't have a bouffant hairstyle, and even with Toni's trick of sewing in a small hairpiece, I spent the next year adjusting and readjusting my crown. And even though I hand-stitched my banner to repair the tear, it still bore the scars from that first disastrous appearance.

I never felt comfortable when people asked for my autograph. Although I learned to sign my name quickly, it seemed strange for someone to want my signature on anything but a test paper. The undivided attention I received whenever I entered a room was overwhelming, and my first reaction was always one of embarrassment. My head would spin when an entire crowd hushed, stood, and applauded. Eventually, however, I always found myself smiling, and I soon learned to accept these moments in stride, returning the audience's affection with endless smiles and waves. None of this had happened to me as a presidential scholar. Being beautiful, I thought, must be more prestigious than being intelligent. At least that's how everyone acted!

✳ ✳ ✳

Toni invited me to move in with her family for my makeover before Atlantic City. They lived in southeast Tulsa, on the nice side of town, with great views, a huge back deck, and lots of trees around an oversized lot. Toni's family took me into their hearts too, treating me like a surrogate daughter and even putting me on their Christmas card that year. It was a strange twist of fate that strangers were kinder to me than some of my own relations, but that's how my life has been: other people have always helped me out. Toni continued to work with me through the summer, knowing I had no idea what to expect.[6] It was a long and difficult task for her, and I often thought of her as Professor Higgins and myself as Eliza Doolittle.[7] It was like *My Fair Lady* all over again, this time with an Indian: Toni was going to try to pass me off as a viable contestant for the Miss America pageant.[8] Unlike Eliza and Professor Higgins, however, I couldn't have found a more compassionate teacher.

*   *   *

I never realized the benefits associated with being Miss Oklahoma. One big benefit was a car: I drove a Satellite Sebring Plus, compliments of Tink's Auto Mart in Tulsa.[9] It wasn't too long before I was out driving down country roads, testing the speed and maneuverability of my new car. I was pushing eighty miles per hour when I came quickly upon another car on the road. Instead of slowing down I decided to pass the car and stepped on the gas. The "Plus" in the engine kicked in, and my car effortlessly sailed around the other one, spraying dust as it faded into the distance.

As I was checking the rearview mirror I noticed the car was gaining on me, a small flashing light coming from inside it. I suddenly realized I had passed an unmarked police car. He was signaling me to pull over, so I slowed and gradually stopped. The policeman cautiously walked up to my car and looked at the decals on it: bright blue circles with a huge silver crown in the middle. Around the top of the circle were the words "Miss

21. Susie's official Miss Oklahoma photograph was used by the pageant throughout the year and was printed in bulk for her to sign at appearances. *Photo by Bob McCormack, permission obtained from Bob McCormack photographic studio archive (2008.049), Department of Special Collections and University Archives, McFarlin Library, University of Tulsa, Tulsa OK.*

America Pageant," at the bottom "Miss Oklahoma." A paint-
ing on the door declared, "Susan Supernaw, Miss Oklahoma." I
watched the policeman walk around the car and read the other
side. He looked inside then came around and asked to see my
driver's license. I handed it to him.

"Are you really Miss Oklahoma?"

"Oh, I'm the real thing!" I smiled my plastic smile. "Here, let
me show you." I got out of the car and walked around to the trunk.
I was dressed in cutoffs and wearing a white crop top. If I'd had
my straw hat I would have looked like a Tractor Queen. I took
out a small briefcase. Inside were my official pageant pictures,
the ones I autographed at public appearances.

"See?" I explained. "Doesn't this look like me?" I held up a
picture next to my face.

He saw the resemblance and smiled. "My daughter would love
to have your autograph," he confided, looking sheepish.

"No problem at all. Here, let me sign a couple of them. How
about if I make one out to your wife or sister?" I took out several
pictures and a felt pen and began writing. "Okay, what's your
daughter's name?" In a few minutes I had completed signing
several pictures. I straightened the stack and handed them to
him. "Anything else?"

"Yeah," he sighed. "Please slow down. We'd like to keep you
the whole year."

After that day I referred to those Miss America decals on my
car as "radar passes" and always carried along a good supply of
pictures. The way I drove, I was certainly going to need them.

A new wardrobe was another unexpected benefit of the posi-
tion. One of the first things Toni asked to see was my wardrobe.
She needed to know what she had to work with in planning for
Atlantic City.

She knew she was in trouble when I responded, "What wardrobe?" I had no wardrobe, just jeans and T-shirts. I had borrowed most of the things I wore in the Miss Phillips pageant,
and although I'd bought a new swimsuit and evening gown for

the Miss Oklahoma pageant, I'd still borrowed the other nice clothes I wore. Realizing she was going to have to design an entirely new wardrobe for me, Toni introduced me to Marge Wright Clarke. Marge was the owner of a very nice clothing store in downtown Tulsa called Clarke's Good Clothes. I was going to need at least three outfits a day for three weeks, all of them carefully coordinated with matching accessories and shoes. I never knew dressing could get so complicated.

Marge's store provided me with a wardrobe, and in return I modeled many of their clothes for the next year in television commercials.[10] Besides all my new store-bought clothes, Toni arranged to have my competition evening gown hand-tailored. Everything I wore, whether taken off the rack at Clarke's or Neiman Marcus or individually designed by a specialist, took into account my size and coloring. Since Toni couldn't change my height, everything was designed to make me look taller, and she wanted me to wear the highest heels possible.

Toni had lots of ideas to help me be a better contestant. One thing she didn't worry about was press conferences. She said with a laugh, "You don't need much work for your interviews because you're outspoken and intelligent. Your opinions are based on facts. Did you register to vote? That will be one of the subjects they'll talk about in Atlantic City, since eighteen-year-olds are now allowed to vote."[11]

"Yes, I registered as part of the Project Oklahoma drive to enlist eighteen- to twenty-one-year-old voters. The press was there, remember? What else do I need to work on?"[12]

"You'll need to gain some weight, so you'll get a variety of wonderful food and an intense exercise program to make sure the weight goes to the right places."

"Gain weight? How much weight?" Most contestants would have liked that, but for me it seemed impossible. Unlike a lot of people who eat more under stress, I always lose my appetite. Perhaps I have too much adrenaline and can't slow down enough to eat.

"About ten pounds, strategically located."

"And?"

"Some dancing lessons and a grooming program."

In order to get me to eat Toni talked with Kathy and found out all of my favorite foods. When I wasn't hungry she would tempt me to eat with rare steak, fresh baked macaroni and cheese, fried okra, corn on the cob, tomatoes, or baked potatoes smothered with sour cream and cheese. Toni also made me a special milk-shake with sugar, vanilla, and a raw egg. Between the exercise program and a diet consisting of raw and cooked foods, I gained seven pounds (strategically located) in three months.

I was delighted to realize that the wonderful dancer I'd met during the pageant was Toni's oldest daughter, Gaye. She would become my dance instructor. She worked me pretty hard and helped me choreograph a new dance for the Miss America pageant. My dancing up until that point consisted of a classical-ballet floor exercise–style dance with lots of tumbling. The music I wrote was slow and lethargic, conjuring up images of a butterfly floating on a soft summer breeze. Classical ballet, however, was now out, along with the plain black leotard and tunic.

My new talent dance was modified to modern jazz, so I wrote a new song with a heavy drumbeat. Gaye had three months to make me a jazz dancer. When I wasn't working with her on back layout kicks, I was busy writing music to go with my new dance. Instead of featuring two pianos and a string quartet, my new music would be played by an entire orchestra. I worked with Irwin Wagner, who wrote the complete forty-piece orchestra arrangement.[13] Toni designed my new talent costume, all silver with fringe down the arms and across the back. My new dance looked more like the jamming dance of the bear cub.

Gaye also worked with me on modeling in high heels because my stage presence still needed work. She taught me to turn in my evening gown with an extra step backward. As she'd turn and step she'd say, "One step back gives the gown extra time to flow around; slide the foot back real slow—to give them time to look once more." I was beginning to feel like a professional model, even if I was short.

My days were never dull, and they were always focused on me. If I wasn't eating or sleeping, I was dancing or outside tumbling. Only the rain made me see what was happening inside. It saddened my heart to watch Toni try to use her hands: she had rheumatoid arthritis, and her hands were distorted into shapes unable to hold anything. She tried not to show her pain, but I often saw her trying to write with little success. When I saw her trying to sew jewels on my competition gown, I took the dress and finished the delicate sewing, reminding her she'd done more than enough.

As the Miss America pageant drew near my appearances became more frequent. Those I liked best were the ones involving the press. I liked being outspoken and was passionate about my feelings. I liked listening to other views and then defending my own with additional facts. That may be the one thing I had in common with Phyllis George, who was very outspoken. I think that many times the Miss America pageant personnel were unsure how to control her. You couldn't argue with her because she could capture you with her smile. I admired her charming spunk and openness.

During the summer I made a lot of appearances: everything from grand openings, powwows, and TV commercials, to local events.[14] Since the Oklahoma pageant came before the Texas pageant, each new Miss Oklahoma was invited to be a guest star at the Miss Texas pageant. Other state queens were also invited to the Miss Texas pageant, including Miss Kentucky, Miss Louisiana, Miss Arizona, and Miss Wyoming. The Miss Texas pageant is one of the latest of all fifty state pageants. It is also the biggest, with over sixty contestants—more than the Miss America pageant. The Miss Oklahoma pageant had only thirty-six contestants.

Miss Texas pageant officials chartered a plane to pick me up in Tulsa and fly me and my official chaperone, Francis Campbell, directly to Dallas.[15] A limo was waiting when we arrived in the Dallas/Fort Worth area, and much to our surprise we were given a police escort to the convention center. I felt like a real celebrity.

The Miss Texas pageant personnel put us to work immediately. We had a photo session with the press so the papers could publish our pictures in connection with the Miss Texas pageant.[16] I loved the picture in the paper because I was standing closest to the camera and looked just as tall as those long-legged beauties behind me.

Finally the rehearsal started, and Phyllis George arrived. Phyllis had been Miss Texas before becoming Miss America, so just as Oklahomans adored Jane Ann Jayroe, Texans loved Phyllis. She always got a standing ovation whenever she entered a room.

The Miss Texas pageant was far more grandiose than the Miss Oklahoma pageant. It sure seemed like there were more Texans with tons of oil money than there were Oklahomans with oil money.

A pageant is a very different event if you're a performing guest star than if you're a contestant. There is no nervousness or that sinking feeling in your stomach before you perform. For guest stars all singing and music are prerecorded, and tapes are played the nights of the performance. I thought it ironic that the entertainment professionals should have such an advantage over the nonprofessional contestants. A lot can happen on stage when you do things live.

As an introduction to the evening gown competition, the five invited state queens danced with a male partner dressed in a tuxedo. I really enjoyed waltzing around the stage, each step and twirl carefully choreographed. During a break at the dress rehearsal the day before the pageant competition began, I was clowning around backstage. I started singing the music and waltzing in a circle backstage. Unfortunately there wasn't as much room as I thought, and one of my turns brought me face-to-face with a large metal clothing rack. I managed to keep from hitting my head, but my foot rammed into the metal at the bottom of the rack. My dancing immediately stopped, and I yelped and started jumping on one leg, holding my damaged foot in my hands. I hopped over to a chair and sat down. I hadn't been wearing any shoes at the time, since heels were not comfortable, and I took them off every chance I got. Now I finished the rehearsal barefoot, an ice pack wrapped around my toe.

The next morning my toe was badly bruised and swollen. The pageant personnel sent me to a doctor to have it checked. A few x-rays showed that it wasn't broken, just badly bruised. If it had been broken, I wouldn't have been able to perform onstage. I kept my foot on ice and elevated all day, hoping the swelling would go down enough for me to wear my shoe. By the time I got to the pageant and dressed, I had devised a way to walk without limping: I simply held my toe off the ground. But I still couldn't get my foot into my shoe, so I had to get a larger pair.

My evening gown dragged slightly on the floor since my new shoes had lower heels, but I convinced myself that no one would even notice. So as the state queens appeared onstage and began dancing, I elegantly danced among them, waltzing and twirling without much of a limp. When the number was over and the stage lights faded, Phyllis's appearance brought the crowd to its feet. She motioned for them to sit down, and they obediently complied. My mind faded a little until she said the words "state queens." Phyllis then introduced us one at a time. When I heard my name and the words "Miss Oklahoma," I glided over to the microphone. She started telling the audience about first meeting me at the Miss Phillips pageant. My mind visualized those days at Phillips. They seemed so long ago. She then told a story about me at the Miss Oklahoma pageant.

As Miss America, Phyllis had been the primary guest star at the Miss Oklahoma pageant. During opening rehearsals different girls had been selected to pretend to be Phyllis. Each Phyllis pretender appeared at the top of a huge staircase, gracefully descended, and waltzed over to the piano, where she pretended to play.

Finally, my turn came. The rehearsal music began, and the

announcer spoke: "And here she is, ladies and gentlemen. Miss America, 1971, Phyllis George." I stepped out on the staircase, and a few people applauded symbolically. I carefully walked down the endless steps and waltzed in big circles on the stage toward the piano. Then I sat down and spun around on the seat. In a moment I pulled my dress up, lifted my feet up on the piano, and started playing "Mary had a little lamb . . ." with my toes. Everyone had cracked up, and for a moment the rehearsal had stopped.

"Now, we'll be together again in Atlantic City," Phyllis finished the story for the audience. "I was wondering," she said innocently. "Were you planning on doing your imitation of me again in Atlantic City?"

"Well, no, not really. I doubt they'll give me the chance." The crowd howled with laughter.

Then without warning she said, "Susie and I have a secret we'd like to share with you." The audience applauded and then hushed in anticipation. Phyllis paused. "Yesterday at rehearsal Susie hurt her foot because she wasn't wearing any shoes. Isn't that just like an Okie?" She turned to me with a huge smile on her face. "She's a barefoot queen."

Caught off guard, I had nothing to say in response. I raised my eyebrows and gave a silly grin. I reluctantly lifted the skirt of my gown off the ground and exposed my feet. My left toe was wrapped with a large bandage that stuck out of my shoe, and my right foot had extra padding that stuck out in the back. The crowd roared with laughter.

In spite of my embarrassment I liked Phyllis's nickname for me and thought how close she was to the truth. Being a member of the Bear Clan, and having the name "Dancing Feet," I really was a Bear Foot Queen. The incident followed me even to Atlantic City. Whenever someone who knew the story saw me, they'd say, "Show me your shoes." I'd pick up my dress and show them my feet, hopefully with shoes. But it never stopped me from kicking off my shoes any time I could.

16

The Indian Queen

I was totally baffled at the effect an Indian Miss Oklahoma had on the Indian tribes in the state. Traditionally the Five Eastern Tribes (often called the Five Civilized Tribes) did not get along the western tribes.[1] We referred to them as "plain" Indians, instead of "Plains Indians." Animosity began in 1867, when many of the Plains Indians were relocated to western Oklahoma.[2] At that time the entire state of Oklahoma (except for the panhandle) was divided among the Five Eastern Tribes.[3] The western two-thirds of each tribe's reservation was taken in order to make room for new tribes such as the Kiowa, Sac and Fox, Comanche, Cheyenne, Arapaho, Pawnee, and many others.[4] That had occurred over a hundred years ago, but the Five Eastern Tribes still remembered it, and although it was a result of the white man's law, they still disliked the newcomers.[5]

Old habits and prejudices die hard. Perhaps the state's tribes had never united before because these old negative memories, caused by the white man, had not been replaced by new positive memories. Non-Indians were often amazed at the constant bickering that occurred among Indian nations. Putting such a variety of Indian nations in one state was like moving all the peoples of Europe into just one area. Each tribe had its own language and culture, just like in Europe. Different languages and religions led to rivalries and blood feuds among the tribes and caused many disagreements. This was hard for many non-Indians to understand, although it shouldn't have been.

My Muscogee (Creek) grandma, Carrie, is a good example. According to her, anyone of any race was better than the Seminole. I found this ironic, since the Seminole and Muscogee (Creek) had once been closely related.[6] Our languages, customs, songs, dress, and food were similar in the old days, before relocation. Still, her prejudice was based on these old days, when the Muscogee (Creek) were in Georgia and Alabama.

It took several years for the Southeastern tribes to lose their lands, but relocation began in 1830 with the Indian Removal Act.[7] At that point President Andrew Jackson ordered the removal of the Indians from the Southeast, in spite of the Supreme Court's earlier ruling that he could not do this.[8] The Supreme Court, however, did not enforce its decision and protect the American Indians from removal, so the U.S. president defied its ruling, forcibly marching many American Indian tribes to Oklahoma, a journey called "The Trail of Tears."[9] Over one third of American Indian people on this march died, mostly the very young and the very old. Many were without even blankets to keep them warm as they walked against the winter wind. Entire clans were wiped out.[10]

Although this had occurred in the 1830s, Grandma Carrie never forgot that many Creek citizens (some of whom had already left the Creek Confederacy) refused to go on the march.[11] They simply ran away. The word *Seminole* in fact means "runaway."[12]

It never bothered me that long ago a bunch of my relatives headed south into the everglades and that the U.S. Army never could remove them all.[13] To be honest I thought it was pretty cool how they had outsmarted the U.S. government and the military. So Grandma's prejudice toward the Seminole seemed unjustified to me, but I could never convince her otherwise.

But, more important than her opinion of the Seminole was the cultural heritage she had given me. Now I was flattered that my tribe recognized my achievements and honored me at an

22. A photograph of Susie dressed in women's buckskin regalia was also printed in bulk for her signature and used as an alternate Miss Oklahoma picture for cultural and American Indian events. The buckskin was loaned to Susie by friends since she did not have one of her own. *Photo by Bob McCormack, permission obtained from Bob McCormack photographic studio archive (2008.049), Department of Special Collections and University Archives, McFarlin Library, University of Tulsa, Tulsa OK.*

official reception held at the Muscogee (Creek) Indian Council House in Okmulgee.[14]

Kenneth Anquoe decided, further, that now was the time to do what had never been done before: the tribes must stand united, even just long enough to support me. I'd endured the prejudice of the majority population, poverty, alcoholism, and domestic violence, and yet remained true to my culture's spiritual teachings. Kenneth believed that I represented the unique Indian spirit and needed only to convince all the other Indian nations to share that belief.

Kenneth thus gathered together representatives from all the tribes and Indian organizations in the state.[15] Their selected representatives met with Toni and other Miss Oklahoma pageant officials. They wanted to do something for me to show their pride. They wanted to make sure Americans knew that I was the not just the state's queen but also the Indian tribes' ambassador, their queen.

Toni had a suggestion: "The tribes could sponsor a page for Susie in the Miss America pageant booklet. A full page costs one thousand dollars."

"You mean the pageant doesn't pay for it?" Kenneth asked.

"No."

"But Susie doesn't have any money. There's no way she can afford a page." Kenneth looked at Toni decided: "Unless the Indian tribes of Oklahoma sponsor it."

Kenneth would make it happen. The Oklahoma tribes, usually unwilling to sit at the same table, were finally going to come together. It was symbolic: Kenneth was from a western tribe, and I belonged to an eastern tribe. Already the west and east had united through the Native American Church, but the big challenge now was to get all the tribes to join on a nonchurch matter. Fortunately Kenneth was a popular and persistent man, and he convinced the tribes to host a statewide powwow in my honor.[16] Oklahoma City was selected for the powwow, not just because it was located in the center of the state but because it represented an unmarked division line between the eastern and western tribes. We called it the 98th Parallel, as if it marked a demilitarized zone.

Kenneth knew how to work with the various tribal differences. Between raffles and blanket dances he was confident that they could raise enough money for my page. I was flabbergasted at all the attention. These people were willing to put their differences aside because of me. With friends and relatives located all around the state Kenneth easily spearheaded the effort of organizing the huge powwow.

Although he now lived in the Tulsa area, Kenneth was originally from Anadarko, Oklahoma. And although he'd attended Riverside School at Anadarko and Bacone College at Muskogee, he'd always retained his cultural heritage. Kenneth had helped me many times, usually in a spiritual way. He'd taught me a little bit of the Kiowa language and a lot of the sign language he used. More important, Kenneth had taught me how to pray in the Native American Church. Now he was sure that no one would consider arguing about tribal differences after singing and praying together all night.

Kenneth invited me to his house before my powwow and reminded me of my childhood dream when I had received my Indian name, Ellia Ponna. He was one of the few people who knew about my dream, although a lot of people now knew my Indian name, which had become popular after I was named Miss Oklahoma. I was Super Sue to people in Tulsa and Super Susie at Phillips University and in the town of Enid.[17] Broken Arrow was known as "Susie Supernaw Territory."[18] Word of my Indian name (as if Supernaw wasn't Indian enough) had also been leaked to the press, and people had started calling me Dancing Feet. Technically I really wasn't Dancing Feet, because I hadn't yet earned my name or received it in a ceremony, but that's not the kind of thing one says to the press. Just about anything would've been better than my earliest nicknames, Jimmy and Bozo, and I never felt comfortable with names like "Super Sue" and "Superstar Supernaw."

Now I asked Kenneth: "What about people and the press calling me Dancing Feet? Is that all right, even though I haven't earned my name?"

He thought a moment. "Let it serve as a reminder to you to fulfill your promise."

"So it doesn't matter that I haven't earned my name?"

"Earning your name is most important, but it's something you keep to yourself. It's a personal journey, not a public one. Remember, your name is Ellia Ponna, not Dancing Feet."

"But they mean the same thing."

"But they're not the same."

I looked puzzled, and he laughed. "Remember, details." I could never understand this distinction logically, but something inside me made it feel right. My name was Ellia Ponna. I liked that better than Dancing Feet anyway.

Kenneth helped prepare me spiritually by sponsoring a small private meeting at his house. Before this meeting took place a Muscogee healer nicknamed Buzz Barnett motioned me to come over. I curiously joined Kenneth standing beside Buzz, who leaned toward me and said, "It's time for you to stop winning awards."

"What you do mean? I thought I was supposed to win awards. Haven't I brought pride to our people?" I felt defensive.

"Replace competition with cooperation. Leave some awards for others to win." I was puzzled by his comments, so he continued: "The more awards you win, the more important you may think you are. Remember to not feel or act more important than others. When we feel superior to others we may embarrass or belittle them." I nodded, understanding the path of *ekvncvpecetv*. Buzz looked serious, but his eyes sparkled.

Kenneth nodded and said, "What is important is that you earn your name." My jaw dropped, but I knew he was right. It wasn't about competing with others; it was about completing my journey.

Buzz continued: "Remember we're all related, and you must

share your energy with everyone. These are the Muscogee values that bring pride to our people."

My eyes watered, and I almost started to cry. Kenneth reminded me: "The opportunity will be provided if you find a way to live in harmony and maintain a balance in your life. Your actions mold your spirit. Your spirit knows the way."

Buzz finished the lesson: "Don't forget your inner strength comes from balancing your body, mind, and spirit. Your spirit grows strong when you share your energy with nature and people because it's a reciprocal exchange."

I visualized a universe of swirling energy and didn't pray about the pageant that evening, feeling it would have been a selfish prayer. Instead I prayed that I could earn my name. Although I hadn't seen him in some time, I prayed for Dad too. I prayed that he'd find the strength inside to make his life better and to help himself. Just once I prayed that he'd accept me now. More important, I prayed that he could accept himself and that I could learn to accept him as he was.

Mom drove me, and we met Kathy at the powwow, since she was living in Oklahoma City. My sister Judy was in Okinawa with her husband and had just had her second child, a girl named Rhonda. Louise never came to powwows, so she and her kids stayed home. Mom brought some lawn chairs and watched our stuff as we danced.

The gourd dancers, joined by Kenneth, danced all afternoon and finally stopped for the evening meal. Kathy and I ate quickly and went inside a tent to change into dancing clothes. I led the Grand Entry, dancing after the flag bearers and before the Head Man and Head Lady dancers. People stood as we danced around the arena. The drum sang a traditional American Indian flag song to honor our country and its veterans. After Kenneth prayed I performed the Lord's Prayer in sign language Kiowa style, and the colors were escorted out of the arena. As the dancers left the arena the emcee announced that the powwow would begin with an honor dance for me. My immediate family was called

23. Susie dances with her dad for the first time during her honor song at the beginning of her Oklahoma City powwow. *Photo by Bob Albright*, The Daily Oklahoman, *July 18, 1971. Copyright © 2009* OPUBCO *Communications Group.*

to gather at the entrance. Since my family had no special song, Kenneth had asked a traditional songwriter to write an honor song for me and to teach it to the other members of the drum.[19] The drum would sing the song the first time, and only my closest family would dance with me. Then on the second round anyone who wanted to could dance behind us.

Just as I walked into the arena to begin dancing my father stepped forward to join the family line, dancing on my right during my honor song.[20] I was shocked to see he was a good dancer, having never seen him at any Indian dances before. This was the only time any of us ever saw him dance in the style of the old ones, which meant he had to be sober.

I remembered what Grandma Carrie had told me about children leading their parents into unknown territory, where they would not go on their own. Kenneth later told me, "Never give up on a person changing. Anyone can change if they want to change, but you can never change them." I nodded, realizing that Dad had changed a little that day, and so had I.

Mom later said that this was the best thing that had ever happened to him. He'd gone out and bought new clothes for his picture in his company paper.[21] His company invited me to visit his office so some pictures could be taken of us together. I was glad he now wanted to be associated with me, in spite of his response when he learned I'd won the pageant: "If Susie won a pageant, there must have been a bad crop." If that was the best he could do, I'd thought at the time, I knew I'd never be able to please him. But now, at least for a while, he quit drinking and actually enjoyed my fame. His presence at the powwow was proof enough that maybe things could change. If not, at least for a day I could pretend that we were a real family and that he really cared.

Another pleasant surprise was a gift from an old high school friend, Johnny Whitecloud.[22] He'd wrapped the bottom of a perfect eagle plume, one from over the eagle's heart, with colored string before handing it to me. Kenneth called it "the real thing."

Honored to receive such a precious gift, I held it gently. Kenneth reminded me: "The bone used to make the eagle whistle comes from the wing that covers its heart. That plume comes from the chest of the eagle and has lots of *dw dw*, special power, if you can learn how to use it. It can carry knowledge or prayers from one world to another."

"Do you remember when Neil Armstrong landed on the moon and said, 'The eagle has landed'?" I liked that he'd called the spacecraft an eagle.

"Of course. What are you getting at?"

"When he called the spacecraft an eagle, do you think that it carried knowledge from one world to another?"

"Symbolically, I suppose. Did you know our shamans have been going to the moon for hundreds of years?" I shook my head, and he continued: "Of course they didn't need a spaceship to do it." We both laughed. I looked around; there were people everywhere, but we still had the moment to ourselves.

I continued a conversation we'd been having for a long time: "Scientists think that there may be multiple universes, even parallel universes. What do you think?"

"There are many worlds besides this one." Kenneth moved his hand upward, indicating the heavens.

"Do you believe these worlds can be right next to us even if we don't perceive them?" Scientists, I knew, believed that there are different dimensions and different worlds.

Kenneth thought for a moment. "Sounds right to me." I started to ask another question, but he held his index finger up to indicate silence. He continued: "Now let's get back to this world. There's still a lot to be done here and now."

More than enough money was raised for the page that night. The extra money was given to Toni so that professional pictures could be taken.[23] She then arranged the photo sessions and designed the page in the pageant booklet, using a variety of pictures. When I looked at the page design, it wasn't the layout or the variety of pictures that caught my eye; it was a small group of

24. Money raised by the Indian Tribes of Oklahoma paid for this page in the 1972 Miss America pageant booklet. *Photos by Bob McCormack, permission obtained from Bob McCormack photographic studio archive (2008.049), Department of Special Collections and University Archives, McFarlin Library, University of Tulsa, Tulsa OK.*

words in the lower right-hand corner: "Presented by the Indian Tribes of Oklahoma."

I had their blessing. Not only my people but all Indian people in Oklahoma shared in my honor. I felt humbled and hoped I wouldn't disappoint them.

I later performed the Lord's Prayer in sign language at the Tulsa Pow-wow assisted by the Boston Avenue Methodist Church Choir.[24] In Indian style my relatives, not to be outdone, decided to use our annual Kihekah Steh Club powwow as another way to spread the word about my future trip to Atlantic City.[25] I felt sorry for the club princess, Raylene Lasley, since my appearance upstaged her, but she was gracious and shared her platform so I that could sit in the arena. Bill Supernaw gave away many things in my name.[26] These gifts were a "thank you" to all the folks who had helped me out in some way. My relatives didn't forget me either, lavishing gifts on me, including shawls, a red Pendleton Kihekah Steh Club blanket, and a uniquely designed hand-beaded crown decorated with both the American and the Oklahoma flags. Again I was honored and hoped I wouldn't let any of these folks down.

My biggest musical debut came not at a powwow, but at Tulsa's football stadium when the Tulsa Philharmonic Orchestra played the new song I'd written for Atlantic City.[27] Kenneth felt I should name it "Dancing Feet," to remind me of my journey, and I reluctantly agreed. When asked by a press agent if I'd written an "American Indian" song, I replied, "Since it was written by an Indian, I guess it's Indian. It's not traditional, but more of a jazzy sound with some really strong drums." He smiled but looked disappointed.

As Kenneth escorted me into the arena for the orchestra's concert, I felt both remorseful and joyous. I was sad because Dad wasn't there: I never quit hoping I could please him. But I shifted my thoughts to the present and realized how lucky I was to have Kenneth in my life. I was blessed with a special fatherlike figure whose words and teachings provided a path for me to follow in

25. Susie waits while Kenneth Anquoe introduces her at the outdoor Tulsa Philharmonic Concert in August 1971. *Photo by Bob McCormack, permission obtained from Bob McCormack photographic studio archive (2008.049), Department of Special Collections and University Archives, McFarlin Library, University of Tulsa, Tulsa OK.*

search of my destiny. My own dad may have abandoned me, but another man had welcomed me as a daughter. My sorrow turned to joy. The Native American Church didn't just preach family values but taught them through the actions of its roadmen.

Kenneth lived in many more worlds than I ever could. He worked in the city for a major chemical company. He was a great singer of both traditional songs and NAC songs. He was a roadman and a spiritual leader. He was a proud father and a good husband. I could only hope that my life would be as meaningful to others as his was to me. People welcomed him everywhere because he made a big difference in their lives.

Kenneth introduced me to the crowd. When I stepped forward to the microphone, the crowd rose to its feet in avid applause. I was shocked, but I smiled and looked around the stadium, waving. There were lots of Indians contributing to the enthusiasm with shouts and hoots; it almost sounded like a powwow introduction, except for the random beating of a drum (sounding like applause) that occurs when folks are introduced Indian style.

After a couple of minutes I signaled the crowd by holding up a single hand and then motioning downward, a trick I'd learned from Phyllis George. That stopped the applause, and the audience obediently sat down. I'd never tried that before, and it felt good, having so many people at my command. A hush of anticipation hovered over the crowd for a moment. Now my song was making its debut. I wasn't going to dance to it because there wasn't enough room. So I made a few motions during the music, visualizing my bear cub dancing.

The tympani drums picked up the rhythm and began their backbone beat. The bass drum began, and then the tom-toms joined in. The sound began to vibrate in the pulsing rhythms of the multiple drumbeats. After a slow crescendo the brass and woodwinds started the melody. Finally the strings joined in on the melody, completing the sound.

The full-bodied music soared from the open football stadium directly into the clear night skies, and I was sure the spirits heard it. The musicians played with expression, and my music delighted the audience. I also became part of the music, jumping up and down at key moments, signaling different instruments to join in. I could hear it all in my head so clearly. The stadium crowd went wild when the drums took over the final beat.

My heart was thumping in time with the drums. Then the spotlight washed my eyes in whiteness, and flashes of my dancing bear cub filled my mind. His movements mimicked part of my new dance routine: "Of course the jazz rhythm completes the picture." My bear cub was not wearing a tunic, dancing ballet to classical music, but was jamming to the drums. I realized then that Atlantic City was giving me the opportunity to finally fulfill my dream and live up to my name of "Dancing Feet." The energy of the rhythm mixed with the enthusiasm of the crowd's reaction, instilling a new confidence in me.

Toni recorded the song that night, so I practiced my Atlantic City routine using the tape. In Atlantic City my music would be performed live by an orchestra. Hearing the crowd's cheers and applause on the tape during my rehearsals reminded me of all the support I had from the city of Tulsa, Oklahoma American Indians, and the state pageant personnel. My determination to not let them down gave me the endurance I needed to continue my preparation for Atlantic City. But I pushed myself a bit too hard in my last workout and pulled my back just before it was time to leave for Atlantic City.[28] I went to the doctor and got some medication. At night I put a heating pad on my back, praying that my injury wasn't a sign that I wasn't going to earn my name.

17

Dancing Feet

In spite of the wonderful effort to get my entire wardrobe into two suitcases, the airline lost them both somewhere in Philadelphia. I spent my first night in Atlantic City wearing the same clothes I'd worn all day, a gray traveling outfit. I stretched my back while I waited for luggage that never arrived. I noticed that Miss West Virginia, Linda Jean Moyer, had arrived just before me in the same outfit.[1] Graciously I complimented her on the dress and how well it fit, secretly glad she wore her belt on the outside while mine was inside the outer jacket, giving the outfit a different look. She smiled and returned the compliment. When you have fifty state queens looking for that perfect dress, it's not unusual to find more than one of them wearing it. This wasn't the last time I witnessed another contestant wearing the same outfit I had on.

Whenever contestants discovered they had identical formal wear, they would work out a schedule together. I had one hot pink chiffon formal that was the same style as two other contestants, so we agreed to wear our gowns on different nights. Or if we wore them on the same night it was at different events. For example, I decided to wear mine in the finale, while another contestant wore hers in the introduction of state queens.

Hotels sponsored the contestants and their chaperones. My hotel sponsor was Howard Johnson's, which sponsored four states: Ohio, Oklahoma, Oregon, and Pennsylvania. Miss Ohio,

Laurie Lea Schaffer, was just down the hall from me, so she and I traveled together to the Convention Hall during the pageant. Laurie was a pageant pro. It took her three hours to get ready each morning because she never left the hotel until her appearance was perfect. It took her two hours just to fix her hair—hair so ratted and rigid from hairspray that I figured it must take her at least that long to comb it out again.

I never understood what the big deal was when we were just going to rehearsals. It wasn't like we were going to an interview or a press conference. It's not that I didn't spend time getting ready: I had a new outfit for each day, complete with nylons, matching shoes, and jewelry. I'd even brought some hot pants, not knowing if I'd be allowed to wear them.[2] Dressing, carefully putting on my makeup, and combing my long hair just didn't take me three hours. Instead I spent my extra time soaking in a hot bath, hoping my back would get better. Maybe I should have taken a little longer getting ready and tried ratting and spraying my hair some. Or I could have tried wearing more makeup. Perhaps I wasn't trying hard enough to fit in.

Besides the death of her father, Laurie's worst life experience had been appearing on stage with her dress unzipped.[3] Laurie was conservative in her morals and fashion, and she believed other young people shared her values, thus fitting the middle-class mold perfectly.[4] Laurie could have taught me a lot about unspoken rules and pageant etiquette: she was a preliminary swimsuit winner.[5]

Many of the contestants thought it was cute that I was an American Indian and treated me more like an oddity than an equal. Some folks thought I shouldn't be there at all, as if the presence of minorities downgraded the pageant. They had a "there goes the neighborhood" attitude. Whenever I'd gotten that attitude from some of the girls in the Miss Oklahoma pageant, I'd tried to ignore it and be friendly. Patricia Patterson, Miss Indiana, was the only African American contestant in Atlantic City, and she thought it was time for a minority woman to be

Miss America.[6] But Cheryl Brown, last year's Miss Iowa and also African American, didn't agree.[7] Miss Hawaii, Aurora Joan Kaawa, was a Native Hawaiian, and we got along really well. Even though Native Hawaiians were not then considered American Indians by the federal government, we instantly connected, sharing a concern for preserving our cultures and traditions.[8] Although I never said so I couldn't see a minority woman winning for some time; she'd have to be someone who was part of the middle-class American "status quo," not someone standing outside looking in.[9]

I'm not sure how they assigned contestants to the various competition groups, but I thought it was interesting that my group of seventeen contestants included the only three minorities: Miss Indiana, Pat Patterson; Miss Hawaii, Aurora Joan Kaawa; and myself. Most of the eventual pageant winners would also come from our group.[10]

When approached by the press I said I wanted to improve the image of the American Indian, not that I thought an American Indian should win, like I'd said about Miss Oklahoma back in June.[11] I also said I wanted to use my background in anthropology to help preserve Indian cultures, not just for Muscogee (Creek) but for all tribes.[12] No one seemed impressed. As if to emphasize my point about the popular image of American Indians, an Associated Press (AP) photo with the cutline "War Cry" was released, its caption declaring that I wanted "the Miss America scalp as a contribution to the American Indian image."[13] The *Anchorage Daily Times* ran the picture, titling it "Real-Live War Whoop."[14] I was devastated. Instead of improving the image of American Indians, the press somehow had me contributing to the stereotype. I was somewhat relieved to see a very complimentary picture of me released by United Press International (UPI), its cutline "Miss Oklahoma, Susan Supernaw, a full-blooded Creek Indian, adjusts her feather during Miss America pageant festivities."[15] At least UPI didn't mention scalping people. Still, I smiled at how the press made me a full-blooded Indian but wondered why they had to say that I was adjusting my feather. In contrast, when the *Navajo Times* ran a short article about me, it used my official American Indian pageant picture, identifying me as a Creek from Oklahoma.[16] A friendly voice echoed from home as the Tulsa journalist Troy Gordon observed: "It doesn't matter that she's charming, intelligent, talented, and beautiful. Whenever the time comes for them to take a picture they'll think . . . what do Indians do? Oh yes, they give war cries."[17]

As if to emphasize Troy's point, in my next picture I was supposed to be showing Priscilla Doyle, Miss Connecticut, how to wear her Indian headdress. Priscilla had been given the Indian name "Princess Soft Sunshine" by the Easter Seal Society, which had no authority to give Indian names.[18] I tried to tell her this was a man's headdress and that even princesses didn't wear them, but she didn't care. Neither did the press: it made a nice picture. I found it ironic that the picture showed a non-Indian woman wearing an American Indian man's headdress while a Muscogee (Creek) Indian smiled in the background. I guess they didn't want my expert advice after all, not that I had any to give, since Muscogee (Creek) don't wear eagle-feather headdresses. Now if they had asked about otter or mink headwear, I could have offered some real advice.

My experience in the 1972 pageant was complicated. The Miss America pageant had begun as the "Atlantic City Bathing Beauty Contest," created in 1921 to bring more tourists to Atlantic City at a time when American Indians weren't even citizens of the United States (which would happen in 1924).[19] Over time the pageant blossomed into a major money-making event focused on middle-class values.[20]

Where did I fit in? The stereotype of American Indians left behind by John Wayne movies had certainly done some damage.[21] To make matters worse Wayne's interview in *Playboy* magazine in May 1971 had angered many minorities, particularly his declaration that he believed in white supremacy.[22] Now I told the press that I was active in the cause for American Indian rights and that out of this passion had come a personal boycott of John Wayne movies that stereotyped American Indians.[23] I thought it would be neat to take one of his "cowboy and Indian" movies and change the ending so that Wayne gets shot off his horse by an Indian arrow as he rides into the sunset.[24]

Unlike Laurie, then, I couldn't say that the majority of young people agreed with me. But also unlike Laurie the members of my race had been depicted over and over again as unclean savages speaking broken English.

When asked by the press if I represented the "ideal American girl," I explained that I was more of an "all-American girl." I wanted to say that I was the "girl-next-door" type, like I had during the Miss Oklahoma pageant, but I doubted that anyone around here lived next door to an American Indian.[25] However, since I was American Indian I could really be an "all-American girl."

But part of the mainstream, I wasn't. The fact that I was a presidential scholar only made me seem more aberrant. The press didn't play this up, except back home, and the judges didn't ask about it. They did, however, ask about my music. Even though I'd assimilated somewhat, conforming to mainstream values much of the time, I still knew I was American Indian, and I knew my unique culture made me think the way I did. That introspection put me too far outside the norm. So I kept my quest secret. How could the "ideal American girl" or even an "all-American girl" be at a pageant to earn her American Indian name? She was supposed to be here to win.

Now my traveling companion, Laurie, was a perfect "ideal American girl." I called her "the no sex, no jeans, no drugs girl." The expression came from a quote she'd made to the press. At the age of twenty-four, she said, she'd never owned a pair of jeans, never had sex, and never taken illegal drugs.[26] Until we met I would not have believed it possible for someone to go through life without wearing jeans. The one thing I discovered that Laurie and I had in common was that we'd both hunted with our fathers. How, I wondered, could she hunt without wearing jeans? It took some time for me to realize that there must be another style of living that I could never imagine. I visualized her riding with the hounds on a British-style fox hunt.

Laurie and I were about as far apart as you could get on the social scale. Yet we were in the same competition, being evaluated according to the same set of values and interviewed by the same set of judges. Laurie's goal was to win. She'd been in her state pageant three times before.[27] For her pageants were serious business, and that tenacious attitude helped her keep winning.

By the time Laurie and I got to the convention center for the first rehearsal rain was falling and showed no signs of letting up. I wore my new raincoat, a tan double-breasted deluxe trench coat with a removable light flannel lining. Bought especially for the Miss America pageant, it was the nicest coat I'd ever had. After shaking the rain from my coat and the excess rain off my hair, I walked to the clothes rack where other coats were hanging. While hanging up my coat I noticed an identical coat on the rack, so I held it up in the air and shouted, "Hey, whose coat is this?" To get some attention I whirled the coat over my head. Suddenly from the other side of the room emerged a Southwestern state queen.

She angrily grabbed the coat from my hand, looking like she wanted to strangle me right there if there weren't so many witnesses. Then she threatened, "Put that down. That's an expensive raincoat. Don't touch my things. Just stay away." She paraded off with her trophy coat in hand.

Some girls looked at me, and a hush fell over the group. My first impulse was to run and tackle her from behind, perhaps even rubbing her nose on the floor (being the true country girl that I was), but Atlantic City required a different kind of strategy. I stood next to the chair, held my coat up high in the air, and countered, "Well, this is *my* raincoat. It's just like yours except that I got mine at the trading post on the reservation." Of course this wasn't true, but I said it anyway. I was surprised at how easy it was to humiliate her and felt guilty.

I learned a long time ago that you can't really change the stereotypes people have. Sometimes you can help open their eyes, but they have to change by themselves. Too often the people who need to change the most are the ones who never will. I wasn't at the pageant to convert anyone, and I wasn't there to win. I just wanted to earn my name and make some new friends. Obviously this state queen wouldn't be one of them. Or could she?

I started to feel guilty about what I'd said, partially because it wasn't true and partially because I'd said it intentionally to humiliate her. I'd fallen off our traditional path of humility and humbleness (*ekvncvpecetv*) by intentionally embarrassing someone. I was no longer living in harmony and had to make amends. The NAC taught me to honor and pray for my enemies: "kill 'em with kindness," not "put 'em down and then laugh." I hung up my coat quietly and slowly walked over to Sissy, the queen in question. She glared at me.

"I'm sorry I said that. It wasn't true. I was just joking." Well, at least it was a start. She looked shocked, but I smiled and reached out my hand. "Please, let me hang up your coat. I didn't get my coat on the reservation; we got it in Dallas. I was teasing you. I'm sorry."

Her reaction startled me. She gave me a great big hug! Some of the girls close by heaved sighs of relief and said "Awwww" in unison as I gave her a peck on her cheek and gently took her raincoat and hung it on the rack next to mine. "*Ekvncvpecetv*," I thought to myself. "It's really a good way to live."

✳ ✳ ✳

A beautifully unique competition evening gown is the most important item in a contestant's wardrobe. Mine was handmade, not like the old church dresses from my youth made of calico material cut from a newspaper pattern, but intricately designed, handmade by professionals with hand-sewn jewels. Another important gown is the one worn in the "Parade of Queens" down the Boardwalk in Atlantic City. In the old 1921 bathing-beauty days this event was called the "Father Neptune Parade." It's a perfect example of the power of a name. Whether the parade was for Father Neptune or for queens, Toni designed me a beautifully unique bright yellow gown with ostrich feathers for the sleeves. We called it my "Big Bird" dress after the big yellow bird on *Sesame Street.*[28]

Our first public appearance as candidates was this parade down the Boardwalk. I sat alone on top of the backseat of a convertible. A huge cardboard sign in the shape of a crown, made with thousands of individual sequins fastened at the top, spelled out "Oklahoma." The sequins shimmered when the slightest breeze touched them. Each queen sat under a sign that bore the name of her state, and the states were presented in alphabetical order.

We rode in our chauffeured cars down the Boardwalk, huge crowds of cheering spectators lined up along both sides. It was like a Macy's Thanksgiving Day parade, only girls in beautiful dresses were the main attractions, not large floating balloons. During the middle of the parade my car began to sputter and jerk. Then it died. My chauffeur started it again, and we proceeded another block before the car choked and died again. This time it stayed dead. The cars behind me slowed to a stop. Some of the local guys in the crowd decided to push my car so the parade could continue, but as they gathered around the car security guards sent them back and got on their radios for help. Then four guards got behind my car and began pushing. The crowd cheered as my car moved once more. One of the security guards started talking on his walkie-talkie, looking up the Boardwalk at another contestant's car.

Her driver had stopped, and we quickly caught up with her car. The guys were breathing heavily through their half-closed mouths, but they tried not to show it.

One said, "Get out of the car and go to that one in front of us." He pointed.

"You mean I'm riding with her? But what about my sign?" I pointed to the Miss Oklahoma sign in my car.

"It stays, there's no time. Quickly now." He extended his hand, and I was escorted to the other car.

"But how will people know which queen is which?"

"Don't worry, they'll figure it out."

I finished the parade as an intruder in Laurie's car. She certainly wasn't thrilled, and while I didn't mind sitting with her under her state crown, it was confusing to the people who saw us. They even wrote about it in Oklahoma.[29]

✳ ✳ ✳

Pageant rehearsals lasted all day, every day, for the entire week, with breaks only for eating. During these short breaks we often split into small groups where we could be more informal. Each year the contestants sang a silly song during the final rehearsals. With the help of a few others and using the same famous tune that each year's class of contestants used, our song proclaimed:

We're the Miss America girls, sweet and jolly . . .
We don't cuss, we just say "golly!"
We don't smoke, drink or screw,
And we don't go with the guys that do.
Now you may think we don't have fun,
Hell, we don't!

Standing in a line we sang loudly while making some large arm motions. Everyone laughed and clapped, except for a couple of the pageant officials, whose mouths were frozen in horrible gasps.

An older woman, masquerading as an official, came up to me and asked, "Can you tell me those words? I don't think I heard it right."

"What do you mean?"

"It sounded like you say the word 'screw,'" she said.

I raised my eyebrows, pretending to be shocked. Hiding a grin I said, "The line was, 'We don't smoke, drink, or CHEW.'" I said the word loudly so she could hear. "You know, like chewing tobacco." It wasn't true, but there was no reason for her to be upset. Sigh: another white lie had emerged, and it kept getting easier to stretch the truth.

✳ ✳ ✳

The press helped build up a tremendous amount of energy with the anticipation and hype generated by photos, articles, and interviews. They also liked to pick their favorites and the possible winner. All the publicity really just got everyone ready for the real thing. When all the judges gathered, it was really time to sweat, because the tough questioning was about to begin.

There are several types of interviews for pageants, and the public is never really aware of what goes on behind the closed doors. Many contestants have competed in beauty pageants for years, and somewhere along the way they have learned how to be marketable. The trick for judges and pageant officials, then, is to find the most marketable girl. Laurie, for example, emphasized that she was a gourmet cook, specializing in fondue, and Campbell's Soup was a big sponsor that year. She was certainly much more marketable than I was, cooking up bread soup and making ketchup sandwiches. I guess I could have used Grandma Carrie's recipe for blue dumplings or the Osage recipe for grape dumplings, but Campbell's would have had to enclose a free sample of baking soda so you could brush your teeth afterward.

✳ ✳ ✳

Looking my best was a daily requirement. Luckily, changing my grooming habits was easier than changing my barefoot habit. I felt most comfortable barefoot with no makeup, my hair pulled back in a ponytail, wearing jeans or cutoffs. Maybe I was a Tractor Queen at heart. Knowing I wasn't back on the farm and needed to act like a big-city girl, I tried my best to look the part. My most frequent question was, "Where are my extra nylons?" The biggest hassle about pageants for me was wearing nylons: I wasn't used to hose and tended to cause huge runs in them, sometimes just by putting them on. My habit of running around barefoot most of the time made the situation even worse. Before I realized it my shoes would be off, and my nylons would have a series of runs starting at each heel.

It didn't take much for me to ruin a pair of nylons even with my shoes on. I could sit at a table and get a run on my upper leg from the wood or metal, or I'd bump into something and get a run on the side of my leg. It got to the point where I began carrying a six-pack of nylons in my purse for emergencies, but there were so many emergencies that I still always seemed to run out. You can take the girl out of the country . . .

* * *

Interviews usually started in groups, so anything on the agenda with the word *social* meant interviews. Success in these interviews was based on your ability to engage in somewhat intelligent small talk while being adorably yourself. Most of the girls would cluster in small groups, and the judges would circulate among the groups in order to make sure they met everyone. There were a few brave souls like me who approached judges to talk individually. By separating myself from the crowd I was assured the judges would remember my face if not my name. It took a lot of nerve to just walk up to a judge and start talking. Still I ventured forth, knowing that when I left, that person was already judging me in ways I'd never know or probably understand.

It took a lot of discipline to force myself to be outgoing, but I did my best, even if it meant learning new behaviors. It was like wearing nylons. When I put on nylons I had to think and act differently. Still, something inside gnawed at my spirit, and I knew I couldn't compete with those social debutantes on their level because I was unwilling to change certain parts of myself. I could be serious about the competition and adopt an attitude focused on winning the pageant at all costs, or I could earn my Indian name. But I could not do both.

The traditional value expressed by *ekvncvpecetv* meant that

I must cooperate rather than compete, so the pressure was off for winning. I remembered what Phillip Deere had said about not being able to walk both paths, that one day I would have to choose. In my personal quest I needed only to adhere to my traditional values and imitate my bear cub's dance in public to be successful. It didn't matter what a judge's scorecard read, as long as I earned my name. I wanted to become Ellia Ponna, and I silently vowed to earn my name.

✳　✳　✳

Each night of the competition the convention center was filled to the brim with a cheering audience. There were also unwanted visitors outside. The pageant finals had been disrupted by protestors since 1970. The most popular group protesting this year was a women's liberation group, asserting that the pageant exploits women. Vietnam Veterans against the War also protested, wearing fatigues and carrying a red-paint-splattered girl on a stretcher, her sash reading "Miss Vietnam." These veterans said that the pageant dehumanizes women just as war dehumanizes people.[30] It didn't seem like the time to tell them that Miss Vietnam should be at the Miss Universe pageant instead.

There were TV cameras at every turn on the stage, along with many in the audience. Over four hundred million people would be watching on TV, in addition to the fifty thousand screaming bodies in the auditorium. Huge monitors were mounted in the halls and the dressing room so that everyone could keep track of what was happening. Contestant after contestant completed her portion of the competition. All the rehearsals and preparations were finally paying off, and the program moved swiftly.

As my turn approached I realized the past seven years of prayers and hard work were now materializing. My back ached, so I arched it gently while I sat. My racing mind was only slowed by deliberate breathing and focused concentration as I relaxed my back for my dance routine and prayed for assistance.

My concerns faded into the background as I ran to position

myself on stage in the darkness. The crowd hushed, and drums boomed from the darkness. Several spotlights focused on my body, partially blinding me with their brightness. But I could hear the music, and my tense body responded as I began to move my feet, then my hips, and finally my arms, pumping to the beat. The beat vibrated inside me as I began spinning and twirling, mesmerized by the familiar rhythm and the melody of my personal song. Time slowed, and the sounds of the audience faded until there was only a solo drumbeat.

Bursting with the energy of the vibrating sounds, I sailed high into the air, flipping and jumping as if the floor itself had become a trampoline. As I performed some jazzy moves, just for a moment I thought I saw my bear cub on the other side of the stage dancing with me. A mysterious peaceful calm came over me, and my back pain faded as I finished my last flip and went into the splits. When I looked again he was gone. As the crowd began to applaud the lights grew brighter until everything was washed out in whiteness. The whiteness slowly transformed into a brief reflection of the Beautiful Lady walking away with a shuffling bear cub. Together they faded, leaving me with a feeling of warmth and comfort.

The whiteness faded, and I slowly adjusted my eyes and looked into the crowd. As people came into focus my heart rejoiced at the look of pride on their faces. I couldn't help but wonder whether anyone else had seen the bear cub. Moments later another wave of questions flooded my mind: did this mean I had earned my name?

Most Indians receive their names as a result of something they have done. I was different: my Indian name had been given to me before I did anything. Perhaps this was because I needed extra strength to change my life. If I earned my name the pageant's outcome wouldn't matter.

The fifty girls were reduced to ten finalists. While the names were being read off I thought about alternate universes and how, scientifically speaking, we were all winners, since Hugh Everett's "many worlds interpretation" made it possible for forty-nine other universes to exist, in each one a different state queen was the winner.[31] I tried to imagine what the universe was like where I had won. Then the ten semifinalists were reduced to the top five finalists, and finally the top five girls were asked a final question on stage. The entire audience listened with anticipation, while I wondered, "Did I earn my name? Did my dancing resemble my bear cub's dance? Was the bear cub really there, and did the Beautiful Lady smile?" Had I seen them both, or was it only my imagination and the bright lights?

Still in a trance as the winners were announced, I heard some screams, and my eyes moved to see Laurie screaming and laughing at the same time. She was the winner. This seemed appropriate, for she certainly fit the "ideal American girl" stereotype. I moved forward into the group to congratulate her. I had won a one-thousand-dollar scholarship called the "Judges Special Award."[32] No one explained what it was for, but Pat Patterson, the African American from Indiana, won the same award. We stood next to each other while we waited to congratulate Laurie, and Pat said she'd never heard of the award before. I was glad Aurora, Miss Hawaii, had won a one-thousand-dollar talent scholarship, because I would have been really upset if the minorities had all won the same "special award."

Laurie's face glowed as she reveled in the moment, for her dream had come true. She had focused on her quest and succeeded: she was a triple-crown winner.[33] When it came my turn to talk with her I genuinely shared in her happiness. We were both forever changed that night.

18

Ellia Ponna

Slowly the light from the glowing embers fades. I look around the tipi to reorient myself. A haunting melody wraps itself around me, and feeling its power I vibrate inside. When the drumming stops I look at Kenneth.

"Bring in the water." He signals with his fan, and a woman enters the tipi, carrying a bucket of water. Wrapped in a shawl she kneels by the tipi door while Kenneth begins to sing the first of four songs to honor the water.

The music fades as I sit dumbfounded, unsure of what I've seen. I wanted an answer about my future but saw my past instead. Distracted by the day's events I didn't pray for my future but asked, "Why are there pain and suffering in my life?" Suddenly I realize that the answer to my question was given to me. I didn't recognize it at first, but now I understand. Much of my spiritual strength is a result of my pain and suffering. I might never have found the church had it not been for my pain and suffering nor met Phillip, Marcellus, and Kenneth. I'm now grateful for my crazy past, humble to be sitting here in this holy church in the presence of God. I understand that the answer to my future is in remembering my past. But how far back in my past must I go?

According to Buddhism suffering is a natural human condition. But because Buddhists believe in life after death and reincarnation, my pain was caused by karma, which means that in another life I must have been a wealthy womanizer or some other kind of terrible person. Am I condemned to suffer in this lifetime in order to atone for my sins in a past life? Did my spirit prearrange all my suffering in this life before my birth? That thought causes me to shiver.

The power in the sound of the eagle whistle makes me realize that my pain and suffering caused me to pray desperately for help many different times. My prayers were answered when after waiting and watching, somebody appeared to help me. Without pain and suffering I would've never ended up here at this moment. Pain and suffering helped me to discover the connection that each spirit shares with the rest of the universe.

When the prayers and songs end Kenneth sets down his gourd and staff. He nods at me, and I pull my yellow-fringed shawl up to my shoulders and hold it tightly with one hand. Using a tipi pole to steady myself I stumble to the front of the altar and face the fire, extending my hands for Kenneth's blessing. He throws cedar into the fire. As the smoke rises he uses his eagle fan to capture a little and then pats it on each hand.

"Everything happens for a reason," he whispers while he swirls smoke over my body. "God does not give us any adversity that we can't handle." As he taps his eagle fan on my shoulders, I realize that he is talking about my life of pain and suffering. How did he know? Then he taps the top of my head with his fan.

"We learn the truth about ourselves and those people around us from adversity." I nod my head in respect.

"You have earned your name. You are Ellia Ponna." Kenneth circles me, praying in Kiowa, fanning more smoke around me. I feel a warm glow inside and smile, thinking how much I've changed since I was called Jimmy. I sigh in relief; now my journey ends.

"Is your journey over now?" Kenneth asks as if reading my mind.

The fire crackles as a timber explodes and flames leap into the air. I look into the coals. For a moment I see something, a scene from the desert. The scene quickly fades, and I realize there's much more to learn.

"No, it's just beginning."

Kenneth smiles and gives my hands a final pat. I shake his hand. Having received my blessing, I walk around the fire to my place and wait for a drink of water. I feel stronger because of my past, but also weaker. I am stronger because I survived, but weaker because I live in fear. I take the water bucket and hold it a moment until the water calms. I silently vow to overcome my fear caused by a violent past so that my spirit can finally be healed.

"A-Ho." I give thanks with a nod, and drink the blessed water, sealing my vow. My new journey begins.

NOTES

FAMILY GENEALOGY

1. Today, Haskell Indian Nations University (a.k.a. Haskell Indian School) is a four-year university located in Lawrence KS. It offers a post–high school education to members of federally recognized American Indian tribes. In 1900 Haskell was a boarding school for elementary and middle-school students with very strict rules. Students had their hair cut and were not allowed to speak their language. They wore uniforms and marched to their classes while the school band played music. Unruly students were locked in a jail located on campus. Losing your tribal identity and assimilating into the dominant society was emphasized. Haskell added high school classes by 1916. See "Haskell: Its History and Its Future," *Brown Quarterly* 1, no. 2 (1996), http://brownvboard.org/brwnqurt/01-2/01-2f.htm (accessed Nov. 17, 2009).

2. The traditional spelling of *Muscogee* is *Mvskoke*, our name for ourselves. The original Muscogee Indians were given the geographic name "Ocheese Creek" (also called the "Ocmulgee Creek") by British traders because they lived along the river. Eventually this name was simplified to "Creeks" and given to other American Indians in the area. The other tribes that became part of the Creek Confederacy were referred to as "tribal towns." During the height of the Creek Confederacy there were over fifty tribal towns. Four groups of Muscogee reside in Oklahoma: the Muscogee (Creek) Nation, the Alabama Quassarte Tribal Town, the Kialegee Tribal Town, and the Thlopthlocco Tribal Town. The Muscogee (Creek) Nation was organized under the Oklahoma Indian Welfare Act of 1936, and it is governed by a principal and a second chief elected every four years and by a national council of representatives elected every two years. See "Creek Indian: An Online Resource on the Historical and Present Day Creek Indians," http://creekindian.com (accessed Dec. 3, 2009).

The name "Eufala" comes from a Mvskoke word traditionally spelled *Y'ufala*, which means "eagle." See "The Yufala 'Star' Clan: A Modern Day Tribe with Traditional Values," http://www.native-american-online.org/LOWER-MUSCOGEE-CREEK-INDIANS.htm (accessed Apr. 6, 2009). The word also refers to an old Muscogee (Creek) town in Alabama called Yufala, meaning "they split up here and went to other places." See Congressman Dan Boren, "McIntosh County," http://www.house.gov/boren/mcintosh.shtml (accessed Apr. 5, 2009).

3. Although Carrie was technically an only child, she grew up with her half siblings. She was closest to her half sister Judy and to her half brother named Reo.

4. Sara got married and moved in 1963 to Texas, where she lives today. She has three daughters: Deborah Ann (Higginson), Kelley Elizabeth (Willingham), and Laura Katherine (Medrano).

5. Charles had a history of several heart attacks, the first one in 1949. He also had diabetes and arthritis.

6. Since the Muscogee (Creek) were a matrilineal culture, the young couple lived with the wife's family. Therefore it was common for a man to marry his wife's sister upon her death.

1. BLESSINGS INSIDE A TIPI

1. William Shakespeare, "Romeo and Juliet," Act 2, scene 2, line 45.

2. "Supernaw" is my family name. The original name was "Suprenant," a French word meaning "surprising" or "amazing." See the "Family Genealogy" section, earlier in the book.

3. Kenneth Anquoe's (1921–89) lifelong goal was to keep Indian youth from forgetting their customs. Before his death Kenneth said, "I finally know what I want to be. I want to be a star so I can watch over everybody and show them the way." He revived the Kiowa Black Legging Warrior Society for veterans and was called Pe-toin-Ahn-Oy, which means "man with many spears." See "Powwow Organizer, Ex-Boxer Kenneth Anquoe Dead at 68," *Tulsa World*, Nov. 20, 1989.

4. The Comanche Quanah Parker brought the Half Moon–style meeting to the Oklahoma Delaware, Caddo, Cheyenne, Arapaho, Ponca, Oto, Pawnee, and Osage. See Jay Fikes, "A Brief History of the Native American Church," in *One Nation under God, The Triumph of the Native American Church*, comp. and ed. Huston Smith and Reuben Snake (Santa Fe: Clear Light Publishers, 1996).

2. JIMMY

1. "Papaw" is a term that means grandfather.

2. "Mamaw" means grandmother.

3. Hank Williams (Sept. 17, 1923–Jan. 1, 1953) was a country singer, writer, and musician famous for his honky-tonk style.

4. Willie Derrisaw, Carrie's father, lived on their allotted land west of Eufaula, near a small town called Fame.

5. Today Eufaula Indian Boarding School is controlled by the Muscogee (Creek) Nation. It was originally established as the Asbury Mission Boarding School in 1849 by the Episcopal Church. When my grandmother went to school there, Eufaula Indian Boarding School was run for Indian girls and controlled by the government. See Congressman Dan Boren, "McIntosh County," http://www.house.gov/boren/mcintosh.shtml (accessed Mar. 25, 2009); Indian Pioneer History Project for Oklahoma, Jefferson Berryhill, "Creek Schools," vol. 102, Apr. 29, 1937, http://www.okgenweb.org/pioneer/ohs/creekschools.html (accessed Mar. 23, 2009). An old photo of the school can be found online: "Mary Josephine Wadsworth in front of Eufaula Boarding School," http://www.ancientfaces.com/research/photo/389561 (accessed Mar. 23, 2009).

6. When Dad, dressed in graduation attire, walked across the stage to receive his diploma at Seminole High School, his four-year-old sister, Sara, said to her parents, "There goes John with his nightgown on."

7. Sometimes nicknamed "flags" or "skivie wavers," signalmen transmitted, received, encoded, and decoded messages using the flag semaphore, visual Morse code, and international flaghoist. The U.S. Navy disestablished the rating of signalman in late 2003. See Nathan Good, "To the Navy Signalman's Page," http://usscurrituck.org/signalman.html (accessed Nov. 14, 2009).

8. "Supe" was my father's lifelong nicknames.

9. An LST (Landing Ship, Tank) is an amphibious vessel designed to land battle-ready tanks, troops, and supplies directly onto enemy shores. Also referred to as "large slow targets," these ships were enormously useful during the war but very vulnerable to enemy submarine attacks.

Flotilla 7 is a formation of warships that may be part of a larger fleet. Flotillas are usually composed of the same class of warship, such as destroyers, torpedo boats, or LSTs. The LST Flotilla 7 was assigned to the Asian-Pacific Theater.

The USS LST 466 was a first-class LST that earned seven battle stars for its World War II service. It was awarded the following medals: the China Service Medal (extended), the American Campaign Medal, the Asiatic-Pacific Campaign Medal (seven), the World War II Victory Medal, the Navy Occupation Service Medal (with Asia clasp), and the Philippines Liberation Medal (two). The LST-466 participated in the following campaigns: the New Guinea operation (Lae and Saidor), the Bismarck Archipelago operation (Cape Gloucester, New Britain, Admiralty Islands landings), the Leyte operation (Leyte landings), the Luzon operation (Lingayen Gulf landing), the Hollandia operation, Western New Guinea operations (Toem-Wakde-Sarmi, Biak Island, Noemfoor Island, and Cape Sansapor), and the Borneo operation (Tarakan Islands and Balikpapan).

Commissioned in 1943, the USS LST-474 earned eight battle stars for World War II service and was awarded the following medals: the Combat Action Ribbon (retroactive, Leyte landing), the American Campaign Medal, the Asiatic-Pacific Campaign Medal (eight), the World War II Victory Medal, the Navy Occupation Service Medal (with Asia clasp), and the Philippines Liberation Medal. During World War II the LST-474 was assigned to the Asian-Pacific Theater and participated in the following Asian-Pacific campaigns: the Eastern New Guinea operation (Lae and Saidor), the Leyte operation (Leyte landings), the Bismarck Archipelago operation (Cape Gloucester, New Britain), the Luzon operation (Lingayen Gulf landings); the Hollandia operation, the consolidation and capture of the Southern Philippines (Mindanao Island landings), Western New Guinea operation (Biak Island, Morotai landings), and the Borneo operation (Balikpapan). LST-474 performed occupation duty in the Far East in 1945 before it was decommissioned in March 1946.

See "Flotilla Definition," *Encarta World English Dictionary*, http://encarta.msn.com/dictionary_1861674206/flotilla.html (accessed Nov. 17, 2009); Gary P. Priolo, "NavSource Online: Amphibious Photo Archive USS LST-466," and "NavSource Online: Amphibious Photo Archive USS LST-474," http://www.navsource.org/archives/10/16/160466.htm and http://www.navsource.org/archives/10/16/160474.htm (both accessed Apr. 2, 2009).

10. An LSM (Landing Ship, Medium) is an amphibious vehicle used to move troops.

The LSM-13 was awarded two battle stars during World War II, when it was assigned to the Asian-Pacific Theater for the Luzon operation (the Lingayen Gulf landing) and the Okinawa Gunto operation (the assault and occupation of Okinawa Gunto). It was decommissioned in May 1946.

The USS *General R. M. Blatchford* (AP-153) was a General G. O. Squier class transport ship, commissioned in January 1945 by the U.S. Navy in World War II. During the war the ship was awarded the Asiatic-Pacific Campaign Medal, the World War II Victory Medal, and the Navy Occupation Service Medal (with Asia clasp).

See Gary P. Priolo, "NavSource Online: Amphibious Photo Archive LSM-13," and "NavSource Online: Service Ship Photo Archive AP-153/USAT/T-AP-153 General R. M. Blatchford," http://www.navsource .org/archives/10/10/14/14013.htm and http://www.navsource.org/ archives/09/22/22153.htm (both accessed Apr. 2, 2009).

11. The World War II Victory Medal was awarded to all members of the military who served on active duty between Dec. 7, 1941, and Dec. 31, 1946. The Navy Good Conduct Medal was first issued in 1869. Each branch of the military issues its own medal; the navy's is awarded to enlisted members who complete three consecutive years of "honorable and faithful service."

The Okinawa Gunto operation was the navy's name for the Battle of Okinawa (an eighty-two-day battle ending in June 1945), which was the largest amphibious assault in the Pacific Theater during World War II. The U.S. Navy sustained more casualties in this operation than in any other battle of the war, due to seven major kamikaze attacks involving more than fifteen hundred planes. The Operational Star is awarded for combat.

The Asiatic-Pacific Campaign Medal was awarded to members of the military who served in the Pacific Theater from 1941 to 1945. A service star denotes participation in an official navy campaign. The three major campaigns in which my father was involved were the New Guinea Operations, the Bismarck Archipelago Operations (in the Admiralties), and Okinawa Gunto. See "WWII Victory Medal," http:// www.gruntsmilitary.com/ww2v.shtml (accessed Nov. 14, 2009); "The Navy Good Conduct Medal," http://www.history.navy.mil/medals/gcm .htm (accessed Nov. 14, 2009.

12. Groups of warriors were called Gourd or War societies among

the Kiowa, and the Gourd Dance was once part of the Kiowa Sun Dance ceremony. An exclusive warrior society called the "Dog Soldiers" was for proven warriors who had visions and dreams of wolves and dogs. Today Gourd Societies are intertribal organizations of military veterans and their families. The "yip" at the end of each song is a tribute to the red wolf, America's indigenous wolf. See Judy Gibbs Robinson, "Gourd Dancers Uphold Their Tradition's Purity," *NewsOK*, July 9, 2006, http://newsok.com/article/1907298/1152311050 (accessed Nov. 17, 2009).

13. Most American Indian reservations in Oklahoma were replaced by allotted land as a result of the Dawes General Allotment Act of Feb. 8, 1887. American Indian tribes lost legal standing, and tribal lands were divided. The government believed that getting rid of common ownership of tribal lands would facilitate the assimilation of Indians; instead it was disastrous for them. The Osages claim their reservation is intact (which is why they retain oil royalties) because of the 1870 Drum Creek Treaty. Osage lands were sold, and the proceeds were used to buy land in northern Oklahoma. The Caddo, along with the Quapaw, were also excluded from the General Allotment Act because their lands had already been established. See "Welcome to the Indian Nations Archives Division of the Oklahoma Archives," http://www.rootsweb.ancestry.com/~usgenweb/ok/nations/osage/index.htm (accessed Nov. 15, 2009).

14. Officially called the "Servicemen's Readjustment Act of 1944," the GI Bill provided for education and a year of unemployment compensation for returning World War II veterans. It also provided loans to buy homes and start businesses. See Department Editors, "A Brief History Of: The GI Bill," *Time Magazine*, May 29, 2008, http://www.time.com/time/magazine/article/0,9171,1810309,00.html (accessed Nov. 15, 2009).

15. The Flower Hospital, Inc., a small, private women's and children's hospital located in north Tulsa County, is now closed.

16. My birth was not verified until three days later.

17. A partial mastectomy is the surgical removal of one breast as treatment for breast cancer. See "Breast Cancer, Lumpectomy, and Partial Mastectomy," http://www.webmd.com/breast-cancer/lumpectomy-partial-mastectomy (accessed Nov. 15, 2009).

18. Superman is a fictional cartoon superhero created in 1932 by the American writer Jerry Siegel and the Canadian artist Joe Shuster. His character inspired television and radio series, films, and video games.

19. Joseph, the son of Jacob, is a biblical figure in Genesis (in the Old Testament), famous for his colorful coat and his ability to interpret dreams. Due to jealousy his brother Judah sold him into slavery for twenty pieces of silver. He eventually was freed in Egypt, after interpreting a pharaoh's dream.

20. The western corn root beetle is about a quarter of an inch long and has alternating black and yellow stripes running lengthwise on its wings. See "Western Corn Rootworm Beetle," http://www.ent.iastate.edu/imagegal/coleoptera/rw/3936.69wcrw.html (accessed Dec. 13, 2009).

21. A guardian angel is believed by some Christians to be an angel assigned to protect and guide a particular person.

3. BOZO

1. The Osage Nation retained its claim to mineral rights while other Indian nations in Oklahoma lost their mineral rights as a result of the Allotment Act of 1887. In 1896, after oil was discovered, the BIA granted the Osage tribe a 10 percent royalty on all sales of petroleum produced on the reservation. In 1906 the U.S. Congress passed the Osage Allotment Act, which allocated a share of the reservation's subsurface natural resources, regardless of blood quantum, to all persons listed on tribal rolls or born before July 1907. The Osage Nation held up Oklahoma statehood in an effort to maintain mineral rights on their new reservation lands. They are the only tribe today to retain a federally recognized reservation within the state of Oklahoma. See Charles J. Kappler, comp. and ed., "Chapter 3572—Osage Indians, Okla. Division of Tribal Land, Etc.," Acts of Fifty-Ninth Congress—First Session, 1906, Indian Affairs: Laws and Treaties, Vol. III, Government Printing Office, 1913, Oklahoma State University Library online, http://digital.library.okstate.edu/kappler/Vol3/HTML_files/SES0252A.html#ch3572 (accessed Nov. 13, 2009).

2. Racial bias was largely due to the fact that by 1930 Osage Indians received large oil royalty checks. Whites began marrying into Osage families and then killed them for their head rights. The non-Indian population thought of Indians as lazy do-nothings who never worked. It didn't matter what tribe you belonged to, only that you were Indian. Those same white folks who hated Indians for not working yet collecting oil money admired the Osages' white counterparts: rich oil men.

3. See details in the "Family Genealogy" section.

4. Assimilation was also called *Americanization*. It was both government law and general public opinion that only one standard set of cultural values should be held in common by all citizens. See Jon Reyhner, "American Indian/Alaska Native Education: An Overview," http://jan .ucc.nau.edu/~jar/AIE/Ind_Ed.html (accessed Nov. 15, 2009).

5. The assimilation of American Indians into mainstream American society was set by an 1850s U.S. government policy called "termination." See Robert J. Miller, "The History of Federal Indian Policy," in *Native America, Discovered and Conquered*, http://lawlib.lclark.edu/blog/ native_america/?page_id=9 (accessed Nov. 15, 2009).

6. A child's right to child support and parents' responsibilities to provide support were not internationally recognized until 1992 under the UN Convention on the Rights of the Child. A noncustodial parent who does not pay the required child support is called a "deadbeat." In the 1950s there was no automatic withdrawal of deposited paychecks for enforcement of child support payments. See "History of Child Support in the USA," http://www.childsupportanalysis.co.uk/information_and_ex planation/world/history_usa.htm (accessed Nov. 17, 2009).

7. Maria Tall Chief was born Jan. 24, 1925, in Fairfax OK, part of the Osage reservation. Maria was the first American prima ballerina. Her father was Osage, and her mother was of Irish and Scottish descent. I met Maria in 1974, when she lived in Chicago, working as the artistic director of the Chicago Lyric Opera Ballet.

4. HORSE CRAZY

1. *Sputnik* 1 was the first artificial satellite launched into a low-altitude elliptical orbit by the Soviet Union, on Oct. 4, 1957. The Russian word *sputnik* means "companion." *Sputnik* 1's success ignited the space race between the United States and the Soviet Union. See Chris Mihos, "Sputnik (1957–1963)," http://burro.astr.cwru.edu/stu/advanced/20th_so viet_sputnik.html (accessed Nov. 17, 2009).

2. During childhood some children receive visions that help them experience the oneness of all life. A vision can reveal one or more guardian spirits, usually in the form of an animal; a natural force like wind, rain, or lightning; or a spirit in human form. These guardian spirits remain to help and protect the child during his or her life.

5. A NEW NAME

1. American Indian spirituality is interwoven into everyday life. Everything—the way you live, the thoughts you think, and your interaction with others—should maintain connections with the natural universe. Dreams and visions provide insights, allowing us to live a life that embodies a reciprocal connection between people and the rest of the universe.

2. The proper spelling in Mvskoke is "Elle Pana," but everyone used the English spelling, "Ellia Ponna."

3. The creator, "Hesaketvmese" (also spelled "Hesagedamesse"), is the Master of Breath or Wind. This entity was called "God" by early Muscogee Christians since he receives our prayers. Traditionally he is an assistant to the powerful creator "Epohfvnkv," who does not get involved in mundane matters.

4. The assassination of John F. Kennedy took place on Friday, Nov. 22, 1963, in Dallas TX.

5. On May 25, 1961, President John F. Kennedy presented a challenge before a joint session of Congress: "I believe that this nation should commit itself to achieving the goal, before this decade is out, of landing a man on the moon and returning him safely to the Earth." See Richard Stenger, "Man on the Moon: Kennedy Speech Ignited the Dream," cNN.com/Space, May 25, 2001, http://archives.cnn.com/2001/TECH/space/05/25/kennedy.moon/ (accessed Dec. 13, 2009).

6. METAMORPHOSIS

1. His name was Woodrow D. Kehl, and he was Caucasian.

2. Woody was a member of the Ancient Mystical Order Rosæ Crucis (AMORC), also called the Rosicrucian Order. It is a philosophical and humanist worldwide organization. See AMORC—Rosicrucian Order, Ancient and Mystical Order Rosae Crucis, English Grand Lodge for the Americas, http://rosicrucian.org/ (accessed Nov. 16, 2009).

3. Robert Louis Stevenson first published *The Strange Case of Dr. Jekyll and Mr. Hyde* in 1886. Known for its vivid portrayal of a split personality, of good and evil within the same person, the novel spawned the phrase "Jekyll and Hyde" to describe a person with vastly different moral character from one situation to the next. See "SparkNote on Dr. Jekyll and Mr. Hyde," 2003, http://www.sparknotes.com/lit/jekyll/themes.html (accessed Nov. 16, 2009).

4. Written and illustrated by Charles M. Schulz, the syndicated comic strip *Peanuts* ran from Oct. 2, 1950, to Feb. 13, 2000, which was the day after Schulz died. It was considered one of the most popular and influential cartoons of all time, and the *Peanuts* television specials won or were nominated for many Emmy Awards. See "Frequently Asked Questions," http://www.schulzmuseum.org/ (accessed Nov. 16, 2009).

5. I didn't see Louise for about eight years after that.

6. Judy lived on the other side of town for about a year, and I saw her only a few times before she married and moved to Oklahoma City. She relocated her family with her husband when he was stationed in Okinawa, Japan. She had three children: Clinton Hill, Rhonda Hill (Sturch), and Clark Hill.

7. He eventually was awarded seven patents and listed as a coinventor on two inventions. He designed computer hardware interfaces for seismic and oil field equipment for Amoco Oil Company.

8. Ham radios are also called amateur radios because the communications are not used for commercial or monetary purposes. Radio operators are called "hams" and use radio equipment to communicate with other radio hams around the world. See Gary Brown, "How Ham Radio Works," http://www.howstuffworks.com/ham-radio.htm (accessed Nov. 17, 2009).

9. John's sister, Sara, said he used to same skull to scare her when she was young, so it couldn't have come from the war.

10. The Creek language, or Mvskoke, is a Muskogean language of the American Southeast. It is a language with complex verbs and a subject-object-verb word order. See "Muskogee (Creek) Language," http://www.native-languages.org/muskogee.htm (accessed Dec. 13, 2009).

11. In the fall Grandma Carrie made sofkey in a metal tub. Dad decided it was a good way to make beer and improved on his equipment and recipe over the years.

12. Blue dumplings are made from white cornmeal and burned hulls from purple field peas. Osage grape dumplings are made from smashed wild grapes mixed with sugar, flour, and butter. Often cooked with pork, they are both sweet and tart.

13. Sofkey was made by removing corn kernels from the cob, soaking them in lye, and then grinding them. The cornmeal was then cooked with water and lye and left to sour (ferment) for a couple of days.

14. Several activities and dances were held on sacred ceremonial

grounds called stomp dance grounds. Stomp dances are danced around a fire with women shaking shells worn around their legs for rhythm while the men take turns leading songs. Stomp dances celebrate many occasions, such as the planting of corn, the coming of traditional healers, local marriages, and the beginning of hunting season. A social form of stomp dancing occurs after-hours at some powwows, such as the Kiheka Steh Pow-wow in Skiatook.

15. Kids butting in line and crowding out adults is still a common complaint at today's social stomp dances.

16. Women traditionally wore turtle shells around their legs and stomped the ground to create the rhythm since no drum is used. Small aluminum cans are frequently used today because they are lighter and easier to shake while dancing. Plus this saves turtles.

17. In our creation myth the Turtle brings light and knowledge to the world. The call of the turtle (*locv locv*) around the fire at a stomp dance honors the female shell shakers and the journey of the turtle, which began in the female energies of earth and water.

18. The Green Corn Dance is the most important ceremony because it celebrates the new corn, which was the life of the tribe. Four logs are placed crosswise to build a new fire because the fire is considered to have great sacred power and therefore is renewed annually. All home fires are put out and started again from the new fire. Traditional leaders fast and purify themselves with black medicine before tasting the new corn. Then the dances and feasts begin.

19. The fire is sacred because it contains the energy of Grandfather Sun. The basic elements of earth, fire, water, and air are represented by the four logs placed in the cardinal directions. Traditionally during busk, when the fire was renewed, it was fed a deer tongue.

20. Marcellus Bear Heart Williams (1918–2008) was one of the last traditionally trained medicine people of the Muscogee (Creek). He was a roadman who often "adopted" people in the church, calling them his nephews, nieces, children, and grandchildren, even though they were not biologically related. See L. T. Amsden, "Marcellus "Bear Heart" Williams," http://www.bearheart.info/bearheart.htm (accessed Feb. 13, 2009).

21. See Jean Chaudhuri and Joyotpaul Chaudhuri, *A Sacred Path: The Way of the Muscogee Creeks* (Los Angeles: UCLA American Indian Studies Center, 2001). The information on the sacred paths is from Chaudhuri

and Chaudhuri's work, which is an excellent source of information on Muscogee beliefs.

22. "Ebofvnka" is also spelled "Ibofanga" (Chaudhuri and Chaudhuri, *Sacred Path*, 15).

23. Another spelling of *anogetka* is *anoghechka* (Chaudhuri and Chaudhuri, *Sacred Path*, 101).

24. Another concept used in conjunction with *ye gun bay geta* (to be less important) is *yee yas gheeda* (to be humble) (Chaudhuri and Chaudhuri, *Sacred Path*, 101).

25. Other words used for *ye ge da* are *yeejagheeda* and *yeehajoyee-geegheeda* (Chaudhuri and Chaudhuri, *Sacred Path*, 101).

26. Phillip Deere (1929–85) was a Muscogee (Creek) traditional elder and spiritual leader. He was a spiritual advisor for the American Indian Movement (AIM) and Indian youths and a speaker at international conferences and national Native rights activities. See "The Winter Camp Chronicles—Phillip Deere, Muskogee Creek Elder," http://mytwobeads worth.com/PhillipDeere.html (accessed Feb. 15, 2009). Phillip and I were part of "The New Indians," a *National Geographic* special produced by Terry Sanders and Freida Mock in 1975.

27. See Chaudhuri and Chaudhuri, *Sacred Path*, 12.

28. A matrilineal society traces inheritance and clan membership through the mother's lineage. For the traditional Muscogee, when a couple married they moved in with the mother's clan, which raised the children while the man worked in his wife's fields. Since my mother was not Muscogee I received my Bear Clan membership from my grandmother.

29. Kenneth Anquoe (1921–89) helped Indians in the Tulsa area in the 1950s and 1960s, even going out in the middle of night. Kenneth's sister said, "He has touched many lives—not just Indians, but all peoples." See Victoria Nininger, "Kiowa Tribe Honoring Kenneth Anquoe: A Lifetime of Service to Indians," *Tulsa World*, Nov. 19, 1989.

30. Quantum physics is the science of things so small that the quantum nature of reality has an effect on them. Quantum means "discrete amount" or "portion"; its effect was discovered by Max Planck in 1900. See "What Is Quantum Physics?" http://library.thinkquest.org/3487/qp.html (accessed Nov. 14, 2009).

31. The double-slit experiment in quantum mechanics demonstrates the dual nature of light particles–wave photons. The English scientist

Tom Young performed it in 1801 to see whether light is composed of particles or of waves. See "Classic Two-Slit Experiment," http://www.colorado.edu/physics/2000/schroedinger/two-slit2.html (accessed Nov. 15, 2009).

32. Because of the Civil Rights Act of 1964 "separate" implied racial segregation, and "separate roles" implied sexual discrimination.

8. BEEF NOODLE

1. Tribal ceremonies around the beginning of menses mark the transition from childhood to adulthood.

2. Charm, Inc., was a modeling school in Tulsa. I took the beginning class and learned quickly that I could never be a model since I was only five-feet-three-inches tall. I still learned how to walk in heels though.

3. The Tulsa State Fair ran from Sept. 29 to Oct. 8, 1967.

4. I did not know that Mom had talked with the folks at Charm, Inc., about nominating me for the contest.

5. The first picture appeared on Sept. 17, 1967, in *Ranch and Farm World*, a magazine that was included monthly in the *Tulsa Sunday World*. The 1967 awards banquet in honor of the Nationwide Junior Tractor Operators was held on Oct. 1, 1967, at the Tulsa State Fairgrounds cafeteria.

9. SUSIE Q

1. The U.S. Congress, as part of the 1994 Crime Bill, enacted legislation called the Violence Against Women Act (VAWA), making violence against women a crime. Until then women and children were offered no protection under the law. See Violence Against Women Act (VAWA), "RL30871, Violence Against Women Act: History and Federal Funding," Open CRS, Congressional Research Reports for the People, Aug. 7, 2008, http://opencrs.com/document/RL30871/ (accessed Nov. 19, 2009).

10. SUPER SUE

1. Edgar Cayce (Mar. 18, 1877–Jan. 3, 1945) was a twentieth-century American psychic who could answer questions while in a self-induced trance. As a child he could memorize the pages of a book by sleeping with his head on it. See "Who Was Edgar Cayce? Twentieth Century Psychic and Medical Clairvoyant," http://www.edgarcayce.org/are/edgarcayce.aspx (accessed Feb. 10, 2009).

2. "Quantum mechanics" describes physical systems at the microscopic scale (the atomic level), whereas "classical mechanics" refers to the motion of objects that can be seen with the naked eye. Quantum principles include the dual-wave and particle-like behavior of matter and energy and the prediction of probabilities in situations where classical physics predicts certainties. Newtonian physics is based on Sir Isaac Newton's three physical laws of motion (the foundation of classical mechanics) and his law of universal gravitation. Newton's laws of motion, together with his laws of gravity and his calculus techniques, provided for the first time a unified explanation for a wide range of physical phenomena. See K. Michielsen and H. De Raedt, "Quantum Mechanics," http://msc.phys.rug.nl/QuantumMechanics/ (accessed Nov. 13, 2009); Alex Paterson, "Newtonian Physics," Mar. 11, 2008, http://www.vision.net.au/~apaterson/science/physics_newtonian.htm (accessed Nov. 18, 2009).

3. The theory of multiple universes is also called the multiverse theory. It states that multiple universes make up reality. These different universes are sometimes called parallel universes, alternative universes, quantum universes, interpenetrating dimensions, parallel worlds, and alternate realities. Continuum theories involve a gradual transition without abrupt changes to explain variations. Einstein's general relativity theory, for example, views the universe as a seamless whole, with space and time as part of the same continuum, rather than as separate entities. The duality of the nature of light—whether light is a particle or a wave—long troubled scientists. Quantum field theory proves light is a particle and then resolves it into a field. In the end light protons are particles that are regarded as excited states of a field. See "Are There Other Universes?" http://www.space.com/science astronomy/generalscience/5mysteries_universes_020205-1.html (accessed Nov. 14, 2009); Janusz J. Charatonik, Pawel Krupski, and Pavel Pyrih, "Examples in Continuum Theory," Feb. 21, 2001, http://www.karlin .mff.cuni.cz/~pyrih/e/e2001v1/c/ect/ect.htm (accessed Nov. 14, 2009); C. R. Nave, "Wave-Particle Duality," http://hyperphysics.phy-astr.gsu .edu/hbase/mod1.html (accessed Nov. 17, 2009).

4. The word *biodiversity* describes the fragile web of life that interconnects everything on earth. Every member of this web helps keep it in balance. See Field Museum, "Biodiversity and Conservation: The

Web of Life," http://www.fieldmuseum.org/biodiversity/intro.html (accessed Feb. 15, 2009).

5. The Danish physicist Niels Bohr (Oct. 7, 1885–Nov. 18, 1962) received the Nobel Prize for Physics in 1922 for his contributions to understanding atomic structure and quantum mechanics. His quote "Anyone who is not shocked by quantum theory has not understood it" appears in *The Philosophical Writings of Niels Bohr*. See also "Niels Bohr Quotes," http://www.brainyquote.com/quotes/authors/n/niels_bohr.html (accessed Nov. 17, 2009).

6. A college entrance exam, the ACT is a multiple-choice test that covers the academic areas of English, mathematics, reading, and science.

7. The 1949 musical *South Pacific* is one of the greatest musicals in history. The story draws from James Michener's novel *Tales of the South Pacific*. The music was written by Richard Rodgers and the lyrics by Oscar Hammerstein II.

8. The Rockettes are a famous precision tap-dance group that has performed for seventy-five years at Radio City Music Hall in New York City. Their trademark finale is a head-high leg kick in the perfect unison of a chorus line.

9. The floor exercise is a gymnastics event performed on floor. The floor in this case is a specially prepared exercise surface with a clearly designated perimeter. Female gymnasts must perform a variety of leaps, jumps, tumbling strings, and turns to music as part of a choreographed routine.

10. Students become candidates for the National Merit Scholarship by taking a national test given by the National Merit Scholarship Corporation.

11. Southern Methodist University is a private university located in Dallas, Texas. The National Cheerleader Association held high school cheerleading clinics across the country at different universities during the summer. The selection process for the National Merit Scholarship involves examining in detail school and test records, honors, and activities.

12. The University of Mississippi's main campus is in Oxford.

13. The telegram was dated May 25, 1969.

14. Created and produced by Allen Funt in 1948, *Candid Camera* used concealed cameras to film ordinary people in unusual situations,

ending the joke with the show's catch phrase, "Smile, you're on *Candid Camera.*"

15. "To Central Senior 'Come to Lunch' Said Mr. Nixon," *Tulsa Tribune*, May 27, 1969.

16. A special commission selects two outstanding students from each state, a boy and a girl. Leadership, scholarship, and school activities are all areas considered in the naming of presidential scholars, but scholarship is the most important criteria.

17. The Atchison, Topeka and Santa Fe Railway Company, through its Santa Fe Freight Agent, J. B. Goodknight, awarded me its Scholarship Certificate in June 1969.

18. Spiro Agnew (Nov. 9, 1918–Sept. 17, 1996) was President Nixon's vice president and a former Maryland governor. In Oct. 1973 Agnew resigned as vice president because of criminal charges.

19. The hippie subculture was well established by 1965. Hippie fashion included long hair, headbands, beads, and going barefoot. In their quest for spiritual enlightenment hippies used mescaline and peyote, but not in the context of the Native American Church.

The American Indian Movement (AIM) is an Indian activist organization and a catalyst for Indian sovereignty, including the protection of Indian rights and traditional culture. Founded in 1968 in Minneapolis–St. Paul, AIM organized Indian people to shield them against police brutality. In 1969 AIM assisted the United Indians of All Tribes in their occupation of Alcatraz Island, reclaiming federal lands. Although AIM activists seek negotiations through nonviolent means, they believe in defending themselves and all Indian people. See Laura Waterman Wittstock and Elaine J. Salinas, "A Brief History of the American Indian Movement," http://www.aimovement.org/ggc/history.html (accessed Nov. 13, 2009).

20. Martin Luther King Jr. (Jan. 15, 1929–Apr. 4, 1968) was a prominent leader of the American Civil Rights Movement. He advocated nonviolence and direct action for social change and won the Nobel Peace Prize in 1964. He was assassinated by James Earl Ray in Memphis, Tennessee, when he was thirty-nine.

21. Senator Robert F. Kennedy was the brother of assassinated President John Kennedy. Robert was assassinated on June 5, 1968, in Los Angeles CA by Sirhan Sirhan, a Palestinian.

22. Title VI of the Civil Rights Act of 1964 prohibits discrimination

on the basis of race, color, or national origin in all federally assisted programs. This affects student admissions, financial aid, athletic and academic programs, and the Presidential Scholarship Program. Title VII prohibits discrimination in employment. See "Indian Civil Rights Act," http://www.answers.com/topic/indian-civil-rights-act (accessed Nov. 14, 2009).

11. TOMORROW'S LEADER

1. The Washington Monument was built between 1848 and 1884 as a memorial to George Washington. It is 555 feet 5 1/8 inches (169.294 m) in height and is the tallest structure in Washington DC. See Robert Mills, "Washington Monument," http://www.greatbuildings.com/buildings/ Washington_Monument.html (accessed Nov. 14, 2009).

2. Charles "Bud" Wilkinson (Apr. 23, 1916–Feb. 9, 1994) was Oklahoma University's (OU) head football coach when the Sooners won national championships in 1950, 1955, and 1956. OU set a NCAA Division I record of forty-seven consecutive wins from 1953 to 1957. During the Nixon administration he was a White House advisor and presidential aide. See Bob Carter, "Wilkinson Created Sooners dynasty," http://espn.go.com/ classic/biography/s/Wilkinson_Bud.html (accessed Nov. 20, 2009).

3. Shirley Chisholm (Nov. 30, 1924–Jan. 1, 2005) was the first black woman elected to the U.S. Congress, representing New York's Congressional District 12 for seven terms from 1969 to 1983.

4. Carl Albert (May 10, 1908–Feb. 4, 2000) represented Oklahoma's Congressional District 3 for thirty years. When Speaker John McCormack retired in Jan. 1971 Mr. Albert replaced him as speaker of the House of Representatives. First elected to Congress in 1947, he was elected House majority whip in 1955 and House majority leader in 1961.

5. The "Old SOB" was short for the Old Senate Office Building, the nickname of the Russell Senate Office Building, first occupied in 1909. The "New SOB" is the New Senate Office Building, opened on Oct. 15, 1958, and named the Dirksen Senate Office Building in 1972. The Hart Senate Office Building, built in the 1970s, is the third Senate office building in today's capital. See U.S. Senate: Visitors Center Home, "Russell Senate Office Building," http://www.senate.gov/pagelayout/ visiting/d_three_sections_with_teasers/russel_senate_office_map_page .htm (accessed Nov. 20, 2009).

6. Edward "Ted" Kennedy (Feb. 22, 1932–Aug. 25, 2009) was a Mas-

sachusetts Democratic senator since Nov. 1962. In 1969 Kennedy became the Senate majority whip. The late president John Kennedy and the late senator Robert Kennedy were his older brothers.

Everett Dirksen (Jan. 4, 1896–Sept. 7, 1969) was an Illinois Republican congressman and senator. He first won the congressional seat in 1932 and was reelected seven times. He was elected to the Senate in 1950, and in 1959 he was elected the Senate minority leader, a position he held until his death.

7. The Midway meeting was designed to align U.S. and South Vietnamese positions for peace negotiations and to recognize the legitimacy of the present government. After his mid-Pacific meeting on the tiny atoll of Midway, Nixon announced the withdrawal of 250,000 U.S. troops. A policy called the "Vietnamization" of the war included turning more of the war effort over to the South Vietnamese. See John M. Rincon, "The Effects of Vietnamization on the Republic of Vietnam's Armed Forces, 1969–1972," http://www.militaryhistoryonline.com/vietnam/vietnamization/default.aspx (accessed Jan. 30, 2009).

8. In 1968 the Indian Civil Rights Act stated that neither the U.S. Constitution nor the Bill of Rights applies to Native American tribal governments and that the federal court system has no jurisdiction over a crime between two Indians on Indian land. However, tribes are ultimately subject to the power of the U.S. Congress and the U.S. Constitution. Actual self-determination was not official U.S. policy until 1970, when Richard Nixon issued his July 8 congressional "Message from the President of the United States Transmitting Recommendations for Indian Policy." This resulted in the eventual passage of the Indian Self-Determination and Education Assistance Act of 1975.

9. In 1978 the American Indian Religious Freedom Act (AIRFA) became law. Protecting the traditional religious rights of American Indians, AIRFA led to a number of changes in government policies regarding access to sacred places and use of sacred items such as eagle feathers and bone whistles. The 1994 amendment to the act made it legal for peyote to be used for ceremonial purposes. See National Park Service, Department of Interior, "American Indian Religious Freedom Act," http://www.nps.gov/history/local-law/FHPL_IndianRelFreAct.pdf (accessed Nov. 16, 2009).

10. George Washington University (GW or GWU) has operated as a private, coeducational university in Washington DC since 1821.

11. Although Carl Albert was born in McAlester OK, his family soon moved to Bugtussle, a small town just north of McAlester. His father was a farmer and coal miner.

12. The *Apollo* 11 mission was the first manned mission to land on the moon and return. On July 20, 1969, Neil Armstrong and Buzz Aldrin Jr. walked on the moon, while Michael Collins orbited above. See Smithsonian National Air and Space Museum, "Apollo 11 (AS-506) Lunar Landing Mission," http://www.nasm.si.edu/collections/imagery/apollo/AS11/a11.htm (accessed Nov. 16, 2009).

13. The Black Panther Party, founded in 1966, was an African American organization whose goals were often overshadowed by its confrontational tactics. Its members supported "Black Power," which encouraged racial pride and the creation of black political and cultural institutions. They were most active in the mid-1960s and 1970s. See "History of the Black Panther Party," http://www.stanford.edu/group/blackpanthers/history.shtml (accessed Nov. 13, 2009).

14. In December 1969 the Selective Service held a lottery to determine the order for men being drafted into the U.S. Army for the Vietnam War. Each day of the year was represented by a number from 1 to 366 (including Feb. 29). Numbers written on slips of paper were placed in plastic capsules and then mixed in a shoebox. After being dumped into a deep glass jar the capsules were drawn out one at a time. See "The Vietnam Lotteries," http://www.sss.gov/lotter1.htm (accessed Nov. 14, 2009).

15. This is a sharp contrast to the large number of Indian men who enlisted for World War I and II.

16. A "hawk" is a supporter of war policy, while a "dove" supports peace.

17. He said this on May 1, 1970. See "Nixon Puts 'Bums' Label on Some College Radicals," *New York Times*, May 2, 1970.

18. On May 4, 1970, four Kent State college students were shot to death and nine students were wounded in thirteen seconds of gunfire by Ohio National Guardsmen during an antiwar protest on the campus. See "Kent State 1970: May 1 through May 4, Description of Events," http://www.may4.org/ (accessed Nov. 14, 2009).

19. On May 9, 1970, about one hundred thousand people attended a peaceful antiwar rally in the Ellipse, across from the White House, to protest the invasion of Cambodia and the killings at Kent State. Nixon spoke with students at the Lincoln Memorial. See Kathryn Collins Philp,

"The President, Politics, and the Police: Consequences of the 1970 'Stoning' of Richard M. Nixon at the San Jose Civic Auditorium," Apr. 15, 2005, http://www.californiapioneers.com/NixonStoningbyPhilp.pdf (accessed Nov. 17, 2009); "War and Protest—the U.S. in Vietnam (1969–1970)," http://www.bbc.co.uk/dna/h2g2/A715042 (accessed Nov. 14, 2009).

20. The Ellipse, located south of the White House, is often called President's Park South. The national Christmas tree was planted there in 1978. See "Washington DC Ellipse," http://www.visitingdc.com/neighbor/washington-dc-ellipse.htm (accessed Mar. 23, 2009).

21. The Watergate complex is an office-apartment-hotel complex nicknamed "White House West" because many White House staffers and cabinet members lived there in 1969. It was later the site of scandals that ultimately resulted in the resignation of President Nixon in 1974. See "Washington-Watergate Complex," http://www.planetware.com/washington-d-c-/washington-watergate-complex-us-dc-water.htm (accessed Nov. 19, 2009).

22. Tear gas is used for riot control. CS gas (2-chlorobenzal malononitrile) is the main ingredient because it is considered nonlethal, although burning skin and vomiting are common side effects of its use.

23. This was a slight exaggeration, since Carl Albert did not become the Speaker until Jan. 1971. However, he had been elected to replace John McCormack and was planning his office move.

24. With the killings of Kent State University students and dissent over the U.S. moving soldiers into Cambodia, a nationwide student strike occurred. Across the country colleges and universities were affected, and many of them closed classes early and resumed them in summer or fall of 1970. Many GW students passionately supported the peace movement, challenging both the Nixon presidency and university president Lloyd Elliot (1965–88). Since GW was only three blocks from the White House the undergraduate dormitory Thurston Hall was believed by some to be a staging ground for student antiwar demonstrations. See "Historical Impact of Kent State and National Student Strike, May, 1970," http://may4.org/12.html (accessed Jan. 31, 2009).

25. Princeton University, known for its academic excellence, is located in Princeton NJ.

12. COMING HOME

1. Union Station, the main train station in Washington DC, was built in 1908 and today is visited by twenty million people a year.

2. Princeton University is one of eight universities referred to as belonging to the Ivy League. In 1969 Princeton University admitted its first women undergraduates. See "The History of Women at Princeton University," http://libguides.princeton.edu/content.php?pid=15189&sid=112631 (accessed Nov. 19, 2009).

3. A Bunsen burner is a gas burner with small holes at the bottom so air can mix with gas to produce a hot blue flame. See "Chemistry Bunsen Burner Diagram," http://education.smarttech.com/ste/en-US/Ed%20 Resource/Lesson%20activities/Notebook%20activities/Browse%20 Notebook/United%20States/Secondary/7-9/Chemistry/Bunsen%20 Burner%20Diagram.htm (accessed Nov. 17, 2009).

4. Phillips University, located in Enid OK, was a private, coeducational college from 1906 to 1998. In June 1999 the college became a satellite campus for Northern Oklahoma College (NOC), which is based in Tonkawa OK. See "Phillips University," http://digital.library.okstate.edu/ encyclopedia/entries/P/PH005.html (accessed Nov. 12, 2009).

13. SCORPIO SUE

1. "Presidential Scholar Will Attend Phillips University," *Enid Daily Eagle*, June 9, 1970.

2. William Cosby Jr. (b. July 12, 1937), born and raised in Philadelphia PA, is a comedian, actor, and author. He began releasing a series of popular comedy albums in 1964 that featured humorous recollections of his childhood. At age seventy-two he continues to contribute to the entertainment industry. See "Bill Cosby, The Artist" http://www .billcosby.com/ (accessed November 17, 2009).

3. When I attended high school during 1966–69, the Tulsa Central Braves football team played all three years and won only one game. Our basketball team, on the other hand, was state champion in 1969.

4. Bill Rice, Dave and Freda Friday, John Wolf, Vicki Pratt, and I were the officers.

5. The "Indian Concerns Seminar," the academic portion of the conference, took place Apr. 20–23, 1971. The guest speakers included Phil Homeratha, Sparlin Norwood, Duane Pratt, Everett Rhodes, and Jim Tartsa. Drumming and dancing were provided by the Kiowa Tiapah Gourd Dance Society.

6. At that time the legal drinking age in Oklahoma was eighteen for women and twenty-one for men. In Dec. 1976 the U.S. Supreme Court

ruled that the law was discriminatory and struck it down, requiring members of both genders to be twenty-one years old. See "Heady Moment: Court Case Challenged Drinking Age," Aug. 22, 2008, http://newsok.com/heady-moment-court-case-challenged-drinking-age/article/3286994/?tm=1219366293 (accessed Mar. 21, 2009).

7. The Miss Universe Pageant is an international pageant that originated in 1952. Its feeder state and national pageants do not require talent as part of the competition. Miss America and its affiliated state pageants have required talent competition since 1938.

8. Jane Ann Jayroe was a former Miss Oklahoma and Miss America 1967.

9. Dr. Robert E. Rhoades was an associate professor at Phillips from 1968 to 1976. Currently a distinguished research professor at the University of Georgia, he helped to establish the field of agricultural anthropology.

10. "Buh" is an expression used by American Indians in Oklahoma to express surprise.

11. The word *powwow* is from the Narragansett word for "spiritual leader." A powwow is a dance where Native American and non–Native American people sing, socialize, and honor American Indian culture. The word is sometimes used to refer to a meeting, especially a meeting of powerful people, but such use is considered disrespectful to Native culture. See Troy Johnson, "Pow-wow, A Collection of Photographs and Video," http://www.csulb.edu/~aisstudy/powwow/ (accessed Nov. 13, 2009).

12. "Susie Supernaw Is Miss Phillips," *Enid Morning News*, Mar. 28, 1971.

13. "Tulsa Girl Honored at Phillips U," *Tulsa Tribune*, Mar. 30, 1971; "Coed Coaches Little-Leaguers," *Tulsa World*, Aug. 23, 1970.

14. "Miss Phillips U," *Tulsa World*, Mar. 31, 1971; "Presidential Scholar Susie Supernaw Makes a Hit with Nixon," *Tulsa Tribune*, June 21, 1969.

15. "Miss Phillips," *Sunday Oklahoman*, March 28, 1971.

16. Kathy attended Northeastern State College in Miami, Oklahoma, from 1967 until 1969.

17. In 1938 the Miss America pageant established a chaperone system whose primary purpose was to keep pageant contestants away from scandal. See "The American Experience, Miss America Timeline,"

http://www.pbs.org/wgbh/amex/missamerica/timeline/timeline2.html (accessed Feb. 15, 2009).

18. My sister was always well groomed, with perfect hair and a beautiful smile. Her elegance and charm naturally drew attention to her rather than me. I never tried to be as polished as my sister.

19. It wasn't called a plastic smile because it was fake but because I naturally smiled really big. It was a "plastic smile" because, as my mom said, "It stretches clean 'cross your face."

14. SUPERSTAR SUPERNAW

1. Rita Hayworth (1918–87) was a 1940s actress and sex symbol. Her most notable film, *Gilda*, was filmed in 1946, costarring Glenn Ford.

2. Russell Gideon, "Your World, Magazine of the Magic Empire," *Tulsa Sunday World*, June 5, 1971. The photo was taken by Don Hamilton of the *World* staff.

3. See Fred Davis, "Making a Splash," *Tulsa Daily World*, June 12, 1971.

4. Fred Davis, "Misses Phillips, Norman Share Spotlight," *Tulsa Daily World*, June 11, 1971.

5. Photo by Dick Grant, "Beauty with Amity (Sculpture)," *Tulsa Tribune*, June 11, 1971.

6. "I didn't think I had a chance in swim suit because I'm short and skinny." See "Beauty Pageant Continues," *Tulsa Tribune*, June 11, 1971.

7. The Grammy Award–winning country singer-songwriter Dolly Parton (b. Jan. 19, 1946) is known for her soprano voice, flamboyant dress, and voluptuous figure on a short frame.

8. The proper swimsuit attire for the Miss America pageant at that time was a one-piece swimsuit that did not show the pubic bone. Swimsuits had an extra panel in front to cover the pubic area. The pageant had recently dropped the requirement for a panel.

9. "Supernaw Is Super Friendly," *Tulsa Tribune*, June 12, 1971.

10. A list of the top ten contestants was in *Sunday World*, World Staff Photo, "Pageant Finalists," June 13, 1971.

11. The phrase "women's liberation" was first used in 1964. In the 1960s the women's movement dealt with cultural and political inequalities, some women protesting against beauty pageants because of the swimsuit competition. See Jo Freeman, "The Women's Liberation Movement: Its Origin, Structures and Ideals," http://scriptorium.lib.duke.edu/wlm/womlib/ (accessed Nov. 14, 2009).

15. THE BAREFOOT QUEEN

1. The Kiwanis Club of Tulsa became a cosponsor of the pageant in 1966 and took over full sponsorship in 1972, with Charles Welch as the executive director. See "Charlie Welch 1927-2009," Miss Oklahoma Pageant, http://www.missoklahoma.org/charlie-welch/ (accessed Dec. 13, 2009).

2. The year 1971 was Toni's last. Charlie Welch assumed her role as executive director for the 1972 Miss Oklahoma pageant.

3. This quote appears in Troy Gordon, "Round the Clock," *Tulsa World*, June 15, 1971.

4. *Hesci* (pronounced "Hess-jay") is a greeting in Mvskoke.

5. Beth Meyerson was Miss America in 1945. See "Miss America—Our Miss Americas," http://www.missamerica.org/our-miss-americas/ (accessed Feb. 15, 2009).

6. Newspaper articles on my preparation for the Miss America pageant included "Miss Oklahoma Exercises Each Day to Keep in Shape," *Tulsa Daily World*, June 14, 1971; "Susan Works Long Hours to Represent Oklahoma," *Sunday Oklahoman*, Aug. 29, 1971; Dayton Blair, "Miss Oklahoma Has Routine Not Designed for Relaxation," *Tulsa Sunday World*, Aug. 29, 1971.

7. The 1964 film *My Fair Lady* is an adaptation of the stage musical based upon the play *Pygmalion*, by George Bernard Shaw. In the story Eliza Doolittle, a poor flower girl, takes speech lessons from Professor Henry Higgins, in hopes that she can pass as a lady.

8. In the 1930s a new pageant rule required contestants to be white, and rule 7 of the contestant contract rules in the 1950s stated, "Contestants must be of good health and of the white race." In 1970 this rule was changed. The first nonwhite (black) contestant in the pageant was Cheryl Brown, Miss Iowa. See *USA Today*, "Miss America Melting Pot," http://www.usatoday.com/news/nation/2002-09-16-miss-america_x .htm (accessed Feb. 15, 2009); "The American Experience, Miss America Timeline," http://www.pbs.org/wgbh/amex/missamerica/timeline/time line2.html (accessed Feb. 15, 2009).

9. "Miss Oklahoma Gets New Car," *Tulsa Tribune*, July 10, 1971.

10. I wanted to model their clothes on the runway, but they agreed that I was just too short.

11. The legal voting age in America was twenty-one until a 1971 reform reduced it to eighteen.

12. "Independent Miss," *Tulsa Daily World*, July 15, 1971; "Miss Oklahoma Registers," *Tulsa Tribune*, July 14, 1971.

13. Dr. Irvin Wagner was a University of Oklahoma music professor. He and his orchestra Now provided the music for the Miss Oklahoma pageant.

14. See "Project Opened with Flair," *Tulsa Tribune*, Aug. 12, 1971; "State Beauty to Perform at Pow Wow," *Tulsa Daily World*, Aug. 7, 1971. One local event was the Third Annual Hydro Plane boat races, held in Claremore on Aug. 20, 1971.

15. Frances Campbell was the official Miss Oklahoma chaperone for many years.

16. "Meacham's Welcomes Five Visiting Queens to Fort Worth and the Miss Texas Pageant," *Fort Worth Star-Telegram*, July 11, 1971.

16. THE INDIAN QUEEN

1. The "Five Civilized Tribes" refers to five American Indian nations: Cherokee, Creek, Choctaw, Chickasaw, and Seminole. They lived in the Southeastern United States before they were relocated west of the Mississippi during many federally legislated removals. They were called "civilized" because they were agricultural societies that tried to get along in their new culture and therefore fought for their lands in the U.S. courts rather than on the battlefield.

2. The 1867 Medicine Lodge Treaty removed Plains Indians from white settlers by establishing reservations for each tribe in the western part of Oklahoma in exchange for their traditional lands.

3. Original Oklahoma lands were called Indian Territory—lands set aside in the Indian Removal Act of 1830. See "New Perspectives on the West," http://www.pbs.org/weta/thewest/places/trails_ter/indian.htm (accessed Feb. 16, 2009).

4. An 1890 map of Oklahoma can be found online at RootsWeb, an Ancestry.Com community. See "1890 Map of Indian Territory," http://www.rootsweb.ancestry.com/~cherokee/1890map.html (accessed Feb. 16, 2009).

5. Ironically the Osage Nation had several skirmishes with both Cherokee and Muscogee (Creek) people when they were first relocated to former Osage lands in Oklahoma. See Richard Kay, Mary Ann Wortman, and William W. Bottorff, "Osage Indian Nation," http://www.ausbcomp.com/~bbott/cowley/Oldnews/Wortmaw/OSAGER.HTM (accessed Nov. 18, 2009).

6. Larry Worthy, "North Georgia Creek History," http://ngeorgia .com/history/creekhistory.html (accessed Nov. 18, 2009).

7. The Indian Removal Act of 1830 authorized establishing treaties with Eastern tribes to exchange their original lands for lands west of the Mississippi. See "Indian Removal 1814–1858," http://www.pbs.org/ wgbh/aia/part4/4p2959.html (accessed Nov. 14, 2009).

8. In *Worcester v. Georgia*, 31 U.S. (6 Pet.) 515 (1832), the Supreme Court ruled that the federal government needed to ensure that the State did not infringe upon the Cherokee tribe's sovereignty. The Supreme Court, however, did not send federal marshals to carry out its decision, therefore permitting Andrew Jackson to remove the Indians avoiding the possibility of a political conflict between the two branches of government. Some people rationalize that since the Supreme Court did not send federal marshals to protect Indians from Andrew Jackson's forced relocation, the Supreme Court was responsible for not enforcing its decision. However, most historians agree that Andrew Jackson defied the Supreme Court order by forcibly relocating all remaining tribes in the Southeast and by launching the second Seminole War in an effort to relocate those who tried to escape. See *Worcester v. Georgia*, 31 U.S. (6 Pet.) 515 (1832), http://www.georgiaencyclopedia.org/nge/ Article.jsp?id=h-2720 (accessed Nov. 13, 2009); "Andrew Jackson, Seventh President—1829–37," http://www.nps.gov/history/history/online_books/ presidents/bio7.htm (accessed Nov. 14, 2009).

9. The "Trail of Tears" refers to the forced relocation of Indians during the 1830s. Although many people commonly think of Cherokee removal in 1838, the Choctaw were actually the first tribe to be removed, in 1831. See Randy Golden, "The Trail of Tears," http://ourgeorgiahistory.com/ indians/cherokee/trail_of_tears.html (accessed Nov. 14, 2009).

10. A map of the Trail of Tears is available online. See "Trail of Tears," http://www.cherokeemuseum.org/html/collections_tot.html (accessed Nov. 17, 2009).

11. The Creek were a confederacy of tribes. The towns of Abika, Coosa, Coweta, and Tuckabutche are considered the four "mother" towns of the Creek Confederacy. The tribes included the Yuchi, Alabama, Coosa, Coweta, Cusseat, Chehaw, Hitchiti, Tuckabatchee, Oakfuskee, and others. See the Oklahoma Historical Society's Encyclopedia of Oklahoma History and Culture, "Creek (Mvskoke)," http://digital .library.okstate.edu/encyclopedia/entries/C/CR006.html (accessed Feb. 16, 2009).

12. The Seminole Indians, originally Creek, were considered desert-
ers by the Creek. The Seminole did not wish to move and live with
the Creek because they might face death for leaving the main band of
Creek Indians in the first place. See "Seminole Nation, I. T., 'The Land
between the Rivers,'" http://www.seminolenation-indianterritory.org/
(accessed Nov. 19, 2009).

13. The U.S. government spent about thirty-five million dollars to
capture and relocate thirty-five hundred Seminoles. Another three
hundred remained in Florida. See "Military Campaigns of the Indian
Wars," http://www.legendsofamerica.com/na-indianwarcampaigns2
.html#Seminoles (accessed Nov. 14, 2009).

14. "Tribe Plans Reception for Susan," *Tulsa Tribune*, Aug. 23, 1971.

15. The group included representatives from the Tulsa Indian Affairs
Commission, the Oklahoma Indian Affairs Commission, the Intertribal
Council of Five Civilized Tribes, and the Tulsa Pow-wow Club. See Bill
Crawford, "Superstar Supernaw—'71 Miss Oklahoma," *Lawton Con-
stitution Morning Press*, June 14, 1971.

16. The powwow took place on July 18, 1971.

17. Bill Crawford, "'Super Sue' Going to Hollywood," *Lawton Constitution Morning Press*, Sept. 12, 1971; "Susan Supernaw Wins Miss Oklahoma
Title," *Enid Morning News*, June 13, 1971.

18. "Creeks Pow Wow for Susie," *Broken Arrow Ledger*, June 24, 1971.
Broken Arrow, part of the old Creek reservation, was home to my dad,
as well as to the Broken Arrow Indian Club.

19. All the singers sitting around a drum are referred to simply as
"the drum."

20. Bob Albright's photo of my dad and me appeared in the *Sunday
Oklahoman*: "Leading a Dance," July 18, 1971.

21. I was given a personalized Amoco hardhat by Mike Waller, the
manager of research in the division where Dad worked as a geophysical
instrument technician. The photo appeared in *Amoco's News Digest*,
Aug. 1971.

22. Johnny was well known for his championship fancy dancing at
powwow competitions.

23. The Intertribal Council of the Five (Civilized) Tribes gave me
honorary membership on the council and one thousand dollars toward
expenses. The Oklahoma Indian Affairs Commission financed the page
in the Miss America Pageant booklet. See "Buckskin Beauty," *Tulsa*

Daily World, July 11, 1971; "Miss Oklahoma Has Routine Not Designed for Relaxation," *Tulsa Daily World*, Aug. 29, 1971.

24. "Miss Oklahoma Repeats the Lord's Prayer," *Tulsa Daily World*, Aug. 9, 1971.

25. "Miss Oklahoma Will Appear in Skiatook This Saturday," *Skiatook News*, Aug. 12, 1971.

26. Bill Supernaw and Charles Supernaw (my grandfather) were brothers.

27. Rochelle Befort, "Shirtsleeve Symphony Attracts 8,000 People," *Tulsa Daily World*, Aug. 6, 1971.

28. "Beauty Conquers Pulled Muscle," *Tulsa Daily World*, Sept. 10, 1971.

17. DANCING FEET

1. "First Pageant Girls Arrive," *Atlantic City Press*, Sept. 4, 1971.

2. "Hot Pants Okay—If in 'Good Taste,'" *Atlantic City Press*, Sept. 8, 1971.

3. "1972 Crown Goes to Miss Ohio," *Sunday Press—Atlantic City*, Sept. 12, 1971.

4. Bill Crawford, "Miss America Can Claim New Record for Tears," *Lawton Constitution*, Sept. 13, 1971.

5. "Kansas, Ohio Take Top Honors," *Atlantic City Press*, Sept. 11, 1971.

6. Judy Simpson, "Time Ripe for Black Queen, Says Bewitching Miss Ind," *Atlantic City Press*, Sept. 6, 1971. In 1968 a Miss Black America contest was held in Atlantic City in protest of the "white" Miss America pageant. In 1970 Cheryl Brown, Miss Iowa, became the first black contestant in Atlantic City. See "The American Experience, Miss America Timeline," http://www.pbs.org/wgbh/amex/missamerica/timeline/timeline3.html (accessed Feb. 15, 2009).

7. "Ex-Iowa Queen: U.S. Not Ready for Black Queen," *Atlantic City Press*, Sept. 11, 1971.

8. It wasn't until 1974 that the Native American Programs Act was amended to include Native Hawaiians. A Native Hawaiian is defined as "an individual any of whose ancestors were natives of the area which consists of the Hawaiian Islands prior to 1778 in Title 45 CFR Part 1336.62." Title 45 CFR Part 1336.62 can be found at "Title 45, Volume 4," Oct. 1, 2005. http://edocket.access.gpo.gov/cfr_2005/octqtr/45cfr1336.10.htm (accessed Nov. 14, 2009).

9. In 1984 Vanessa Williams became the first black woman crowned Miss America. Because of a controversy she resigned, and the first runner-up, Miss New Jersey (Suzette Charles), took the crown. She was also black. See "*Miss America Melting Pot*," *usa Today*, Sept. 16, 2002.

10. The winners from my group included Miss Congeniality (Miss Delaware—Paula Kusmer), two finalists for the crown (Miss Maine—Allyn Warner, fourth runner-up; Miss Massachusetts—Deborah O'Brien, second runner-up), and the overall winner (Miss Ohio—Laurie Lee Schaffer).

11. Dick Utts, "Career Hopes for 'A to Z,'" *Atlantic City Press*, Sept. 6, 1971; "Indian Should Win, She Says," *Tulsa Tribune*, June 14, 1971.

12. "Susan Supernaw Wins Miss Oklahoma Title," *Enid Morning News*, June 13, 1971.

13. "War Cry," *Tulsa Daily World*, Sept. 4, 1971.

14. "Real-Live War Whoop," *Anchorage Daily Times*, Sept. 8, 1971.

15. "Miss America Gals Sound Off," *Pacific Stars and Stripes*, Sept. 7, 1971.

16. I had two official pageant pictures: one in which I was wearing my crown and the other in which I was wearing a buckskin. See "Miss Oklahoma, 1971," *Navajo Times*, Oct. 21, 1971.

17. Troy Gordon, "Round the Clock," *Tulsa Daily World*, Sept. 9, 1971.

18. "Advice from an Expert," *Tulsa Daily World*, Sept. 9, 1971.

19. Known as the Snyder Act, the Indian Citizenship Act of 1924, signed by President Calvin Coolidge, granted full U.S. citizenship to American Indians. Although citizenship had long been broadly granted to persons born in the United States, Indians were not included. Citizenship was granted in the 1924 act because of the desire of some U.S. leaders to see Native Americans absorbed or assimilated into the American mainstream. See "The Indian Citizenship Act of 1924," Feb. 22, 2005, http://www.coppercountry.com/printer_100.php (accessed Nov. 15, 2009).

20. In 1935 the talent competition was added, providing yet other ways money could be made from the beauty pageant, especially in the private lessons industry. Every queen needed a stage talent, so dancing and music schools exploded with business. Shirley Temple's fame, for example, led to many young girls getting tap-dancing lessons, creating a whole generation of tap-dancing state queens. I'd had a few group lessons as part of the Dazette dance group during high school; we'd

done some jazz and tap dancing in heels, resembling the Rockettes more than Shirley Temple.

21. John Wayne (1907–79), born Marion Robert Morrison, was a popular actor in both Westerns and military movies. Ironically, when other stars signed up for World War II Wayne put off enlisting until he was finally exempted from service, using his age and a family deferment as his excuse. See "Memorializing the Deadly Myth of John Wayne," http://www.truthdig.com/report/item/20070526_memorializing_the _deadly_myth_of_john_wayne (accessed Nov. 19, 2009).

22. "I don't feel we did wrong in taking this great country away from them [American Indians] if that's what you're asking. Our so called stealing of this country was just a question of survival. There were great numbers of people who needed new land, and the Indians were selfishly trying to keep it for themselves. . . . But you can't whine and bellyache 'cause somebody else got a break and you didn't, like those Indians are." See Richard Warren Lewis, "Playboy Interview: John Wayne," *Playboy*, May 1, 1971, https://www.playboy.co.uk/life-and-style/ interview/64826/1/Playboy-Interview-John-Wayne/commentsPage/1/ contentPage/4 (accessed Nov. 19, 2009).

23. Each of today's contestants has a "platform": a social topic she wants to address during her reign. For my statements see Thomas Baldwin and Eleanor Lillisand, "For 31 Queens It's Busy . . . Busy," *Atlantic City Press*, Sept. 5, 1971.

24. Bill Crawford, "Miss Oklahoma May Get Movie Role," *Lawton Constitution*, Sept. 12, 1971.

25. Fred Davis, "Tulsan Gets Title," *Tulsa Daily World*, June 13, 1971.

26. Bill Crawford, "Miss America Can Claim New Record for Tears," *Lawton Constitution*, Sept. 13, 1971.

27. Laurie was Miss Southeastern Ohio in 1968, Miss Central Ohio in 1969, and Miss Central Ohio in 1971.

28. A children's educational television series, *Sesame Street* premiered on Nov. 10, 1969, and is the longest-running children's program. Jim Henson created puppet characters called "Muppets." He got the name by combining the words *marionette* and *puppet*. See John B. Padgett, "mwp: Jim Henson (1936–1990)," http://www.olemiss.edu/mwp/dir/ henson_jim/index.html (accessed Nov. 19, 2009).

29. "'Super Sue' Still Optimistic," *Tulsa Daily World*, Sept. 10, 1971.

30. "Auburn-Haired Ohio Entrant Wins Miss America Crown," *Tulsa Daily World*, Sept. 12, 1971.

31. In 1957 Hugh Everett, a quantum physicist, proposed that every possible observation corresponded to a different universe. If this is true, everything that could happen in our universe (but doesn't) happens in another universe(or other universes). See Gevin Giorbran, "Hugh Everett III and the Many Worlds Theory," http://everythingforever.com/everett.htm (accessed Nov. 14, 2009).

32. "Viewing Miss America Pageant Is Likened to Horse Race Betting," *Lawton Constitution*, Sept. 13, 1971.

33. "Kansas, Ohio Take Top Honors," *Atlantic City Press*, Sept. 11, 1971.

To order or obtain more
information on these or
other University of
Nebraska Press titles, visit
www.nebraskapress.unl.edu.